OPEN A CHANNEL

The Women of Star Trek

OPEN A CHANNEL

The Women of Star Trek

NANA VISITOR

INSIGHT
EDITIONS

SAN RAFAEL · LOS ANGELES · LONDON

CONTENTS

INTRODUCTION

This is more than a book about *Star Trek*. It's true that I interviewed countless women who told me about their experiences as writers, actors, and producers working on the show, but they also told me a story of what it was like to work in Hollywood over the last sixty years and how that has changed. So, this is a Hollywood story in a sense. Hollywood is just another system, after all, and most systems have lots of things in common. Hierarchy, cultural rules, and bias exist in many of them. So even more than that, it's a story about society and about how the role of women has changed since Gene Roddenberry wrote his first *Star Trek* memo in 1964.

It's also a story about how much impact *Star Trek* has had on its audience. It's well documented how putting a Black woman on the bridge of the *Enterprise* in the 1960s changed everyone's expectations of the future. Nichelle Nichols has been the North Star that many of the women connected to the show look to, and many of us learned social advocacy from her example.

A DIFFERENT WORLD

Things have changed a lot since Nichelle got that seat on the bridge. The original *Star Trek* had the 1960s written all over it, and however important Uhura was, she was rarely the focus of the story. In fact, women were often scantily dressed, and some of the ideas about them haven't aged well. That makes for a complicated story.

It's easy to look back on the show and spot what's sexist to our ever-evolving eyes. What is harder to see is how the small space that women were given to inhabit could warp or hobble your sense of self, and how big you allow yourself to dream.

Writer and teacher Tara Brach tells a story of going to the oceanside with her husband. There was a nearby island, and priding herself on being a strong swimmer, they set off for it. She felt like an Olympic athlete, easily and smoothly making it to the island with almost no effort. But when they headed back, she could barely make her way through the water. The effort required was huge, and she arrived on the beach totally depleted. Of course, on the way out to the island, the current was with her; on the way back, she had to fight against the current with each stroke.

As I began the work, I wanted to know: What were the cultural currents over the last fifty-odd years that were flowing against women? Did they change with the decades? We can't always see or even feel those cultural tides. Most of the time, women just accept the push against them and determine to simply work harder if they want to succeed.

LIMITED HORIZONS

There's one particular story that has stayed with me. When I was on the *Star Trek* cruise, I interviewed a woman called Alice. "It's 1973," she told me. "It was career day at high school. There were 1,100 kids in my class; I was number twenty-four. I mean, I wasn't valedictorian, but I was in the top 2 percent of my class. So, I can't wait to talk to whoever this counselor is and ask what my options are. Where should I apply for scholarships? This is going to be fun! I sat down with this middle-aged man, and he told me how great it would be if I became a nurse, a teacher, or a secretary. My balloon sort of busted there. I'm thinking, 'No astronauts? Not even in the realm of possibility? No NASA, no scientist? We're nothing?' So, then I'm thinking to myself, 'Yeah, what the hell were you thinking? You are not supposed to do that.' So I became a nurse."

Just so you know, Alice hasn't regretted the forty-three years she spent being a hero—I mean nurse—and knows how many lives she has touched. She *was* inspired by Nurse Chapel, but back then *Star Trek* didn't have any female science or security officers, and the culture of the time didn't even acknowledge how good Alice might have been at those jobs. Both *Star Trek* and society at large are different today. I'm pleased to say I talked to a lot of incredible women who work at NASA and its European equivalent, ESA and, one of them—the wonderful Samantha Cristoforetti—is an astronaut. They were all inspired by *Star Trek*, too.

Star Trek's longevity makes it a unique setting to see how women have fared over all these years. From the highly sexualized young women hanging over Captain Kirk to the evolved and complex women of *Strange New Worlds, Star Trek*'s women have pushed the boundaries of what society allowed and also reflected how the culture of the time viewed women.

Like all the best *Star Trek* stories, it's also been a journey of self-discovery. As I set out to write this book, I expected I would watch the shows and objectively see the ways the characters worked for female representation. I thought with a certain amount of relief that I would be doing work that wouldn't involve introspection. Acting, for me, has always involved the careful examination of what it means to be human, and it's sometimes gut-wrenching work. This would be more straightforward, I assumed. I was wrong.

THE WAY IT WAS

When I was entering adulthood, the rules the culture laid down for women were very clear. Following them in the 1970s and '80s provided you with a narrow lane to stay in, but it seemed like the way to win a place at the table. There was a whole generation of men and women who followed the rules laid out for us and figured "that's just the way it is." Some people around my age haven't looked at that phrase with a critical present-day eye, which would maybe lead them to the realization that those are the words that trap you

like a bug. It traps the next generations, too, when we pass that phrase along.

The writing of this book forced me to examine myself and my own ways of thinking. What I saw was unconscious bias in my actions and cultural adaptations that I had gradually made in response to the constant messaging of the culture. It had, with an imperceptible creep, changed how I thought about myself and other women. It had defined my expectations of how much space we can claim for ourselves in the world. I was shocked. I had emerged from my feminist school a very different kind of woman than the women of my mother's generation. I had always worked for a living, and made choices in my career, and I played a powerful *Star Trek* character. I hadn't noticed that even as I played out my hopes of how I wanted a woman's life to be in my character, there was a kind of crystallization happening around me.

Around the time I turned sixty, an age which I thought would bring with it a modicum of respect from others, one of the heads at my agency took me to lunch. He was planning to drop me from his roster, and wanted to take the time to tell me what my problem was. This was at the height of the Me Too movement. He is a dinosaur from the 1990s, and he spoke to me in a way that was commonplace back then. There was a phrase women in Hollywood knew they had to answer in the positive to get a job, a manager, or an agent: Are you fuckable? He told me, among other outrageous things, that he needed to feel that I was fuckable to him. Once he felt that, he said, he needed to feel comfortable enough to fart in front of me. Then, and only then, could we work together.

I was frozen for the rest of lunch, and planned on telling my manager to fire him when I got home. As we left the restaurant, he looked down at my high heels and said, "Okay, now you're fuckable to me."

I called my manager in a fury. He said to me, "If you say or do anything, he will blackball you in the industry." I had been told that same thing at eighteen because of a director's sexual harassment, and I knew firsthand it wasn't just an empty threat. I did nothing, but I didn't keep in touch the way he had told me to, and he dropped me a few weeks later. To say I felt shame twice—for not walking out of the restaurant, and then again for not firing him—is putting it so very mildly. How did I get here?

We know a lot about ancient life from the creatures that get trapped in amber. Those insects from a different time got caught in the sticky resin that gradually formed into crystal and they became a part of the stone, forever as they once were, perfect specimens, unchanging. Daily messages from the culture are everywhere. In the 1960s, '70s and '80s, I wasn't aware that the commercials between the shows I watched, the shows themselves, the magazines I read, news shows, the people who hired me, advised me, managed me, all of them had a stake in selling me something, commodifying me, or instructing me as to what box I should stay in. Each input was a drop of resin that stuck me in a belief system that has seen its day. Play the game, and you'll get what you are allowed. It thrills me to the core that none of these young women I talked to have experienced the phrase "Are you fuckable?" That's progress.

INSPIRED BY *TREK*

I was also thrilled to discover how big a role *Star Trek* has played in changing individual lives. We actors hear firsthand from audience members what the effect of *Trek* has been on their lives, so we are primed to take on the responsibility for our characters. I've talked to people who have been influenced by *Trek* and my character for over thirty years. They've shared heart-swelling stuff. It's a unique opportunity to understand the importance of the story in the midst of telling it. Hearing what gave women a sense of freedom in their emotional lives has made me an advocate for them.

While writing the book, I heard personal stories from the audience that proved that all the women in all the iterations served as virtual mentors when there was no one else in their lives to embody that. Politician Stacey Abrams told me she asks herself the question "What would Janeway do?" LGBTQIA+ audience members found avatars for themselves in stories through Dax, Kira, and Seven of Nine. Astronaut Samantha Cristoforetti answered the question "Could I be an engineer?" for herself because she saw B'Elanna Torres on her TV in a tiny mountain town in the Alps.

But I didn't come close to understanding the overall impact until I held interview sessions with countless people in England, Europe, and later, on a cruise ship of thousands of people for over fourteen hours (and I still didn't get to talk to everyone who had a story to tell), and in my tiny study via Zoom over the course of several years.

It's a virtuous loop, where the actors can be inspired by the audience. Mary Wiseman, Tilly on *Discovery,* said that even when she couldn't find the courage to feel body positivity for her character herself, she could do it for someone who had told her what the character meant to them.

Thanks to Gene Roddenberry, "Infinite Diversity in Infinite Combinations," respect, focus on STEAM, collaboration, and hope for the future are all in *Trek*'s DNA. The impact is global because Gene Roddenberry added something else to the mix. Even if you don't watch *Trek,* almost everyone shares the awareness of its existence. Why? Along with all the discourse on social and ethical issues, all the science, and all the hopeful imaginings for everyone in the future, it's entertaining. It allows for a wide bandwidth that so many disparate humans can use to find commonality.

At *Star Trek* conventions, I have spoken to all ages, all colors, all ethnicities, all sexual orientations, neurotypical and neurodivergent people, people with and without disabilities, and people on all levels of society. I smile at them, and they smile at me when we meet. It's such a good starting point. Roddenberry's values form the bandwidth for the frequency many of us actors find to enter our relationships with the audience, and they with us.

There are too many women's voices out there to think there won't be different opinions on all of this. Writing the book has changed me in a palpable way, but this is only one woman's eyes and ears on the subject. Think of it like this: I'm opening a channel. Let's talk on the bandwidth that for me, through all these years, has started with a smile of recognition for each other.

ABOVE: Today's shows have made a real effort to show different kinds of women in roles that would have been unthinkable even twenty years ago. If the future is like Tilly, then it will be very bright.

LEFT: Captain Janeway was a huge step forward and showed a generation of women that they could take command.

OPPOSITE TOP LEFT: Susan Oliver's green-skinned slave girl was literally a male fantasy brought to life.

OPPOSITE TOP RIGHT: Putting Uhura on the bridge was one of *Trek*'s greatest achievements.

OPPOSITE BOTTOM RIGHT: When *Star Trek* returned with TNG, women were prominent, but still fell into traditional female roles.

OPPOSITE BOTTOM LEFT: The original *Star Trek* is often remembered as a show with beautiful (and available) female guest stars.

INTRODUCING *STAR TREK*

Click. Click. Click. My mother walked very fast in very high heels on Manhattan's Upper East Side in 1966, the year Star Trek *premiered, while my nine-year-old self struggled to keep up in my school-sanctioned penny loafers.*

As exceptional as she was, in many ways she was typical of many women in that decade. She lived by her father's dictate that women should never be seen without lipstick, and carefully fixed my father's martini each night at five, usually followed by a three-course meal. (Although it's hard for me to imagine most women did that!) If things were chaotic for the family, it was her job to smooth it, as was the laundry and most of the housework. Yet, she was the steady breadwinner, turning over the money she earned to preserve my father's sense of being the "man" of the family. "Women's work is never done" was more than just a saying. But it was a tumultuous decade in America, in spite of my mother's efforts to control our little part of it.

World War II had filled the jobs left open by the men fighting the war with the women left behind. When the men returned, the women, who had tasted productivity and a life beyond four walls, were now told to stay home and care for the family, with the traumatized men sent back to work with little or no psychological help. Man up and get on with it. But by 1966, everything was changing. Women hadn't all gone back to their old roles, the youth movement was in full swing, and civil rights were a major issue. There was no going back.

That's the world *Star Trek* came into, and Gene Roddenberry wanted it to be a part of this massive change. Well, some aspects of it anyway. Martinis and women in lipstick still seemed like a good idea. The scene in the first pilot, "The Cage," where the doctor pulls out a martini to "treat" Captain Pike bears this out. Looking at the original *Star Trek*

is like looking at the best progress brewing at this time, along with a big helping of 1960s views on women, with a dash of World War II military culture thrown in. Here was the ship, which hummed along like a submarine, filled with people who seemed to follow a military protocol. Reactivity to the bigotry of the time put Uhura and Sulu on the bridge, and the question of the Cold War was laid to rest with the inclusion of Chekov in our future.

Nineteen sixty-six was a time of ideas. The counterculture was born out of a record number of people attending college, and learning to apply intellectualism, philosophy, and history to the problems of the day. Television now allowed us to watch what was going on in the world, and we began to experience war and inequality like a gut punch. I remember watching the Vietnam War during dinnertime, and it made me understand brutality in a way nothing else could have.

TV could also offer a respite from the pressure-cooker realities. Shows such as *Bonanza* took us back to the Wild West, and Andy Griffith was a bucolic dream of small-town life. Most of the TV shows revealed where we had been. *Star Trek*, which would premiere in September 1966, was something different and would become a franchise that not only had a huge effect on pop culture but that also helped lead our way, with hope and inclusion, to the future. It did that by not simply being about an imaginary future, but by also dealing with the issues of the day—and there were lots of them.

Race issues were exploding, and leaders such as the Reverend Martin Luther King Jr. and Malcolm X were raising awareness and looking for solutions from each of their perspectives. Young people were rebelling, with different views on war, drugs, materialism, and sex. They were a powerful force. There was a Cold War between America and Russia (then known as the Soviet Union), and both raced to be the first to get a person into space. It would be good PR to prove military superiority, and NASA was loaded with ex-military and fighter pilots training to be astronauts. The birth control pill suddenly gave women the freedom to choose when to have children, which allowed them to make a choice to be in the workplace and delay marriage, instead of going from their father's home straight to a husband's. But with a job came attempts from men to lock them out, harassment, and reduced pay. This gave energy to the growing women's movement, which attempted to level the playing field and wake women up from the trance of cultural adaptation and acceptance of a status quo.

The big ideas bred by the counterculture were reflected by Roddenberry's rule that in the centuries to come, humanity would have no need for war. The colonialism of the Vietnam War was evident in the messaging of the Prime Directive, which insisted that while we were exploring new worlds, we should do them no intentional harm. The examination of ethics was going on in colleges at the same time that Spock was finding human behavior "fascinating."

One aspect that might appear sexist through today's lens was actually a nod to the women's movement, a choice made by Grace Lee Whitney. She refused to wear pants in favor of a miniskirt. The decision might have come partly from her strong desire to use her sexuality, the primary power that was allowed to women in Hollywood back then. But it was also a reflection of the changing times. Women were getting out of girdles and elaborate and expensive wardrobes. The miniskirt was freedom, and it became a symbol of the movement.

Star Trek was on TV, and TV was a powerful tool that could be a hugely effective disseminator of information, if it was used in the right way. It needed to be entertaining to have a large reach, and not scare people who were nervous about all the changes taking place in the world. Setting the show in the future allowed people to see change without feeling threatened, and it imagined a world way less frenetic and threatening than the time period it was born in.

But you can see the narrow lane that culturally acceptable women were allowed to take. In 1963, President Kennedy had encouraged the nation to "ensure" that women were being used effectively to "provide a better life for our people," but added that this would be "in addition to meeting their primary responsibility, which is their home." After the housework and the husband and the children, you used your extra time to pursue something that served society. To me, I see this translated in the show as having women included in the workplace but with very 1960s expectations. Hair and makeup in place, with romance on their minds.

Yes, all the women could be carbon-dated by their elaborate hair and makeup, as well as the very time-coded need for women to be performatively sexy. In "Shore Leave," Yeoman Barrows is thrilled at the idea of wearing a flowing gown and being "a lady to be protected and fought for." It was a learned thing. Be soft, seem sexually willing, sensually connected at all times to your body, and have all your attention directed to the men in the scene. They all did it: all the women guest stars. Except perhaps France Nuyen, in "Elaan of Troyius." Her role was a version of Katherine in Shakespeare's *The Taming of the Shrew*, the out-of-control woman (she had a mind of her own) who is "tamed" into being a good wife. Being a Romulan commander also gave Joanne Linville a pass from being performative. She is every bit Kirk's equal and demonstrates that it was the cultural requirements, not the abilities of the women back then, that put women in subordinate positions. Being an alien had definite benefits.

But the Romulan commander was the exception in these early years, not the norm. In the episode "Who Mourns for Adonais?," Kirk and McCoy discuss Lt. Carolyn Palamas, the ship's anthropology and archeology officer. We can stop for a moment to appreciate the inclusion of a woman officer in the plot. That's enough of a moment, though, because she's there to serve the story and to fall for a not-so-benign god.

In the opening scene of the episode, McCoy and Kirk discuss her personal options with fatherly concern. McCoy says, "She's a woman. All woman." (What does that even mean?) "One day she'll find the right man and off she'll go, out of the service." It was as if a woman's career was a placeholder until her real purpose—being married and having a family—came along.

In this respect, *Star Trek* was no different to the real space program. In many ways, Kirk is a flyboy astronaut—the kind of man who has ice in his veins and a beautiful girl on his arm. The ex-military men in charge of NASA believed women had a place in the space agency, just not as astronauts. This flew in the face of common sense. The head of NASA's Life Sciences, Dr. William Randolph Lovelace, saw women's smaller size as useful in cramped rockets, and thought that they were comparable to men in every other way. He started a program to train them for space travel. Of course, he was looking ahead to colonizing space and saw female astronauts as necessary for homesteading; they would join men, but their actual jobs would stay traditionally gendered. Women were eventually barred from becoming astronauts by it becoming a requirement to have had experience flying jets—experience they weren't allowed in the military.

OPPOSITE: Gene Roddenberry clearly wanted *Star Trek* to have a lot of sex appeal. As a result, the show often featured scantily dressed, beautiful young women.

ABOVE: In Roddenberry's first attempt at *Star Trek*, women wore pants and were ready to take command.

There were subcommittee hearings to debate a woman's right to train as an astronaut. Brendan Casserly, in an article in the *Irish Examiner*, quotes astronaut John Glenn's opinion on the subject: "A real crude analogy is, we have here in Washington the Redskins football team. My mother could probably pass the physical exam they give pre-season for the team but I doubt she would play many games for them. Men go off to war and fly airplanes; women are not astronauts because of our social order; that's the way of life." Women could participate in the space industry, they just couldn't actually go to space. NASA was filled with women in support positions, such as lab technicians and telephone operators.

We would see this echoed in *Star Trek*. The yeoman, the communications officer, the nurse, all support staff, reflected this. But as an ex-military pilot himself, Roddenberry's attempt to make Number One a woman in "The Cage" is a pretty impressive run at progress that was ahead of its time. When Majel Barrett was replaced by a man for the second pilot, it mirrored the way NASA eventually shut down the women's astronaut training facility. It may have been test audiences' disapproval or network executives saying no to hiring the producer's girlfriend, but it would be almost thirty years before another woman got a swing at that role.

In people's minds at the time, military experience and space travel were inextricably linked and the idea of women warriors was still a big step. Watching *Star Trek*'s first pilot, "The Cage," I was struck by how easily the plot could be shifted to the story of a battle-weary pilot in World War II. Like John Glenn and Neil Armstrong, Kirk, Spock, and McCoy are cast in hero roles. The women are there not for their own sake or with their own stories, but to make them look good.

Star Trek wasn't unusual in this respect. All too often, femininity and professionalism seemed incompatible. In her book *Where the Girls Are*, Susan A. Douglas points out the social significance of a popular show at the time. *I Dream of Jeannie* depicted an astronaut who becomes the "master" of a beautiful if ditzy genie who lives in a bottle and loves him. She, however, causes chaos in his life with her feminine ways and is always one step away from getting him fired from NASA. It seems it was a done deal that men were to be the heroes, in *Trek* and in NASA. The culture at large had decided it.

Although *Star Trek* put women in Kirk's crew, a worrying number of them are portrayed as unreliable—focused on the superficial and attracted to powerful men. The story rarely—if ever—stops to consider what they want, besides the man. In "Space Seed," the ship's historian Marla McGivers (what is it with historians?) is seen in her quarters painting picture after picture of powerful historical men with questionable ethics. When she meets Khan, the man engineered to be a superpower from the 1990s, she is instantly ready to submit.

In one of their scenes together, you see him psychologically grooming her to acquiesce. It made me think this was maybe more a story about cult followers than weak-minded women. That there is a discussion between Kirk and Bones trying to understand her level of attraction to Khan, to ascertain how much of a danger she would be, leads me to believe that the assumption was that the more her emotions were engaged, the less reliable she would become. This, unfortunately, is the turn the story takes—she betrays the crew to help Khan, although she ultimately saves Kirk's life. In the final scene, when she is faced with the prospect of either a court-martial or a scary planet with her man, she follows her man.

In "Who Mourns for Adonais?," Carolyn Palamas meets and rapidly falls in love with the god Apollo. He is threatening the crew, but when he magically changes her uniform into a revealing, strategically draped gown, she isn't alarmed, but instead displays the cape gracefully, exclaiming, "Oh, isn't it beautiful!"

NO AGENCY

Once she decides to stay with Apollo, Kirk tells her she must reject him and align herself with her crew. She does, and facing Apollo's stormy wrath, she falls on her back on the ground as the spurned lover grows huge over her. When we next see her, she is physically and mentally devastated. It certainly implied to me an off-camera rape, a violence that felt like a manipulation to make sure we side with Kirk's decision for her life. See? Apollo was the bad guy and Kirk was justified. Pulled one way by her emotions, but martyring herself because authority told her to, this intelligent woman had no agency whatsoever.

The implication is that women only exist in relation to men. When they try to step out of their supporting role and take the lead, they demonstrate that they are not to be trusted. This is evident in the last original *Star Trek* episode, "Turnabout Intruder." A former lover of Kirk pretends to be in distress to lure him to a planet where she has found an ancient mechanism that can switch their bodies.

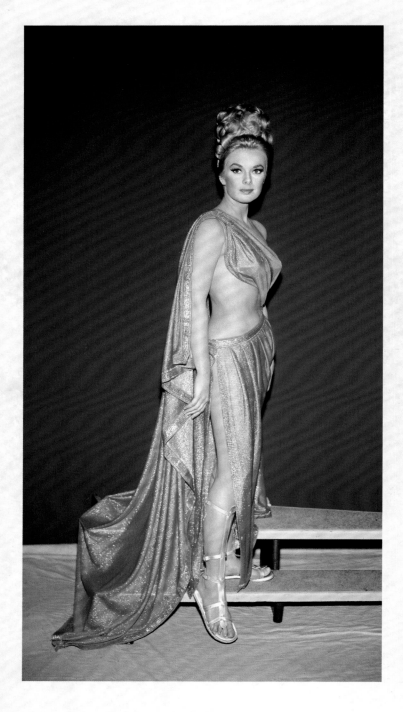

ABOVE: The original *Star Trek* was famous for putting female guest stars in remarkable clothes. Leslie Parrish's dress can only have stayed on with a lot of help from sticky tape.

OPPOSITE: Occasionally, the show had some very worrying ideas about men and women. When Khan dominates Marla McGivers, she responds positively rather than running for the hills.

Once a member of Starfleet, she wants desperately to be a captain, and because that kind of senior position isn't allowed for a woman, she decides to experience it through Kirk's body. "It's better to be dead than to live alone in the body of a woman," she says. Wow, that's pretty misogynistic.

But we are supposed to be experiencing her, I think, as a woman pushing herself into a man's position where she isn't wanted because she is full of self-hate. This was a view some people had of feminists at the time. To Kirk's credit, when Dr. Janice Lester tells him, "Your world of Starfleet captains doesn't allow women...it isn't fair!" he answers, "No, it isn't." And William Shatner's delivery makes it sincere.

But with the body exchange, things move to the male perspective and the writing falls into the trap of portraying a woman frustrated with limitations as evil. Kirk says, "The intense hatred of her own womanhood made life with her impossible." But did she hate her woman's body, or the restrictions she had because of it?

A MAN'S WORLD

The whole show seems to be a cautionary tale of what would happen if women had equality with men. In Kirk's body, Lester is vicious, cruel, and self-serving, bringing no mental control to performing the work or even achieving her own goals. She files her nails in a meeting with McCoy, and meeting resistance from the crew mates who are growing suspicious that something is amiss with their captain, responds with out-of-control rage. Scotty says he's seen Kirk in many different mental states, but "I've never seen him red-faced with hysteria." Just as a reminder, hysteria was treated as a psychological condition for women up until the 1980s.

Once she is put back into her own body, just before she sends half the crew to their death for mutiny, she is broken and childlike. She is sent to a planet in the care of a man. Just to drive the message home that women should stay where society was telling them they belonged, Kirk says, "Her life could have been as rich as any woman, if only..."

Both Shatner and Sandra Smith as Dr. Lester do wonderful jobs in their roles. As Kirk, before she is required to lose control, she is measured and powerful, proving that some qualities that are thought of as male are performative, too. As Dr. Lester, Shatner underplays when it's an almost irresistible opportunity for an actor to overplay in a woman's role.

The choice of the actor to play Lester was interesting to me, as was her wardrobe. She wasn't the typical *Star Trek* sexpot, and she was dressed in a sort of loose, unattractive pants suit with tassels as a vague nod to femininity. I see two possible reasons for this. One could be that there was a sensitivity to imagining when our hero plays the woman, and a tight sequin gown would be distracting, even if it wasn't by choice. The other would be the idea that if you were a woman who cared about being in a man's world, it made you uninterested in your sexuality. This episode was like seeing a message to women in the 1960s, frozen in amber. Stay in your lane.

To be fair to Roddenberry, he was barely involved with *Star Trek* by this point. His show had already been cancelled, and he probably didn't pay too much attention to the script. He might have stepped in and said that in his future, women could captain a starship. *Star Trek*'s most celebrated female writer, Dorothy Fontana, had left too, and I'm sure she would have had something to say about this messaging.

As is often the case, in *Star Trek* you are better off being an alien. In "The Enterprise Incident," written by Fontana, Kirk and Spock go up against the female commander of a Romulan starship. She is played by Joanne Linville and is imperious and effective. When the showrunner at the time ramped up her romantic interest in Spock, Fontana was furious, and feeling that they made her character foolish, she walked away and stopped writing for the show.

What *Star Trek*—and, to be fair, society at large—was comfortable with at the time was women as objects of desire. With the approval of the birth control pill, women suddenly had choice. Sex could come before marriage, and motherhood could be delayed to make time for other pursuits. Gene Roddenberry embraced the idea that sex without commitment was okay. Perhaps, given the currency sexual attractiveness held for women, he saw objectifying them as a compliment and a way to share the power—an idea best left as a relic in the cultural amber of that time.

The show seemed to feature young, beautiful, and adoring barely clad women on every planet. We see these women through our heroes' eyes, in soft focus and romanticized. In a technique used to soften and blur out imperfections, the women we were meant to see as sexually desirable (to our heroes) were lit differently from the men. Being idealized, with romantic music swelling with every close-up, has its drawbacks, though.

In "The Cage," the beautiful Vina is shown in soft focus until Captain Pike is treated to cold reality. When the Talosians' illusions are stripped away, we learn that she is older than she first appeared and stitched together badly after an accident—not the male ideal of beauty. Pike immediately understands why she can't join her fellow humans on the *Enterprise* and instead chooses to stay on a planet with her alien keepers. This takes complete precedence in the story over her being isolated and used by the Talosians like a lab animal. The message seems to be that ugliness is shameful and hiding it is kinder for all involved. He says goodbye with a plea to the Talosians to give Vina back her fantasy of beauty.

That said, *Star Trek* employed many female guest stars and wrote interesting storylines for women. Susan Oliver as Vina got about as much screen time as Pike, played by Jeffrey Hunter, and knocked her varied scenes out of the park.

The message that women should be beautiful was everywhere. At five years old in 1962, I fought against having my hair pulled and set in rollers. "You have to suffer to be beautiful," my mother said with a smile and no irony. The media and their images of little girls in sausage curls sold my mother the curlers, and my mother sold me the message that would stick with me long after the curlers were history.

In "Mudd's Women," Evie, Magda, and Ruth take the Venus drug, believing that it makes them beautiful and therefore valuable. I think *Star Trek*'s message here is an evolved one for the time, even if the finale is less so.

One of them, Evie, eventually stops taking the drug and instantly loses its benefits. It's interesting to note that her supposed unloveliness is simply being makeup free; it suggested to me that the writers were using the pill as an

analogy for the pressure women felt to meet the culture's standard of beauty.

Without her pill, Evie's prospective mate finds her unlovely and she argues for herself. This, in itself, is amusing. The man is a lonely, grubby miner without any options, ready to reject a pretty woman in a pink sequin gown. But this is *Star Trek,* and there's a point here to be made. Kirk makes her take the pill against her protests. She does and is once again fully made-up and glamorous. She asks the man considering her as a wife if he wants one who is selfish, vain, and useless (pretty) or if he wanted "someone to help you, cook and sew and cry and need you" (without the benefit of hair and makeup). Not only is it a forgone conclusion that women are dependent, but also that they really want the drudgery that is the transactional baggage that comes with it. And, of course, being pretty doesn't equate with being useless. In fairness, not having a husband really was something to worry about: Women were economically dependent on men. Writer Kenneth T. Walsh states that until 1970, a single

RIGHT: The message from "Mudd's Women" is that beauty comes from within, but it also says that a woman's real value is as a housewife.

OPPOSITE: Susan Oliver gives a wonderful performance as Vina, but ultimately the message is that because the character is horribly scarred, she has no place in the world.

woman couldn't open a bank account or even hold a credit card without her husband's signature. Women with children were most of the time as dependent as their offspring.

But the lovely Evie is forced by Kirk to see her false dependence on the Venus drug. The pill was a placebo, and her beauty now is due to the fact that "there's only one kind of woman, you either believe in yourself or you don't." That's a nice "beauty comes from the inside" conclusion.

But like the fairy tales in which princesses wait to be rescued by a handsome prince, these stories are a slow, constant drip that tells women what they are supposed to want. This aspect of *Star Trek* trapped it in the 1960s. For most of history, we were told that a woman was safest and most successful in life when connected to a man.

But the *Enterprise* was a big ship carrying some of the biggest issues and hopes of the 1960s with it: counterculture's examination of the big questions, an end to war, exploration instead of colonialism, and racial equality. Sitting at the communications station, a Black woman in the form of Lt. Uhura would be an essential crew member with absolutely unquestionable professionalism. The message was heard loud and clear by little girls and women: In the future, Black women, the most discriminated group of all, would have a place on the bridge of a starship. Like so many other cases of intersectionality have proved, this would be a win for all women. The soft-focus camera shots might have hung around for a while, but the example of how to be a woman in space was always Uhura, not the 1960s performative females. That went for actors and for little girls alike who started to dream of being astronauts.

LUCILLE BALL

Star Trek owes its existence to one of the most famous women in television history: Lucille Ball. Without her backing, the show would never have gotten off the ground. She was responsible for a lot of firsts in Hollywood, and yet, as her daughter Lucie Arnaz said in Amy Poehler's documentary Lucy *and* Desi, *"She didn't care about being the first woman anything."*

She may not have labeled herself a feminist, but she had a far-reaching impact on women, both through her position as head of a studio and as the world's favorite redhead, Lucy Ricardo. The character she got the world to love and accept into their homes every week was a wonderful rebel disguised as the typical American 1950s housewife. *I Love Lucy* was a groundbreaking concept for a TV sitcom. The two married stars changed the way television sitcoms were done by recording on film, live in front of a studio audience. Lucy was the comedic centerpiece as a housewife married to bandleader Ricky. Each episode was built around the idea that Ricky Ricardo was a star, and his wife would do anything to be a star, too.

In actuality, Ball was the bigger star. At the time, building a show around her marriage to a Cuban was risky, but their chemistry was so delightful that people forgot to be scandalized. The character Lucy played seemed at first glance like the typical 1950s housewife; her husband was the head of the family, she was worried about displeasing him, and she would get scolded by him when she did. But here was the radical thing about her: As Bette Midler said, "She was so beautiful and not afraid to look ugly," which was antithetical to where a woman's power was supposed to lie. As Carol Burnett said, "She was fearless": Her character made mistakes and was always more focused on what she wanted rather than what the consequences would be, which were usually Lucy ending up looking ridiculous.

Norman Lear said that "she was the dominant character" of the show, and a broad comedic one at that—another

rarity for a woman. And, she wasn't married to a White man. On national TV. None of these qualities added up to the optics of the performatively "good girl" wife at the time. And people adored her. Housewives and little girls took notes. She ran a studio. She became a solid mentor to many young women in the business as she grew older. She may not have identified herself as a champion of a paradigm shift for women; she simply was.

Back in the 1950s, Lucy and her husband, Desi, ploughed the money they made from *I Love Lucy* into buying RKO and setting up their own studio, which they named Desilu. Arnaz was a brilliant producer and innovator, but the work of running what was now a Hollywood empire included long hours and enormous stress. Some believe the difficulty of running the business ruined Arnaz's health and contributed to the couple's breakup. Because he was eventually too ill to run Desilu, Lucy became head of the studio, all the while wishing someone else was doing it so that she could get back to the creative side of the business that she loved so much.

Watching video of her explaining to a lighting director what she needed from him in a scene is an interesting insight into how hard it must have been for her. She is speaking with obvious knowledge, explaining what needs to be done, while the man tells her why it can't happen without really hearing what she said. She walks away, controlled but frustrated. There are no womanly ways at play in how she speaks to him—she is a professional, expecting to be treated as such. Lucy had said this was why, in the business world, the "s" was added to her last name. A professional woman who knew her stuff and didn't bother to take care of men's egos while she did her work could get a reputation as a ballbuster.

In the 1960s, Lucy decided to invest in TV shows that had nothing to do with her own famous sitcom. The results included *Star Trek, Mission: Impossible,* and *Mannix.* It was far from obvious that making *Star Trek* was a good idea, but Ball saw it as a good candidate for reruns, a new concept invented because Arnaz had insisted on the shows being filmed. Because they owned these films outright, they could sell them again and keep the audience happy by having the show run multiple times a season. I know I happily waited for my favorite moments to happen again as I sat in bed at home, off sick from school. I watched them, as many of us did, over and over. There was power in repeatedly coming into people's living rooms and becoming a beloved friend. By making money off of several broadcast showings instead of just one, not only did they increase profits but they also built a bigger and more devoted audience long after the show stopped filming. That was the long view for profit, but at the time, the money that NBC paid for each episode didn't cover the cost of making it. This made the board nervous, but Lucy—with the tenacity her character showed when she believed in something—overrode the board's objections and decided the studio would back *Star Trek.*

Although there is a legend that Lucy herself swept the floor of the stage after the completion of the second pilot in preparation for a celebratory toast, she wasn't involved in *Star Trek* on a day-to-day basis. She didn't read the scripts or dictate what should be in the stories. That's a gift to creatives, whose vision often gets watered down by too many cooks when the studio executives get involved. By all accounts, Lucille Ball had little time for "nonsense" but was adored by her staff.

One story is revealing: The cost of making all those shows put an enormous burden on Desilu and must have contributed to Lucy's decision to sell the studio to Paramount. When she did that, she negotiated a guarantee that the staff's jobs would be protected for two years. To me, that says that Desilu had a studio head who took accountability for her employees—not a move many studio heads have made. But putting aside her example of a housewife who defies being controlled and is adored in spite or even because of it, her contribution to the culture has been huge. Just imagine if *Star Trek* had been shown only once on broadcast TV, instead of a constant loop you could reliably find throughout the years. Lucille Ball kept *Star Trek* afloat through two pilots, but arguably her most important contribution to assuring the show's longevity was helping us to watch it like an old, familiar friend long after it first aired.

ABOVE: Lucille Ball owned and ran the studio that created *Star Trek.* Although she wouldn't have considered herself to be a feminist, she was living proof that women could do anything a man could.

Majel Barrett-Roddenberry as

NUMBER ONE

When I heard the first lady of Star Trek *was going to be on our show, I expected—frankly—a diva. But the woman who liked to call the audience "friends of* Star Trek*" (as opposed to fans) said convention goers wanted the same thing she did: connection. I saw that firsthand. She was warm and inclusive, and invited me out to dinner.*

We went to the legendary Matsuhisa restaurant on La Cienega, where she seemed to be a regular. I remember the food being incredible, but not much else. The staff knew her favorite way to drink champagne—in oversized brandy snifters filled to the top—and she quickly drank me under the table.

The only time I remember focusing is when she announced we would be splitting the bill, which was one of the most enormous I had ever seen. But my overall impression of Majel Barrett-Roddenberry was a down-to-earth woman, who was as practical about the business as she was focused on it. I understand, in a way now that I didn't then, the significance Major Kira held for her. I got to play the first officer with a complicated past, a definite agenda of her own, and a real character arc—the kind of role that back in 1964 she thought would be hers. In the first *Star Trek* pilot, the *Enterprise* has a female first officer—Number One. Majel said that the role was written with her

in mind, and was, in fact, the very first piece of *Star Trek* that Gene Roddenberry created.

Let's wind back a bit. Majel got her first stage experience in school performances, before studying radio and television arts in college. She worked in summer stock theaters, which are great training grounds for actors; while you perform one show at night, you are learning the next show during the day. After a little Broadway, she got a job at Pasadena Playhouse and stayed in L.A., where she worked her way up to supporting roles in movies, and guested on TV shows—the typical life of a working actor.

She became a contract player with Desilu, the Hollywood studio run by Lucille Ball, which would ultimately make *Star Trek*. Majel trained under Lucy herself. She described Ball as unpredictable: lovely one moment, tough the next. After appearing on several Desilu shows, including *Bonanza* and *The Lucy Show*, Majel met her future husband, Gene Roddenberry, when she guested on his show *The Lieutenant.* She became his friend and soon the other woman, as he was married with two children at the time. They were already a couple when he started work on *Star Trek*, and the role he created for her was as good a gift as any writer could give an actor.

She was called Number One not because she was the first officer but because she was the best her people had to offer.

Number One seems like a real missed opportunity, not just for Majel but also for *Star Trek* and women in general: When Captain Pike left the ship, she assumed command, something that presumably would have happened in most episodes. Back then, it was Number One rather than Spock who "didn't really have any emotions." The Writer's Bible describes her as being "an extraordinarily efficient officer," who is probably the captain's "superior in detailed knowledge of the multiple equipment systems, departments and crew members aboard the vessel." She sounds impressive to me.

Majel even developed a backstory for her, which explained that she had been genetically engineered to have as much intelligence as possible and that she was called Number One not because she was the first officer but because she was the best her people had to offer.

But when the NBC studio executives saw "The Cage," they demanded changes. Gene Roddenberry always said that the network ordered him to get rid of two characters: Majel's Number One and Nimoy's alien, Spock. The way he told the story, the studio wasn't comfortable with an alien or with a woman in a position of authority. So, Roddenberry said, he decided to marry the girl and keep Nimoy, as Nimoy probably wouldn't have liked it the other way around. It was only years later that the studio executives told their side of the story: They simply didn't like Majel in the role.

COLD AND EMOTIONLESS

Watching "The Cage," I can understand why the executives didn't think she worked, but it seems to me she didn't have a chance. Her role was a stereotypically brainy woman, who was deprived of the sex appeal and charisma that were so important to Hollywood in 1964. In order to not be a sexy distraction and to justify her position on the bridge, she couldn't have any of the qualities that Pike (and presumably, therefore Roddenberry) thought made a woman desirable. Roddenberry even had Pike say that he forgot she was a woman. "I can't get used to having a woman on the bridge. No offense, Lieutenant. You're different, of course."

All she could be was an emotionally suppressed brain, and it's hard to turn that into a fully fleshed out character. If likability was what earned you the right to be in people's living rooms week after week, she had the cards stacked against her. When Nimoy played Spock, he was given the conflict of being half-human, with a powerful sense of curiosity—two gifts to any actor—helping him to appear alive and in the moment, as well as deeply human and interesting to watch. Majel was given none of that.

Majel said that being dropped was a crushing blow. "It was," she said, "going to be a marvelous part. Can you imagine where that part would have gone if it had stayed in?"

After being dropped, Majel scoured the first few scripts of the show's first season, looking for a role for herself. She found it in the part of Nurse Christine Chapel, who first appears in "What Are Little Girls Made Of?" She obviously knew doing so could cause trouble. She told a story in several interviews of dyeing her hair from black to blonde and sitting in her lover's office to see if he recognized her. When Roddenberry walked right by her, she was able to convince him the executives wouldn't recognize her either, and she changed her name from Hudec to Barrett to further fool them.

According to Herbert Solow, the Desilu executive who was in charge of production at *Star Trek*, Ball was incensed. She didn't like the deception, nor did she like the fact that Gene and Majel were involved in an extramarital affair, as Desi Arnaz had been unfaithful to her. She wanted them both fired but was talked down from it with help from Solow.

SECOND BEST

Majel had a role and appeared in twenty-six episodes of the original series. But in the end, Nurse Chapel wasn't what she wanted. Whereas Number One was an intelligent and independent woman, Nurse Chapel has much less agency. When she features in stories, she is almost always pining after a man, frequently breaking down in tears. Majel quipped that the fiancé Chapel searched the Galaxy for turned out to be an android, and the man she falls for on the *Enterprise* was a Vulcan with no emotions.

"This woman's not too smart," Majel would say. "We played her out and everything, and there were some great moments, but each time I used to think, 'Oh boy, if only Number One were here.'"

OPPOSITE: The *Enterprise* nearly had a female first officer, who had many of Spock's qualities, but the network wasn't convinced by Majel.

TOP: Majel's relationship with Gene meant she was involved from the beginning, including with costume and makeup tests.

ABOVE: It was a sign of the times that Chapel was the ship's nurse rather than a doctor like McCoy. She would eventually be promoted but not until *Star Trek: The Motion Picture.*

PAGE 25: After the role of Number One was cut, Majel was cast as Nurse Chapel, a woman who was hopelessly devoted to Spock.

Grace Lee Whitney as
YEOMAN RAND

When Grace Lee Whitney came in to audition for Star Trek, *Gene Roddenberry described the part of Yeoman Rand as one of the leads. As she remembered, he told her that he envisioned the relationship between Kirk and Rand as one of unrequited love, and described it as similar to the sexual tension between Matt Dillon and Miss Kitty in the beloved Western* Gunsmoke.

Both those characters were strong, independent people. Miss Kitty ran a saloon. She was a respected and capable member of her community, was no one's fool, and seemed to be Marshal Dillon's equal in every way.

Yeoman Rand, however, often seemed to be a glorified secretary, who pined after her captain, secretly wishing that he would look at her legs. Desilu executive Herb Solow described Roddenberry's vision of the part as "cute and shapely, cute and bubbly, and cute and not too bright." Miss Kitty was most certainly not cute. Nor did she run to her paramour at any sign of trouble.

The character of the captain's yeoman had featured in Roddenberry's plans for *Star Trek* since the beginning, but he kept changing his mind about the casting. In the first pilot, she was Yeoman Colt, before morphing into Yeoman Smith in "Where No Man Has Gone Before" and eventually Yeoman Rand in "The Corbomite Maneuver." In each case, Roddenberry cast an attractive woman, who was clearly designed to appeal to the male gaze. This was an important role, and early publicity shots of her between Shatner and Nimoy, holding vaguely futuristic colored lights, prove that Whitney was thought of as one of the leads.

The memos make it clear that the yeoman fit right in with 1960s male fantasies about the alluring secretary, who offers all sorts of temptations to her boss. One of the earliest pitches says Yeoman Colt serves as the captain's "secretary, reporter, bookkeeper and undoubtably hopes she could serve him in more personal departments." By the time Whitney was cast, the character had evolved a bit, and the Writer's Bible puts the emphasis on her professionalism and says that she "suspends the feminine and is a yeoman without the qualifications of gender." The implication is clear: There is a tension between being professional and being feminine.

A WOMAN'S WORK

Rand is still very much a secretary. The tricorder was invented so she could take notes and, potentially, to create a suitable toy for little girls. In "The Corbormite Maneuver," she delivers Kirk's coffee, and when she exits, he complains to McCoy about being assigned a female crewman, clearly worried that it will be a distraction.

Grace Lee Whitney had been brought up to fulfill all those fantasies. Like other women of the era, she was valued for the way she looked and how sexy she was, with too few people around her valuing her for anything else. Reading her book *The Longest Trek: My Tour of the Galaxy*, you discover that she had a number of cards stacked against her from the beginning.

In my experience, traumatic events can be like a game of Jenga with one's well-being. You start off with a tall, stable

pile of wooden blocks, and then, one by one, random blocks are removed. The player loses when the structure can no longer stand. Whitney started life with some emotional disadvantages. Adopted by a mother who seemed determined to let her know she wasn't as important as a "real" child of hers would have been, she states in her book that she started drinking alcohol in earnest at thirteen.

Show business can seem like a balm for someone in need of loving attention. Whitney's drive, she claims, came from an attitude of "I'll show them! I'll be rich and famous! I'll be somebody! I'll show my birth mother that she was wrong to reject me!"

Looking for social and emotional acceptance with low self-esteem made her vulnerable. She started out as a young singer in Chicago and was soon trying out for her dream job: a Broadway play. After early rejections, she was cast in *Top Banana*, a burlesque show, which I guarantee you featured tall, beautiful women being broadly objectified by the male comics. She played Miss Holland and wore a revealing costume with twin propellers on her breasts. As someone who once dressed as a giant sexy cigar in a Broadway number, I can empathize. It's a job.

A few years later, she moved to Hollywood with her husband and became a working actor. Whitney wrote of being chased by men constantly—in the offices of Hollywood as well as its streets. She said "that's just Hollywood" to herself. Two Jenga blocks removed. She turned down billionaire

ABOVE: Grace Lee Whitney claimed she was responsible for introducing *Star Trek* to the miniskirt because she wanted to show off her legs.

ABOVE RIGHT: Rand was very much the captain's secretary, and the first time we see her, she is making sure he is eating properly.

OPPOSITE: Incredibly, the studio actually sent this picture of Grace Lee Whitney out to promote *Star Trek* even though it had nothing to do with her character.

Howard Hughes's proposition to become his mistress, and saw turning him down for her husband's sake as a foolish decision.

When she was asked to go under contract with Universal, her husband told her she could choose the contract or him. Another Jenga block. She chose him again, but continued her career, appearing in the movies *Some Like It Hot* (1959) and *Irma la Douce* (1963), in both cases as part of a corps of beautiful blondes. During this time, she had two children and was a functioning alcoholic but was unaware that her drinking was taking its toll.

A guest role on a short-lived Gene Roddenberry show, *The Lieutenant*, led to her being cast on *Star Trek*. When she arrived for filming, she was unhappy to see that Rand would be dressed in a turtleneck and pants. She told Roddenberry and costume designer William Ware Theiss that they were covering up "her best assets" and suggested they put her in a miniskirt to show off her legs. It's easy to forget that in the 1960s the miniskirt was a symbol of power and liberation...

But it also suited Roddenberry, who enthusiastically embraced the idea and from that point on dressed all the female crew members in increasingly short skirts. In Whitney's case it was accompanied by precarious basket-weave hair, which consisted of two blonde wigs that Roddenberry seemed determined to get ever taller to seem even more futuristic.

OBJECT OF DESIRE

The portrayal of Yeoman Rand has not aged well. With a tiny miniskirt, vulnerable pout, and a propensity for running to the captain for protection, she was the picture of performative female sexuality. Tellingly in *Star Trek: Strange New Worlds*, the idea that the captain would have an attractive yeoman has been abandoned.

> The portrayal of Yeoman Rand has not aged well. With a tiny miniskirt, vulnerable pout, and a propensity for running to the captain for protection, she was the picture of performative female sexuality.

In the original series, Rand often seems to be there as an object of desire. In "Charlie X," she is the recipient of the powerful teen's crush. She lets him know how to treat a lady (don't slap her on the butt), but refers him to the captain for more instruction. There is a strange moment when the angry, powerful boy makes her disappear from her quarters, wearing a one-shouldered negligee, only to have her suddenly appear later, on the bridge. Even though circumstances are dire, there is a moment where she is ashamed to be dressed in her negligee. Kirk quickly reassures her, which I read to mean that he forgave her for being on the bridge in her nightgown. What else could she have done under

the circumstances? Other than not wear an elaborate, pink one-shouldered negligee while sleeping alone?

Most worrying is a sexual assault scene in "The Enemy Within," where Kirk is split into Good Kirk and Evil Kirk (I know that's an oversimplification and if you know, you

know). He attacks her in her quarters, and she fights him off. Nonetheless, at the end of the episode, Spock is certain that there are aspects of the bestial Kirk that she will miss.

Far more upsetting to me is the way Whitney recounts the filming of the scene that follows the assault. It was a close-up of Rand emotionally recounting the assault to Good Kirk, Spock, and McCoy. It was the last scene before lunch. Everyone always wants to get it done as fast as possible and be able to move to the next scene after the break. Whitney recounts that just before she started her close-up, Shatner came forward and slapped her across the face. The shock made her weep and she was grateful. In her mind, Shatner knew instinctively what she "needed" and helped her give a good performance by making her cry. A film crew eager to get to lunch praised her for being a one-take wonder, reinforcing the moment as good with positive attention. I wonder what would have happened if the roles had been reversed and she had struck him.

The closest we get to seeing Rand's inner life is in "Miri." She, Kirk, and McCoy are part of a landing party that is trapped on a planet when they catch a disease that produces horrible lesions. Horrified by the marks on her body, she confesses that she used to want the captain to look at her legs, but not now when they are hideous.

CONSTANT PRESSURE

Throughout her career, Whitney was cast in the kind of roles that depended on her appearance, so who can blame her for worrying about it as much as Yeoman Rand? Early in filming, Theiss told her that she was too heavy so his costumes weren't looking as good as they should. He suggested she go to a doctor and get a prescription for diet pills. She did, and began a routine of amphetamines during the day and drinking alcohol at night to be able to sleep. Remove a whole bunch of Jenga blocks.

There were other problems, too. According to Majel Barrett, Roddenberry found that giving the captain an almost-girlfriend on the ship restricted the kind of storylines

Star Trek could tell. If the captain had an encounter with a beautiful alien woman, the audience might feel he was being unfaithful to Rand.

It's common knowledge that during a Friday night wrap party, someone she only refers to as "the Executive" got Whitney alone in an empty office. With promises of expanding her part, he asked her to improvise sexy scenes with him. She recounts that at first she was excited by the possibility of career advancement, but it quickly turned into a frightening situation. They had both been drinking, and the Executive got aggressive and demanding when she tried to talk her way out of the situation. She was too scared to do anything but comply with his demand for oral sex.

On the following Tuesday, Grace Lee Whitney was informed that she was being dropped by *Star Trek*. At the time, she was convinced that the two events were directly related. Years later, she said she was less certain. Could the Executive have caused her dismissal to cover up what he'd done? Yes. Could it have been that the creatives made a mistake by trying to have a powerful dynamic between two characters who aren't equally grounded? Yes. Could it have been that the diet pills and drinking affected her professionalism on set? Yes.

The tragic part to me is Whitney's complete cultural adaptation to the male-oriented world she was trying to survive. In her words: "Getting ahead in Hollywood is often a matter of knowing who holds the power, then finding a way to get close to that power, and even in bed with that power.

I had refused to get in bed with the power. It may have been a morally defensible choice—but it was tactically stupid, in terms of my career. Inwardly, I kicked myself for not playing along, because in the end I was just as violated and exploited by this man as if I had—yet I had no career advancement to show for it. Bad move, Whitney, I thought. You've done it to yourself again." She saw it as her mistake for playing the game wrong.

She went into a deep spiral after being fired. It took her years to recover, but by the time *Star Trek* made its big-screen debut in 1979, she was sober and had found God. Those two things gave her a purpose that Hollywood hadn't. She makes a brief appearance in the first movie, now promoted to transporter operator, and returned in three of the sequels. She made her last *Star Trek* appearance in "Flashback," a *Voyager* episode that revisits Tuvok's time on the *U.S.S. Excelsior* under Captain Sulu. We discover that Rand has become the ship's communications officer—like Uhura, a character who *Star Trek* and the culture at large had treated much better.

OPPOSITE TOP: Rand is embarrassed to find herself on the bridge in her negligee after Charlie Evans makes her vanish because she isn't attracted to him.

OPPOSITE BOTTOM: Like so many of the original series women, Rand is distressed by anything that affects her appearance.

ABOVE: The captain's yeoman was originally going to be a major character, but plans changed and Rand was dropped early on.

Nichelle Nichols as
LT. UHURA

You felt it right away. The first time I met Nichelle was many years ago at a convention. She was dignified, gracious, and warm and, unlike others, remembered my name the next time we met. The stereotype of the older woman actor protecting her position from the younger ones is a real thing in Hollywood, but Nichelle was only inclusive and encouraging, and I saw that her interactions with the fans were purposeful and kind. I believe a lot of us that came after her learned about the social responsibility that comes with being a part of the franchise from her.

Uhura is one of the most important female characters who ever appeared in *Star Trek*—in fact, not only in *Star Trek* but in all of television. In 1966, putting a Black woman in a starship was a big step forward. Roddenberry's decision to make her an officer was important. It was rare for any woman to be shown in a position of authority, and it was virtually unheard of for a Black woman. Just seeing Uhura on the bridge inspired a generation of Black girls and women.

When Nichelle auditioned for *Star Trek*, she was an accomplished singer-dancer-actor—what Broadway calls a triple threat. Born in 1934, she had dreams of being a ballerina, but ballet companies only allowed women of color to join in 1955, by which time she was twenty-one and considered too old to start a career in ballet, so she found another route to her passion.

At sixteen, she was already touring with Duke Ellington. She had a child at eighteen, and continued to sing in clubs, performed in productions local to Chicago, and danced in the 1959 film *Porgy and Bess*. She has been quoted as saying that the ultimate for a performer like her was Broadway, and she was ambitious and determined to get there. In a filmed interview with William Miles for his documentary *Black Stars in Orbit* in 1989, she describes her dreams of stardom with a smile: "I'll get a Jaguar, I'll wear pretty clothes..." but

"a funny thing happened" on the way to those dreams. She says she didn't set out to change the world, but, "I got a job." Lt. Uhura changed not only the trajectory of her life, but also the trajectory of many others'.

An officer who was fourth in command, Uhura was an immediate visual indicator that it wasn't exclusively a White man's world set three hundred years in the future.

ON THE BRIDGE

As the communications officer, she has been called the *Enterprise*'s telephone operator, but Tamia Harper of the *SYFY Sistas* podcast writes that seeing a woman like her changed everything. Harper was a science-fiction fan but had never read or seen a Black person included in a story. Not only did she prove women should work alongside men, but also when Lt. Uhura had a message to give her crew mates, they listened attentively.

Nichelle's performance in "Charlie X" shows she has the authority to interrupt the captain when she needs a signature, but it's her singing while Spock plays the lute that really proves her talent. It's a scene that, if not performed with the right tone, could be ridiculous and take you right out of the story. If she had made it an opportunistic showcase of her talents, it would have looked over-the-top and unbelievable that the communications officer was suddenly doing a cabaret performance. Instead, she manages to convey a playful naturalism that sells the lighthearted moment.

In another scene, she takes the news of the death of a crew member with a stoicism you would expect from an explorer. In every scene, she was treated with respect and didn't have to reduce herself to gaining the men's acceptance by behaving in stereotypically gendered ways. There was no batting of the eyes—just a calm, measured professionalism.

Women, from astronaut Mae Jemison to political leader Stacey Abrams to actor Whoopi Goldberg, cite Nichelle Nichols as inspiring them and expanding their vision of what the future could be. I interviewed Vicki Payne, who told me she watched the show as a child in 1966 and she was struck by a Black woman on TV who was "dressed nice. She wasn't a slave. She wasn't a buffoon, and she wasn't a servant, and that was very impressive to us because back then in the Sixties, the darkest person I ever saw on television was Desi Arnaz in a nice role."

Uhura was a catalyst for the storyline in "The Trouble with Tribbles," she is competent and necessary in "Who Mourns for Adonais?" when she uses her duotronic repair tool (a woman with technical skills!), and she is an alluring and formidable woman in "Mirror, Mirror." I watched "Plato's Stepchildren," in which Nichelle was one half of television's first interracial kiss, with real admiration for all our heroes. The physicality of moving as if another entity had taken control requires commitment and a willingness to look foolish, especially considering the time that was given to these sequences. Toward the end, Lt. Uhura and Nurse Chapel are beamed to the mind controller's planet, and what happened next seemed inevitable. The storyline was designed to make the captain and lieutenant guiltless in crossing a 1960s cultural line—they were being controlled! They didn't want to!—and the first televised kiss between a White man and a Black woman made history. According to Nichelle, this was such a radical event for TV that several takes of the scene were done so they could have a version without the kiss in case the network balked. Shatner and Nichols evidently made sure only the take with the kiss could be used by messing up all the others.

Being a pioneer isn't easy. Discrimination, and her frustration with not being given enough to sink her creative teeth into, made the first year of *Star Trek* difficult for Nichelle. Life in TV is hierarchical, with people under contract (hired for a season) being treated as more essential, and therefore treated better, than those with recurring roles (people hired for one show at a time). In order to slip Nichols past *Trek*'s tight budget, Roddenberry made her a day player, promising to get her as many shows as possible. This meant she was only guaranteed employment for one day at a time, which would lead to a real feeling of job insecurity. Getting lines

ABOVE: TV shows were under pressure to cast Black actors, but *Star Trek* went into new territory when it put a Black woman on the bridge in a senior position.

OPPOSITE: Nichelle Nichols looking amazing out of costume.

NICHELLE NICHOLS AS LT. UHURA

cut would add to a feeling of not mattering, as would the daily doses of thoughtless disrespect she received—from someone telling the mailroom not to bother to deliver her mail to being denied entry to the studio by a guard at the gate.

Nichelle asked Roddenberry to let her out of her contract so that she could pursue Broadway. She always told the story that he asked her to take the weekend to think over her decision. It seems fateful that this same weekend she was invited to an NAACP function, where she was asked to give some time to a fan. The fan turned out to be Dr. Martin Luther King Jr., who told her *Star Trek* was the show he and his wife Coretta let their children stay up to see. When she told him her plans to leave the show, he said, "You cannot. Three hundred years from now, we are here. When we see you, we see ourselves, and we see ourselves as intelligent and beautiful and proud."

She told Roddenberry what King had said, and decided to stay. He gave her a contract of nine out of sixteen episodes, a massive step up from day player. But now, from just striving for the good life of a successful actor, she had a bigger purpose. She understood the responsibility that had been given to her as a representative of her people, and she took it on.

LASTING IMPACT

Five years after the show was canceled, Nichelle traveled to a convention, where, for the first time, a NASA scientist was given a panel. His name was Dr. Von Puttkamer, and as she listened to him outlining NASA's long-range plans, she realized that people like her didn't feature in the plan he was outlining. "I didn't see myself as a Black and I didn't see myself as a woman."

She felt disenfranchised from "something that had the potential to affect our lives in the most incredible ways and I wanted to be there, not in fantasy but in reality."

> She understood the responsibility that had been given to her as a representative of her people, and she took it on.

She visited the headquarters of NASA in Washington, and realized that in all other capacities, other than astronauts, there was in fact great diversity. In an effort to get the word out that women and people of color were actually involved in the space program, she started writing articles.

Her relationship with the space program grew as she developed a youth symposium and wrote educational musicals to encourage children to cultivate an interest in science. In 1977, a shuttle launch was planned that would be the first of its kind with male and female scientists being recruited instead of simply pilots. When the word went out, few people of color responded.

Nichelle told the administrators that it would take a celebrity who people trusted implicitly to get the word out that NASA was serious about diversity. She suggested Coretta King, John Denver, and Bill Cosby as possibilities. When they chose her instead, she picked up the gauntlet, and the numbers told the story of her success.

Before Nichols was spokesperson, there were one hundred applications sent in from women and thirty-four from minorities. After she started work, those numbers jumped

to 1,649 women and one thousand minority applications. *Star Trek* was a platform Nichelle used to launch diversity into space. From a performer who dreamed about Jaguars and pretty clothes, she cultivated activism in herself and changed how people saw and dreamed of the future.

Upon her passing in 2022, President Joe Biden said, "Our nation is forever indebted to inspiring artists like Nichelle Nichols, who showed us a future where unity, dignity, and respect are cornerstones of every society." Her grace and activism form a ground that all the women of *Star Trek* who have come after her stand on.

OPPOSITE: Uhura was given an inner life that made use of Nichelle's abilities as a singer.

ABOVE: Uhura (and Nichelle) would inspire a generation of women, who were shown that there was a place for them in the future.

STAR TREK'S GUEST STARS

Hollywood in the 1960s

The women who wore the costumes that looked ready to malfunction at any moment were young, thin, and beautiful. Evidently, in space, you never gained weight and you thoughtfully died at forty.

Beauty was an asset for them, for sure—even for Sandy Gimpel, who played the Salt Vampire in "The Man Trap" and one of the Talosians in "The Cage." She was fully covered with prosthetics and didn't need to be attractive to do the job, but she too was beautiful and remains so to this day. I assumed these were actresses who did this epic show and had built a career around this one credit. I was more than naive.

I was able to gather these original *Star Trek* women because BarBara Luna, who played the sultry Lt. Marlena Moreau in "Mirror, Mirror," has formed a network with them all. From what I could gather, it serves as friendship, information-sharing, and solidarity at conventions. With the organization of a general, she kept us all on track to

make this meeting happen. I invited them to lunch.

As the day approached, as well as preparing the food and baking a cake, I went on IMDb to learn a bit more about BarBara Luna, France Nuyen (Elaan in "Elaan of Troyius"), Sandy Gimpel, Tanya Lemani George (Kara in "Wolf in the Fold"), and Irene Tsu. Irene was not in the original series but in *Voyager*, playing Harry Kim's mother, Mary Kim. But Irene was active in the 1960s as an actress, and I wanted to hear her experiences, too. These were women with extensive careers outside of *Star Trek*. They had been stars and working actors in the Sixties, and I asked about casting couches, being treated fairly, and if being a woman had limited their ability to navigate Hollywood at that time.

Tanya spoke candidly and told me that there were definitely situations in which men expected sex from her, although she always managed to stay ahead of it. She said there were bad men active at the time, but that there were men who were supportive and decent too. She told a story of one man who demonstrated to her how to walk like a woman, swaying his hips just so. It reminded me of a time when director J.D. Swackhammer showed me how to move my hand from my waist to my hip as I got out of the elevator to heighten the allure of the moment. J.D. was a big man but became a seductive sylph as he demonstrated the move. Being a sexy woman is often performative, and who better than a man to teach you what they want? Luna said that no one must have found her attractive because she had never had a problem with sexual demands in the business. She went on, however, to say that an old character actor gave her a phrase to use if anyone ever tried anything with her. It must have been salty because she refused to repeat it, but when she used it in the moment before being accosted, it worked, and the man backed down and let her go. France, through most of this, remained completely quiet.

It seemed to me to be the last thing they wanted to speak about, and that if unwanted things happened to them, they felt they had been weak, stupid, or worse. Finally, Sandy spoke up. She described being backed into a corner by a

man while they were in his office after he had removed his pants. She looked him fiercely in the eye and threatened to scream so loud it would bring the whole studio running. He took her threat seriously and ended the standoff. It wasn't the only time she defended herself. But this was Hollywood at the time, and no one said that anything like this happened on *Trek*.

When I asked *Star Trek*'s casting director Joe D'Agosta if actresses in the 1960s were thought of as party girls ready to have a transactional relationship in exchange for a job, Joe said he had to give me a yes and no answer: "When I came in, a woman was about her skill as an actress. But there was a guy in MGM, he kept a script and the directions said, 'She takes off her blouse.' And he would insert that page into the script he was casting, show it to an actress, and say, 'We'll have to see you.'" The habit of bartering with actresses—a line or two in a project in return for a quickie—was a reality. Not one that

OPPOSITE LEFT: BarBara Luna played the captain's woman in the Mirror Universe.

OPPOSITE RIGHT: Actresses such as Luna had masses of talent, but wouldn't have been cast if they weren't alluring.

ABOVE: In the 1960s, Tanya Lemani George made a career as a belly dancer, making appearances in several TV shows, including *Star Trek*.

Mr. D'Agosta took advantage of. When one young woman read for a part, she told Joe, "I'm told that to make it, you have to sleep with somebody. And if I got to sleep with someone, I'd rather sleep with you." Joe told her no. He gave her the part on her ability.

Andreea Kindryd, Gene L. Coon's assistant on the original *Trek*, flatly said, "The Casting Couch was not a joke. It was real, and it was accepted." I got a sense that these women had gotten so accustomed to the flow of the current against them that they no longer questioned why it was there. They just worked harder against it. To make it as a woman in Hollywood, you needed double competency.

Their strength and discipline is so ingrained that you see it to this day. When I offered to stop for bathroom breaks,

Luna told me, "No, keep going." She had arrived at my house in movie-star mode, with high heels, hair and makeup, and a skintight sequin dress. Her dress would take too long to get out of and would hold everyone up. I suddenly understood why she ate nothing at lunch, and why she asked for only small amounts of water. Where another person would have shown up in comfortable clothes, or inconvenienced a crew, she did neither. She showed up in the image of a glittery star, and the only person who would suffer for it would be her.

I was reminded of my attitude in *Deep Space Nine*: I was a woman with a job and two children, but if anyone was going to suffer, it would be me. Having children and a career was too much to ask the world for, and I did whatever I needed to—usually to the physical and emotional detriment of myself.

I sensed this with all these women—an acceptance of the rules and the real need to play by them if you wanted a seat at the Hollywood table. Unless they had to defend themselves. Then, they took the "chance." But each one who had fought off a man then said how frightened they were afterward of being fired. When they weren't fired as a result of saying no, their relief was as if it was a bullet they managed to dodge yet again. Irene mentioned that she was safe from this: Other men in the business knew that she was Frank Sinatra's girl, and they were mindful of his ability to cause problems for them. She was left alone. It seems that the threat from certain men was real, but no one was expecting the current to change, so the alternative was being an even stronger swimmer. Fight back, or have a powerful man in your life.

OPPOSITE: France Nuyen's character, Elaan, was imperious and beautiful. She had several costume changes, all of which were revealing. This silver outfit was so fragile that it tore repeatedly.

LEFT: Sandy Gimpel was inside the Salt Monster in *Star Trek*'s first episode, "The Man Trap." Stuntwomen were rare in 1966, and Sandy was also a dancer, who appeared alongside Elvis.

DOROTHY FONTANA

Few people have had as big an effect on Star Trek *as Dorothy Fontana. It was Dorothy who Roddenberry handed an early draft of the first* Star Trek *script to, with the command, "Read that, give me your opinion." She went on to write or co-write ten episodes of the original series and was the story editor from the latter part of the first season until the end of the second—meaning that she commented on, or even rewrote, every episode made during that time.*

After *Trek* ended, she returned to produce the animated series and came back for the first half a season of *Star Trek: The Next Generation*. Outside of *Star Trek,* she was a prolific writer, with credits on everything from *Ben Casey* to *The Six Million Dollar Man*.

As a young girl, she dreamed of being a novelist and wrote for her "own amusement." Like so many young women at the time, she did the sensible thing and went to college and got a degree, as an executive secretary, but she was always writing on the side. One of her first jobs when she got to Hollywood was as secretary to Samuel L. Peebles, who bought a script from her when she was only twenty-one. In their time together, she sold him even more script ideas and saw him as a mentor.

When Fontana started as a secretary for Roddenberry, she would read every script that came through the office and offer her comments. Roddenberry obviously recognized her experience and abilities. He gave her the chance to write episodes and eventually offered her the job of story editor. As writer Hannah Louise Shearer told me: "We [women writers] don't need to be elevated, we need to be allowed in. Unlock the door. Get out of the way." All Fontana needed was to be let in. Her love of writing seemed to take precedence over ego or position. As Andreea Kindryd told me, Dorothy loved "rodeos, cowboys, and writing for the show." That *Star Trek* was "the wagon train to the stars" must have suited her just fine. She excelled at writing Westerns, and said: "Fairly often there was a woman who wasn't helpless and that was nice."

But she was operating in a world where being a woman put you at an obvious professional disadvantage. Only 10 percent of the Writer's Guild were women at the time. "If there was a choice between a man and a woman" for a job, "the man would get it." Most women who were able to work as writers stayed in the lane of comedies or soap operas, or teamed with a man who would give them the required entrée. When she discovered her scripts wouldn't get read because a woman's name graced the cover, Dorothy changed her name to D.C. Fontana. She found that once a producer read her material, they were less inclined to be bothered that it came from a woman. Dorothy became one of a handful of women in Hollywood who wrote action-adventure, and her down-to-earth attitudes and passion for writing stood her in good stead. It couldn't have been easy to be a woman in that environment, but Dorothy earned her place at the table.

Because Fontana was at the heart of the writing team, she infused *Trek* with her view of the world. It's impossible to pull the threads apart and see how the show would have been different without her—to know what was her, what was Gene Roddenberry, and what was Gene Coon—but there's no question that she played a huge part in shaping *Star Trek*. She wrote some of the original series' most important episodes, giving Spock his first love affair in "This Side of Paradise" and parents in "Journey to Babel"— not just a father, as you might have seen in a lot of TV shows, but also a mother.

EMPOWERING WOMEN

She was clear that she wanted to give the female characters more to do, and her episodes often had strong roles for women, but looking back they rarely seem that liberated by modern standards. For example, in "This Side of Paradise," Leila Kalomi feels her life is incomplete without Spock. Maybe Dorothy was trapped in the amber of her time, trying to give women stronger roles but still seeing the world, and women's place in it, the way a male-dominated culture had taught her to. Or, more likely, she knew what would be accepted and what wouldn't by the people in charge. A case in point was what she wanted to do in "Friday's Child." This was an attempt to show the kind of woman who was never seen on TV. Eleen was, in Fontana's words, "a selfish woman" who was willing to sacrifice her child to preserve her own life. That turned out to be too radical for Roddenberry.

One of Fontana's big contributions to the original series was also one of her last. In the third season, she decided that the Romulans should be a matriarchal society and put a woman in charge. In "The Enterprise Incident," Kirk takes his ship into the Neutral Zone. He appears to have some kind of breakdown that leads to Spock changing sides and apparently killing his friend and captain. It turns out it's all a ruse to steal a cloaking device.

The character of the Romulan commander, played brilliantly by Joanne Linville, was meant to be every bit Kirk's equal. She's shrewd, intelligent, and authoritative. Or at least that's the way Fontana envisaged her. When rewrites played up her romantic interest in Spock, Fontana was furious. She had set out to create a strong woman only to see her rewritten as gullible. Fontana was so annoyed that she took her name off the script. She wanted to write a script in which we learn McCoy has a daughter, but was told that would be impossible, as the doctor was Kirk and Spock's contemporary. It infuriated her that the new producer, Fred Freiberger, insisted that McCoy was the same age as Kirk. He was ignoring the first two seasons, in which the writers and actors had always understood McCoy to be ten years older.

That Fontana was never considered as a possible head writer for a show whose conception she had been witness to is a tell of the times. Five years after the original series ended, it was revived as an animated show, and Fontana took control of the writing. By all accounts, Roddenberry would step in from time to time but mostly he left her to it. You can see that she made an effort to give the women stronger roles. Nurse Chapel, in particular, gets more screen time, and in one famous scene, Uhura takes the helm of the ship.

For all Fontana's successes, that animated series was the only time she got to actually run a show as the producer. However good her scripts were, the TV industry of her era wasn't prepared to put a woman in charge. In fact, many of the women writers I talked to told me that you were lucky if there was one slot for a woman writer—a state of affairs that persisted into the 1990s.

Those women writers all told me how much they admired Dorothy Fontana, who they saw as a pioneer. She showed them what was possible and laid the groundwork for all the women writers who came after her.

ABOVE: As a woman writing episodic television in the 1960s and 1970s, Dorothy Fontana was a true pioneer. She had a huge impact on *Star Trek* and inspired many of the women writers who followed her.

STAR TREK RETURNS

Star Trek: The Next Generation and the 1980s

Big hair, big shoulders, big credit card debt. Yes, I was there in the 1980s. Star Trek had been away, though. There had been movies—four of them, by that point—but now in 1987, the Enterprise was about to make its return to TV. Things had changed for everyone since Kirk, Spock, and McCoy had left the small screen in 1969, and particularly for women.

Ronald Reagan became the US president in 1981, and the wild 1970s turned into the conservative 1980s. Women accomplished a lot of firsts in politics and business but struggled with the difficulties of being pioneers when they got there. The right to an abortion, the ruling in 1973 of Roe v. Wade, had given women freedom and autonomy over their bodies. The pill was widespread, and marriage was no longer a given. Sexuality wasn't just something that men liked and women submitted to—it could be equally enjoyed by both sexes without consequences for the trajectory of a woman's life.

CHANGING TIMES

Popular TV offered us *Designing Women*, *The Cosby Show*, and *L.A. Law*. Oprah's daytime talk show gave us women who questioned the patriarchy they lived in. More women were graduating college than ever before, and as a result, the Eighties saw a lot of progress for women. Sandra Day O'Connor became the first woman on the Supreme Court, Geraldine Ferraro was nominated to run as a vice presidential candidate in 1984, and Sally Ride became the first American woman in space (Valentina Tereshkova had become the first woman in space, in 1963, but was not trained as an astronaut. It seems that this was a publicity opportunity for the Soviet Union).

Star Trek had played a role in encouraging women to enter the space program. Despite her limited screen time in the series, Nichelle Nichols spearheaded a NASA program to recruit women and minorities. It was a huge lesson that being invited to the party worked to increase opportunity and diversity.

When Paramount asked Gene Roddenberry to create a new *Star Trek* TV show, it was a given that women would play a bigger role. But in 1986, the world was still run by men who'd been brought up before anyone even knew the word "feminism." Reagan was born in 1911, and much of his worldview was formed before World War II. He referred to women in politics as "pretty aggressive gals" or "good little girls." They were aggressive if they disagreed with him, good little girls if they didn't. Writer Françoise Coste describes Reagan as an old-time conservative who believed in the old gender stereotypes.

Roddenberry was born ten years after Reagan, in 1921, and I can't help believing that the two men shared some of their ideas about women, but that's where the similarity ended. Reagan aligned himself firmly with the religious right, whereas Roddenberry took regular potshots at organized religion and embraced elements of the counterculture. Coste describes a line Reagan walked: against abortion and the Equal Rights Amendment (ERA), but aware that he needed the votes of these new fangled feminists.

Coste quotes him as saying that when he married his wife Nancy, who was an actor, it was ingrained in her to simply say, "If you try to make two careers work, one of them has to suffer." At the time of their marriage, they were both actors with vibrant careers, and Ronald Reagan was on the board of the Screen Actors Guild. She became a housewife who did charitable work. This, of course, is a viable and personal choice, but one he implied was necessary to make a life with him.

Gene's wife Majel played a leading role in the family business, organizing Lincoln Enterprises, the company they used to sell *Star Trek* merchandise. Gene could envision a world in which women could be starship captains, but he also liked to raise a hemline.

The 1980s were full of contradictions for women. Reagan managed to see that the ERA was not ratified, but for optical purposes, he and his advisers changed their language toward women ("homemaker" as opposed to "housewife"—a woman isn't married to a house). He added Sandra Day O'Connor to the Supreme Court, and formed a Women's Policy Committee, but it turned out to be a group of women handpicked for the religious right's approval.

STAR TREK SAVIOR

This was the world *Star Trek: The Next Generation* would be born into. And, just as it had in the 1960s, it happened because of a woman called Lucie. In the 1960s, Lucille Ball had put the series into development at her company Desilu. In 1985, Lucie Salhany saved the show when it was in development by suggesting that it could be made for first-run syndication. At the time, this idea was unheard of.

Salhany was the executive in charge of domestic television for Paramount and a bona fide *Trek* fan. If it hadn't been for her inspired suggestion, there's no question in my mind that *Star Trek* would have ended with the movies, but she throws all the credit back to Roddenberry and the creatives. She is one of the success stories for women in the Eighties, but described to me the hell it took to stay there.

She wanted to be clear that she understood and appreciated the privilege of her position, and that her treatment would have been worse if she were a woman of color, but she was excluded, sexually harassed, and had to fight for every inch she climbed.

Speaking of her time working with Rupert Murdoch at Fox, she said that "the battering was emotional, it was personal. 'You're a feminazi, you sided with Hillary Clinton.' Rupert would ask a question, and he'd say, 'Why don't you go home and ask what your husband thinks?'" *Vogue* was full of young models in power suits with kick-ass expressions. The real women in business were making strides, but if their expressions were grim, maybe it was the pure exhaustion of doing your job while having to prove, every step of the way, that you had the right to do it.

Of course, *Star Trek* was a TV show set in the future, so it didn't have to reflect the reality of the day. But it was still a TV show, and I knew all about those from personal experience.

I came to Hollywood the same year Lucie Salhany moved to Paramount, and I soon learned to live the schizophrenic life the culture of the time was serving up for women. My first meeting with a Los Angeles agent had him analyzing me with a pained expression. "I just don't know what box to put you in, Nana. I need to put you in a box so we can get you cast, but you...Are you pretty? Are you the girl next door? The best friend? You aren't enough of anything really." I naively said I could act, and that should get

OPPOSITE: Troi's ability to sense emotions played to traditional ideas about women's strengths.

LEFT: Dr. Crusher was both a physician and a mother, something *Star Trek* has rarely touched on since.

me jobs. But it wouldn't get me in the door, and I learned how to morph to be easily identifiable as a type.

Dynasty was a wildly popular TV show at the time that had two women pitted against each other in catfights that mirrored the binary way women were viewed. One was Krystle, a sweet, beautiful blonde wife; the other was Alexis, a morally questionable classic career bitch. As writer Susan J. Douglas put it, "Krystle just wanted to make her husband happy; Alexis wanted to control the world." Sweet traditional supportive woman or career bitch: What stereotype did you need for your story? I was ready to do what was required.

One look in my Nissan Sentra's back seat during the week told the story of the stereotypes in demand during this time. Back then, I could have as many as five auditions a day all over town, and I would pack a bag with changes

of clothes for each of them. For a sexy role for *Jake and the Fatman*, a tight skirt and low-cut top. For the unassuming, sweet girl (I was meant to intuit that this description meant "plain") who turns out to be evil on *Matlock*, a baby-doll dress plus cardigan and awkward glasses. Audition for *L.A. Law*? I had the power suit with the big shoulders hanging in the back seat. If I dyed my hair dark, I played evil temptresses. If I dyed it blonde, I played mothers and victims. It was a code I cracked to stereotype myself for the convenience of the executives in the business, and it got me work.

So how would *Star Trek* fit into these stereotypes? The actors delivering the lines may be the ones to stay in viewers' minds, but it's the writers and producers who decide what stories to tell. Roddenberry had assembled a team who, like him, hailed from a different era. Bob Justman, Dorothy Fontana, and David Gerrold were veterans of the original series. Bob Lewin was a year older than Roddenberry and had written for *Rawhide*, *Mannix*, and *Dr. Kildare*. Together, this group of people set about creating a new crew for their new *Enterprise*.

Roddenberry wasn't going to put Krystle or Alexis on the bridge, but the writers still had boxes they wanted to tick. One of the first ideas they had was that there would be a cool science officer, who was inspired by Sean Young's character in *Blade Runner*. They even wondered if they could get her for the role. The *Enterprise*'s security officer, who in those days was called Macha Hernandez, was based on the female marine Vasquez in *Aliens*. For one brief period, Wesley Crusher became Leslie Crusher—still a genius and presumably a captain in waiting, but now a young girl. How different would *Star Trek* have been if those ideas had stuck around?

As the development process went on, the characters started to change. The science officer morphed into the ship's counselor, and Roddenberry decide to add a doctor, who was a woman and Wesley's mother.

For all the writers' ambition, there was still an emphasis on what were seen as the characters' "feminine" qualities. The science officer's "cool exterior" belies "her inner emotionality." The casting notes for Dr. Crusher say she has a "natural beauty that is...incredibly compelling." Macha is seen as a contradiction. Her "standard of beauty would have been a shock to the beholder. She is a strong, wiry woman; muscular and beautiful at the same time. She keeps her hair cut short, almost in a (you should pardon the expression) 'butch' haircut."

That wasn't the worst of it. At one point, they thought about giving Troi four breasts, prompting Dorothy Fontana to ask how they planned to arrange them.

Roddenberry wanted to write about an idealized future, but he knew his staff were products of the twentieth century. He even wrote a memo warning them that "all of us have accumulated by now during our 20th Century lives a staggering burden of soon-to-be-outmoded values and political ideas." It's one thing to know what you should be trying to do; it's quite another to actually deliver it.

Looking back from thirty years in the future, it's as if *Star Trek*'s female characters couldn't be strong and in control without being like a man. At the time, feminism was as splintered as women's fashion. The movement was growing and fragmenting as underserved groups banded together to see to their own needs. Women of color were questioning racism in the movement. Equality Feminism sought to emphasize the way men and women were physically and mentally similar to prove that women deserved a seat at the patriarchal table. Their point was that

> Equality feminism sought to emphasize the way men and women were physically and mentally similar to prove that women deserved a seat at the patriarchal table.

OPPOSITE: In 1987, the idea of making the head of security a woman was still seen as "edgy." I can't help wondering how different the show would have been if Denise Crosby had stayed and Tasha hadn't been killed off.

ABOVE: TNG acknowledged that plenty of starships were commanded by women. Tryla Scott was the youngest person to ever make captain, but the show wasn't ready for her to be more than a guest star.

a woman could cultivate traditionally male attributes and have control over her emotions in order to make business decisions just like a man. With a little self-control and discipline, she can have a rock-hard Jane Fonda body that can do the same physical jobs a man does. Difference Feminism fought this idea that implied a woman's strengths weren't as valid as a man's. By adopting typically male attributes, such as aggression and ambition, female strengths like empathy and caring for loved ones would be lost. Instead of attempting to work within the patriarchy, Difference Feminism sought to tear it down and rebuild a new social order.

Actresses of that generation had learned the hard way that Hollywood was only interested in particular ideas of womanhood. I had spent eleven years in a feminist-bent girls' school in Manhattan. If I had gone to Princeton, I might have increased my resilience, but I didn't. I entered the business at seventeen, and my expectations of equality and my own ability started to seem like a naive idea in the face of how things really worked. In Hollywood, it became clear: pick a box. You can be cute, but then you better have a hard body to go with that attitude. You could be amiable and funny, but then it's a given your body is larger, and although you have sexual urges, they will be played for laughs or groans. You can be a leading lady, but that requires big breasts and lots of hair, or a career woman, which probably means you're a bitch as well. I'm using the word "bitch" a lot, because it was used a lot. But when I would see the word in a breakdown for a character I was auditioning for, I would get excited. It meant I could draw outside the lines and not have to be obsequious to the men in the story. Unfortunately, I never played one that was also supportive of other women.

It seemed like there was a lot of attention, not only in Hollywood, to how women presented themselves in the 1980s. And, of course, being focused on appearance and pushing the fun of a catfight didn't leave a lot of time for women to support each other. There were targeted consciousness-raising gatherings to wake up women to how the culture was biased, but how much could they do against the phenomena of MTV and *Dynasty*? There were

all these boxes for women to fit in. There wasn't a thought that all of it could exist on a spectrum of each woman's choosing. You had to jump in a box.

There would be no bitches in *Star Trek*, though. Roddenberry established a new rule: In the future, no one would argue. Everyone would be enlightened and cooperative. I'd be amazed if it was what he wanted, but that instantly cut out all those interesting women.

If you did decide to become a career woman, it came with the cultural caveat that assumed you were ready to do it all. One of the most ubiquitous commercials of the day was a perfume ad that could be hummed by most women in the Eighties. I took the bait and saw it as an empowering anthem that meant we were not only capable of living up to our potential in the workforce but also could be nurturing mothers and sexy wives. Yahoo, yes! We could do it *all*, and have it all.

> *"I can bring home the bacon, fry it up in a pan*
> *And never let you forget you're a man*
> *I can work till five o'clock*
> *Come home and read you 'Tickety Tock'*
> [A man's voice was added in a second version to please those women's libbers:]
> *Tonight, I'm gonna cook for the kids*
> [Wait, but not for me? I still do that too?]
> *And if it's loving you want*
> *I can give you the shivering fits*
> *Cause I'm a woman"*

—Enjoli perfume commercial, 1982

So, my feeling was, if you weren't meeting these goals, or if you got tired or grumpy, or needed care or sleep while you were attempting to be Enjoli's twenty-four-hour woman, something was wrong with you. Not the expectations, you. Do it all, and be nurturing and sweet about it, too. Pick a box, pick a feminism, and listen to what the media is selling you. The overall message? Whatever and whoever you are, if you're a woman, you're just not quite enough.

ABOVE: The miniskirt was so closely associated with *Star Trek* that it almost made a return with TNG. Some of the other ideas for the women's uniforms involved exposing unexpected areas of flesh.

THERE IS A NUMBER in the Broadway musical *Gypsy* where three strippers sing their advice to a young amateur. "You gotta get a gimmick, if you want to be a star." The joke is each of them shows their "star worthy" routines, which turn out to be identical in content; only the costumes change.

In the Eighties, fashion sometimes felt like dress-up. With the emergence of cable networks, MTV was able to show videos of rock stars dressed to extremes to make their unique mark on the world, and the world copied these styles en masse. Big hair, punk rock, glam bands; the sexual freedom and the blurring of gender stereotypes caused the fashion that defined them to sweep across the culture. Madonna dressed like a schoolgirl who had found her grandmother's clothes trunk, if that grandmother happened to have a chorus-girl past. Feminine, empowered, and sexual in her "Material Girl" music video, she was the boss of all those male dancers.

This was one brand of female empowerment, but there was also the Reagan-era message of wealth equals personal value in the video. She was making the empowered choice of who to date, but the song came to the conclusion that it was men with cash. In all her videos, her look dramatically changed, so it seemed to me she was falling into the same trap of jumping into various boxes of performative femininity, trying on all the different aspects of womanhood, one by one, but never integrated.

Another huge celebrity influencer was Jane Fonda. Her workout ethic democratized having physical strength and made workout wear, complete with headband, a fashion trend, and yet another standard for women to meet. Women in the workplace as a force to be dealt with was reflected in power suit dressing, which could be sleekly feminine or an iteration of a man's suit. But either way, they always came with exaggerated shoulder pads. After work as a dancer on Broadway, I would stand in line to be able to dance at Studio 54. After being rejected by the bouncer several times, I bought a tuxedo, slicked my short hair back with my show makeup still on, and got in every time. In the Eighties, a gimmick definitely helped.

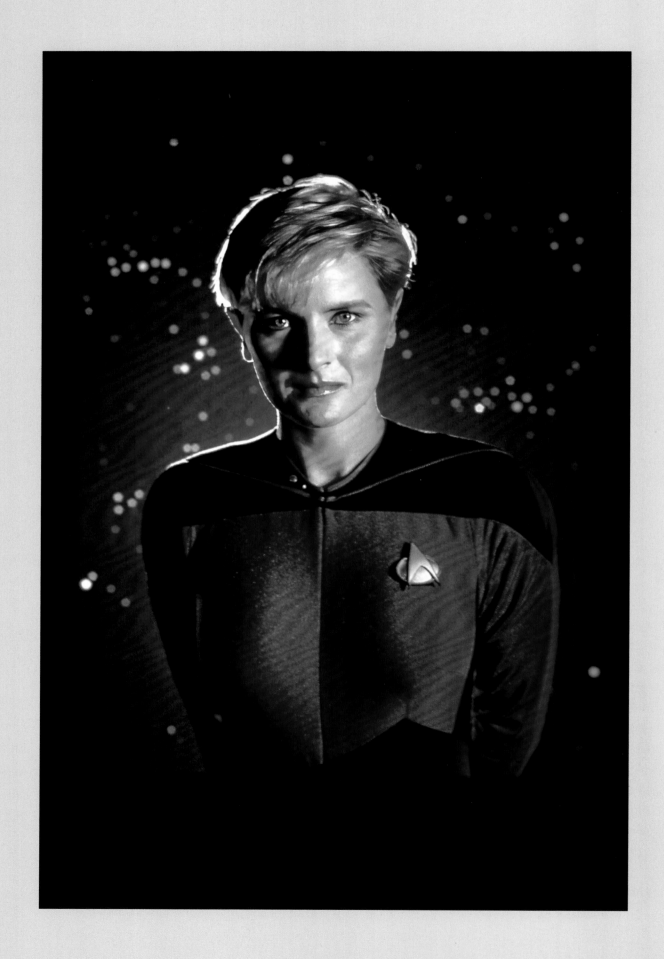

Denise Crosby as
LT. TASHA YAR

The character of Tasha Yar started life as Diabla "Macha" Hernandez, a muscular woman inspired by Jenette Goldstein's female marine in Aliens. *Looking back over the memos, you can see that in a very 1980s way, the* Enterprise's *female security officer was meant to challenge gender stereotypes. Macha was a tough woman who could hold her own with the men. But, oh boy, nobody forgot that she was a woman.*

The Writer's Guide (an internal document given to new writers) describes her as having "a very female body, she is capable of pinning most crewmen to the mat—or being just an exciting sensual and intellectual challenge to the males who enjoy (win or lose) full equality between the genders." The words sound right-minded, but the haze of objectification hangs over them.

Producers of *Star Trek: The Next Generation* were looking at different ethnicities, and Macha could have been Asian or Hispanic. In fact, Marina Sirtis, who has Greek origins, was originally in the running for the role, while Denise Crosby was up for Troi, who was seen as a sophisticated and "mysterious" character.

At some point during the casting process, Roddenberry decided to switch the actors around, and Denise became Yar, who by now was of Ukrainian descent. Today, the idea of a warrior who looks like Denise is commonplace, but in 1987, it must have seemed radical. The Writer's Guide promised that Yar would be a regular member of the away teams, so Denise had high hopes for her new role.

I first met Denise in 1987 when we both guest-starred in Pat Morita's series *Ohara*. The lovely blonde who was stealing my TV husband was an open and charming young woman I sat next to at the catered meal somewhere near Pacific Coast Highway, where we were shooting. She was different from the typical young women I met in the business. There was no sense of competition between us, and she was kind, supportive, even curious about me and my life in and out of the business. Unselfconsciously beautiful, Denise was a real professional on set, ready to collaborate and do what it took to make the piece better. There wasn't a lot of time spent ingratiating herself to power, which is a thing that's easier to spot than one might think. There were plenty of actresses who would transform in response to the sudden appearance of a star, producer, or studio executive.

Denise is a free spirit who follows her own instincts. She is the daughter of a single mother, Marilyn Miller, who became pregnant during a relationship with Dennis Crosby, son of the legendary star Bing Crosby. Marilyn brought up her daughter alone, however, so Denise barely knew her father and never met her famous grandfather. With no real emotional connection from her father's side, she greatly benefited from having a mother who supported her without reservation.

> In 1987, a warrior woman was very much a forward-looking idea. But Tasha is a product of her time.

At twenty-two, an opportunity came up for her to pose for *Playboy*, and her mother encouraged her to pursue it. Denise had long curly hair at the time, and the photographer set up test shots to look like a pastoral painting, complete with bare breasts, a corset, flowing skirts, and animals in a field. Denise felt it was antithetical to who she was and to how she wanted to be represented. But how can a young woman wield any kind of control over her image with a powerful photographer, a big corporation like *Playboy*, a legend such as Hugh Hefner? Back then, certainly, you didn't. There was no possibility of control for a woman in this scenario other than saying no and stepping aside to make room for the hundreds of eager women behind her. So, she took control of the one thing that was in her power. She went to the Vidal Sassoon Salon in Beverly Hills and told them to cut off all her hair.

When she met with the photographer again, he was incensed and told her she had ruined her chances. After all,

OPPOSITE: Most of Tasha's interactions were with the captain, and we didn't learn much about what she did with her private life.

PAGE 55: Having a female warrior like Tasha was something new for *Star Trek*. Tasha was an important step along the way to characters like Major Kira and La'An Noonien-Singh.

she had signed contracts, they had already done test shots. The magazine's star photographer happened to be at the offices and was witness to all this. He was inspired to take more test shots, this time with a theme that felt more natural to Denise. If Hefner liked them, he said, they would do a shoot. Hefner liked them so much that the tests were put into the magazine. Instead of presenting a "naughty milkmaid" idea of her sexuality, Denise was able to stay truthful to herself in the pictures, and to do it on her terms. It worked not just for the male gaze, but her own as well.

Years later, she would take charge of her career again. Landing *Star Trek: The Next Generation* was exciting for Denise. She hoped that being cast as the chief of security would break down stereotypes of what jobs a woman was capable of. But she came to feel that Yar was becoming a place card for a character instead of a three-dimensional person with agency. Roddenberry saw each character as a part of something bigger. In his mind, each of the series regulars represented an aspect of human personality. At the beginning, that was a concept that both writers and actors struggled with. The actors weren't let in on the plan, and often felt that their characters were somehow incomplete.

The show was in flux at the time, as the producers tried to work out who their stars were. They saw Jonathan Frakes's Riker as the equivalent of Kirk, with Data as his Spock, but they weren't sure who would fill the McCoy role or how Picard played into all of this.

NO CONTROL

Roddenberry had told Denise that once she was cast, it was up to her to make the role live. However, she didn't have the opportunity to influence the scripts and soon found that she only got significant screen time in a handful of episodes.

When her part in *The Next Generation* failed to develop the way she had hoped, she decided to take control and leave. She had been studying with legendary teacher Milton Katselas for years, and aspired to indie film work and theater. "[TNG] started out very new and fresh...and it begins to

DENISE CROSBY AS LT. TASHA YAR

settle. So hours and hours were going by each day, and days and days were going by where I was in the same uniform, in the same position, with absolutely nothing to say or do."

What added to her frustration was that this new *Star Trek* in the 1980s was being created by Gene, whose cultural references were still in the 1960s. Interestingly, Denise was very aware of Michael Dorn. "I would look over my right shoulder, and there would be Worf. And it was like, 'Are you doing it or am I doing it?' Certainly, when I stepped off the show, he became chief of security. Go figure."

Watching episodes of the first season, I can understand Denise's frustration. The intention was clearly to create a character who pushed the boundaries of what was normal for a woman. In 1987, a warrior woman was very much a forward-looking idea. But Tasha is a product of her time. I get the sense that the writers keep thinking, "Look! A woman is doing what you think of as a man's job, but it's kind of sexy, right?"

In the much-maligned episode "Code of Honor," Tasha is kidnapped by Lutan, the leader of the planet Ligon 2. The women control land and physical wealth, and hand it to the man of their choosing. Lutan has decided that Yar will be his new "First One," causing his current "First One" to challenge her to a fight to the death. He is fascinated by Tasha's martial arts skills, which he finds, of course, to be sexy.

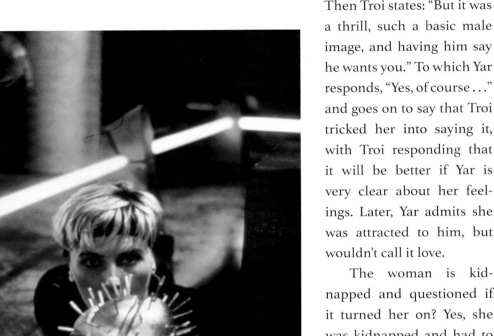

Yar gets to demonstrate her fighting skills, and she does make the choice to fight, but there is a disconcerting conversation between Yar, Picard, and Troi after she is kidnapped. In a scene that borders on a "blame the victim" scenario, Picard asks Yar what she knew about the plan to make her Lutan's First One. She has to tell him she knew nothing about it. Then Troi states: "But it was a thrill, such a basic male image, and having him say he wants you." To which Yar responds, "Yes, of course . . ." and goes on to say that Troi tricked her into saying it, with Troi responding that it will be better if Yar is very clear about her feelings. Later, Yar admits she was attracted to him, but wouldn't call it love.

The woman is kidnapped and questioned if it turned her on? Yes, she was kidnapped and had to fight for her life, but we will never know what that experience cost her, or if she will harbor resentment for a fellow woman crew mate that would suggest, "Yeah, but a part of you wanted it, didn't you?" For me, it is a bleed through of 1960s White male titillation. No wonder I have heard almost every cast member disavow this episode.

Roddenberry clearly saw sexuality as a very important part of a character's identity. Tasha's tough exterior masks a very 1960s view of femininity. For Gene, it seemed inevitable that when men and women work together, sex will become an issue, and it often seems to be more of an issue for the women than for the men. In "The Naked Now," the crew members are infected with a virus that affects them like a powerful alcohol, revealing what is underneath the surface for each character. For Crusher, it's an attraction to the captain; for Troi, it's attraction to Riker; and for Yar, it seems like an uncontrollable need for sex that ends with her seducing Data. It seems like the cocktail parties after filming in the 1960s find their way into scripts that can get some naughty fun out of the fact that there are women on board, without having to look too closely at the actual dynamics of getting drunk and having encounters with an imbalance of power. But I am seeing this in retrospect, of course. For those too young to have been there, this behavior was "just how things were."

The seduction of Data starts with Yar making herself vulnerable by telling him about how she was abandoned at five and learned to survive by avoiding the rape gangs, only to find herself in a place now where all she wants is love and tenderness.

If this had been a disposable guest star, it may have seemed acceptable to the Sixties mindset obviously still in place in this show, that sometimes a woman just wants sex. But we are told she just wants love so we can be titillated by her revealing costume and cat-in-heat behavior, but actually still buy her as one of our heroes and a warrior to boot. In Data's case, we learn that he is sexually fully functional, and he has a small "Why not?" smile on his face as Yar leads him to the bedroom. When the crew recovers, Yar is distraught and seems ashamed of the encounter. "Data, I'm only going to tell you this just once—it never happened." In the end, Picard states that he believes he will have a fine crew, as long as they can avoid temptation.

This speaks to me of how things were in the late 1980s. Women were entering the workplace in significant numbers, and a lot of people imagined that this was going to lead to nonstop sexual escapades, leading to lots of adultery and divorce—which, in turn, could upend society. Women in the workplace could be dangerous! It's as if men were believed to have no self-control or code of ethics after a day in an office that included female employees. In 1987's *Fatal Attraction*, a successful married lawyer has an affair with a book

editor, and she turns out to be literally crazy to have him. Have an affair with a working woman, and your daughter's bunny could get boiled. Take heed.

Having Yar behave sexually without any personal choice seems to me an opportunistic way for the male gaze to have its cake and eat it, too. Here is a situation in which our

OPPOSITE: Having a woman who could fight was still considered unusual. "Code of Honor" even revolved around aliens being amazed by her martial prowess.

ABOVE: Denise was frustrated that we didn't get to see a more rounded picture of Tasha and made the decision to leave the show. But it was the producers who decided to kill her character off, making it all but impossible for her to return.

heroes can have a sexual encounter without any blame, but the woman remains responsible for how the men respond to temptation. If sex is offered up, it's because the woman behaved like a sex siren, rendering them powerless and therefore faultless. If she does it because she isn't in actual control, we can forgive her. She can stay on the series.

ATTRACTIVE WARRIOR

That first season of TNG was much more concerned with sex and with being sexy than the rest of the run. From what I hear, that was Roddenberry's influence. Sixties *Star Trek* had been known for its sexiness, and it was clearly part of the formula he intended to revive. It's possible that, like Uhura on the bridge in a miniskirt, Tasha's sex appeal was meant to distract from the fact that she was a powerful warrior for men who might not be ready for that.

There is another problem for Tasha. She was designed to be the warrior in a show that was determined to emphasize the virtues of thoughtfulness and peaceful solutions. Sometimes this made her come off like a hothead asking for trouble. In "Encounter at Farpoint," she passionately suggests they plan an attack, to which Picard offers a withering response that they could never be successful against the powerful Q. "I'd like to hear your advice," Picard challenges coldly. "I spoke before I thought, sir," is her shamed reply. When she rashly responds to Q and is frozen by him for her impetuousness, Picard saves her. In "The Last Outpost," when Picard asks his crew for suggestions to deal with the Ferengi, Yar suggests attack. Worf agrees that they should "hit them hard and hit them fast." "Impractical!" says Picard. The only other shot of Yar is in reaction to the captain. She didn't seem to be of much use to him, other than serving to make him seem a lot more thoughtful in comparison.

I'm not sure this has much to do with Tasha being a woman. The first season makes it clear that there is one character that we are meant to understand above the others: Picard. It is his struggles with various aliens while adhering to the Prime Directive, his philosophies, his personal growth that we are meant to engage with. If Tasha Yar wasn't developed as a character, she wasn't the only one; Worf and Geordi remain a mystery, as well.

It can't be overstated how courageous leaving a series is. If there were such a thing as bonfires that actors gathered around to tell each other cautionary tales, up at the top of the list of most impactful stories would be: don't quit a running series. The chances of getting one are slim, the thinking goes, and if you get the reputation of being "difficult" by leaving, no one will hire you again. There is also the unsaid judgment that you must think a lot of yourself (another actor sin that you will karmically pay for) if you leave a job when there are so many actors unemployed.

When Crosby had a meeting with Roddenberry to see if she could encourage more focus for Yar, he was understanding concerning her frustrations, and let her out of her contract by killing the character. I watched this episode, and I expected a Yar-based story that maybe saw her battling to the end, with a big close-up to help us enter her emotional reality and feel the loss. Instead, she is killed quickly, and the close-up at the end of the episode goes to Picard. When Troi crash-lands on a deserted island, the away team of Yar, Riker, Data, and Dr. Crusher go to rescue her and the pilot of her shuttlecraft. There, the team meets an alien life form named Armus. He is the physical remains of the evil an entire race of people shed and left on the planet. When Tasha gets impatient with not being able to get to the shuttlecraft, she is unceremoniously killed—no last words, no heroic struggle.

When Dr. Crusher tries to revive her in sickbay, it made me laugh in shock to see that the alien had not only killed Yar but managed to remove all her makeup in the process— there was a lot of lip gloss involved in the previous scenes, but now Tasha is on her way out the door. Interestingly, as soon as Worf is told he will take over Yar's post, he gains some kind of insight beyond his usual warring ways and tells the crew he is most useful on the *Enterprise*, as his presence might be seen as threatening. Picard approves. The emotional intelligence upgrade will serve the character well and allow for more input and trust from the captain. Tasha should have thought of that.

Once everyone is saved, there is a ceremony for Tasha that is best described by Data when he tells the captain that he worries he has missed the point of this human ritual because he is thinking more of his feelings than he is thinking about Yar. Picard tells him he got the point exactly right. It's what we are directed to feel as well. A hologram of Tasha Yar tells each of the remaining crew what she got from them or admires about them. It's a little like a Dorothy in *The Wizard of Oz* moment in which Tasha tells us Troi taught her she "could be feminine without losing anything," (Are you listening, pant-suited feminists?) and that Picard was the closest thing she had as a father (See? She *liked* the patriarchy!). She is shot without a close-up, but we get close-ups of the remaining crew, offering us intimate understanding of their emotions and the workings of their brains.

I can't help feeling it's a missed opportunity. By allowing Yar a dignified and emotional death, we would understand the loss the heroes feel by feeling our own. Instead, we are encouraged to emotionally move along, nothing to see here. Because I can't imagine that Data, Riker, Picard, or Worf would be dispatched with the same carelessness, I see this as indicative of the lack of value the women had in this story *of* men *for* men at this particular point in time.

But...Tasha's eulogy was written by a woman—Hannah Shearer. Hannah is nobody's fool and a real role model for women. She made her way as a female writer when female writers were a rarity in the business. Today, we'd be alive to the danger of seeing Tasha as a character who serviced others and not who she was as an individual, but this was 1988.

In any institution, and this is true today, you can only deliver socially evolved ideas that reflect those of its titular head. This is another reason women in powerful positions make a difference—as do modern content creators such as Mike McMahan, Terry Matalas, and Alex Kurtzman.

I was there in the 1980s, too, and at the time would never have seen any of this as questionable for women. I didn't have the information the present culture has now afforded me. With hindsight, I see that if the men at the top chose to make the effort with the women actors, there could have been balance. Without that generosity, all other attempts from the women to better their deal would be thwarted or granted, depending on their whim.

Because Denise chose to leave, Tasha was gone before the end of TNG's first year. Whatever problems there were with the execution, Tasha wasn't in a traditional female role,

ABOVE: "The Naked Now" set out to show other sides to Tasha's character, but it focused on her desire to explore her more traditionally feminine characteristics and gave her an exaggerated sex drive. I can't imagine Kira having similar thoughts.

the *Enterprise*-D. It's now a warship, and our crew is battling the Klingons in a war that has lasted decades, and one that Starfleet is losing. Worf and Troi are gone, and Tasha Yar is back at her tactical station. The *Enterprise*-C, a ship long thought lost, appears from the past and Picard has the ethical question of how to knowingly send a crew back in time, to face almost certain death in order to restore history and possibly avoid the costly Klingon War.

The opportunity to give Yar the death she deserved started with a script Eric Stillwell, a TNG production assistant, was working on with Trent Christopher Ganino. Stillwell had run into Crosby at a convention in San Jose, where she suggested he write a script to bring her back as a guest star. The production offices had evidently been considering the same thing, and the story was bought and reworked by Michael Piller, Ron D. Moore, Ira Steven Behr, Richard Manning, and Hans Beimler.

This is a great episode for women, who are key to the developing story from beginning to end. Guinan is the only person who is aware that the timeline has changed, and she warns the captain. She also tells Yar that she shouldn't be aboard the *Enterprise*, that she had died what Guinan understood was a senseless death. Even when her words aren't well received by the captain, Guinan insists on her truth being heard and considered. Even though her information sends Yar to a probable death, she does what she believes is right, and then honors Tasha's memory by asking Geordi, "Now tell me about Tasha Yar." With an actor like Whoopi Goldberg, the respect for the woman she never knew is built into the sentence.

Another wonderful woman character is the *Enterprise*-C's captain Rachel Garret, played by Tricia O'Neil. Brave, determined, and dedicated to her crew, she is in every way Picard's equal. She chooses to return to certain death in her timeline, understanding that to do so may prevent the war with the Klingon Empire. It was thrilling to hear her say, "The Romulans will get a good fight. We'll make it one for the history books," and believe her. It made her death incredibly impactful and caused me to reflect on how heroic women in combat have been. It was a role that could have been played by

and losing that character changed the balance of the show. The two female series regulars who were left were both in caring roles: the ship's doctor and counselor. If Tasha had hung around, things might have been very different.

A DIFFERENT TASHA

Denise did get to come back in an episode that gave us a glimpse of how her character might have grown and changed. In season three's excellent episode "Yesterday's Enterprise," a rift in the space-time continuum causes a huge change in any gender. That it was a character who just happened to be a woman made the writing of this role feel like instruction on how storytelling helps in shifting cultural expectations.

HEROIC DEATH

Tasha Yar gets to be a hero, too. There is a romance with the *Enterprise*-C's new Commander Castillo, played by Christopher McDonald. However, I never get the feeling that she requests the transfer to the *Enterprise*-C because she likes a man. It's clear that she understands the chances of survival are slim at best, but she tells Picard she has the training that their tactical team doesn't, and even a few seconds of survival could count toward changing history back to its original timeline. When she joins Castillo on the *Enterprise*-C, there's a quiet dignity that speaks more to Starfleet members following their ethical calling, rather than lovers choosing to die together.

Crosby beats the odds of quitting a series by again returning in season four's "Redemption, Part I," and season five's opener, "Redemption, Part II." Picard is asked to mediate when a Klingon civil war is threatened, only to find that the heartless half-Romulan daughter of Tasha Yar is behind the Duras family's attempt to overthrow Gowron as leader. Not only do we get the powerful Lursa and B'Etor, played by Barbara March and Gwynyth Walsh as Klingon sisters, but also a wonderful enemy for Picard in Crosby's Commander Sela.

Given the opportunity—as she is in this script—Denise turns in a dimensional, powerful, chess-playing antagonist who requires every bit of Picard's focus to defeat. To me, it points to the advantage alien guest stars had. Without the need to meet expectations of a human woman, the actors are allowed a wide spectrum of behaviors.

Some have said the opportunity for episodes featuring Crosby would have happened if she had only stayed. When TNG made its debut, the assumption was that most people would miss a lot of episodes, so there was a lingering anxiety about having the characters grow and therefore change.

In the "Female Warrior" box in a hierarchy led by a father figure, I'm not sure she would have ever had the opportunity to show the range and power as Yar that she had as Commander Sela. In space, the opportunity to be an alien and stay out of the usual array of female human boxes gives women a chance to expand. Denise Crosby got the chance, in the end, to do just that.

OPPOSITE: I love Denise's performance as Sela, which allowed her more scope than Tasha had.

ABOVE: In an alternative universe, Tasha got a heroic death. When the timeline is altered in "Yesterday's Enterprise," she willingly sacrifices herself to put things right. For me, this was the best version of Tasha.

Gates McFadden as
DR. BEVERLY CRUSHER

Gates McFadden fought for decades of her life to be seen as more than just a pretty face, and she's not afraid to look back and examine the culture she lived in and how she dealt with it. Uncomfortable with being performatively female, she entered Hollywood at a time when her looks would put her in the limiting "Beauty" box, and she fought against the restraints.

When I asked her what she would want young people to learn from her, she said: "To find the strength to be the best of themselves, to not be held back by society, and to really look at themselves like a scientist. Why do I feel that way? Why does this upset me? Always remain curious, always wanting to learn."

What she wishes for others is how I have experienced her: willing to question not only authority but herself as well. Fighting to be heard as a whole person surely played a role in her absence during the second season of *Star Trek: The Next Generation*, but audience support, and the shifting power struggles of what she calls the "throne room" (the production offices), brought her back for the remaining five years of the show as well as the TNG movies and the third season of *Star Trek: Picard*.

According to the casting memos, Gates was always one of the front-runners for Beverly Crusher, but it took Gene Roddenberry and his writing staff a while to come up with the role. In the earliest story notes, Wesley's mother, unnamed, simply drops him off on the ship. Even at that point she was seen as a potential love interest for Captain Picard. To quote the notes, "Picard is strongly attracted to her (as she is to him)." But she departs before the end of the episode, handing Wesley over to Picard, who will clearly be his surrogate father. Troi and Yar (at that point Macha) were already in place, but there's just

a note that says the writers will probably need a chief medical officer.

By the time we get to the Writer's Bible in March, Beverly has evolved to become the ship's doctor. The notes say that she is "first and foremost, a brilliant ship's doctor." But, as with all the female characters, they also make it clear that she is devastatingly attractive. The bible describes her as "a beautiful woman," which it says is "an additional asset," and adds that her "very female form" hasn't escaped the captain's eye. Interestingly, it also says that the ship's chief medical officer is in "no way considered an inferior to the captain" and points out that she has the authority to relieve him of duty. The idea was there, but in the end they rarely put Beverly in that position.

With her intelligence, looks, and focused energy, it's no wonder that Gates was a favorite for the role. She grew up in what she calls "Wonder Bread" Ohio, meaning that there was virtually no diversity in her neighborhood. There were no little girls, either, and the boys on her street taught her very quickly that "you're going to be stepped on and ignored if you don't speak up." She would carry that lesson with her.

Her mother started taking her to dance school at a young age. She was struck by the way the dancers at the studio used sexuality, and she recognized that it was a powerful tool for them. However, neither the rough boys in her neighborhood nor the sexualized girls in dance class felt compatible to who she intrinsically *was*. When her mother started to take her to auditions, she was cast at fourteen as a dancer in a nightclub in Erie, Pennsylvania. She would do two shows a night, wearing falsies to fill out her costumes. "I was an object when I was doing that," she told me. "I was pretending, and people loved the pretense." She felt split in two: She had the intellectual side where she felt engaged and natural, and the side that knew how to ape a kind of prescribed sexuality, and the latter felt like it had nothing to do with who she inherently was as a human. It was a power she made a conscious decision not to use.

Once she entered the creative world as an adult, she says she "wanted to change the world." By the time she graduated college, she had learned about feminism, equality, and civil rights, "and it's really about giving everybody the freedom to make choices."

She took a life-changing course of study with Jacques Lecoq in Paris, studying his technique for theater, movement,

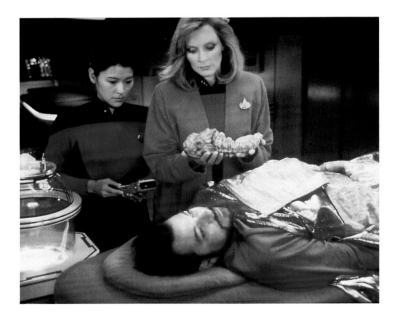

ABOVE: "The Host" introduced the Trill and asked the question about whether love can transcend gender.

OPPOSITE: In early episodes, the writers established that there could be a romance between Picard and Crusher, but the emphasis is always on Picard's experience, and we have very little sense of how she feels.

and mime. Remembering the boys from her neighborhood, she spoke up to Lecoq for equal treatment in the classes: to look her in the eyes and call her by her last name in note sessions as he did the men. It was a world of collaborative theater, and he responded by doing as she asked. She became his assistant and was eventually called upon by universities such as NYU to teach his method. Eventually, she became Jim Henson's choreographer for several movies, casting and staging elaborate scenes.

When she arrived in Hollywood in the late 1980s, sexual harassment was a regular and disturbing occurrence for her. Even in academia, men would expect sexual favors in exchange for opportunities. What would begin as a boost to her confidence would end with her feeling erased as a person when she realized the offer had not been about her abilities but had been transactional all along. This happened to her "all the time."

Hollywood was a shock to her on many levels. Not only the strict hierarchy, which meant you were only allowed an opinion if you ranked high enough on the ladder, but also the amount of personal grooming that was expected of women actors. Talent wasn't enough, and according to her agents, she lost jobs based on producers' displeasure with how she had fixed her hair and makeup. She told me of a *Cosmopolitan* article she used in a show she directed that instructed young women to keep a small mirror and makeup under your bed so that you could fix your makeup before your boyfriend woke up. "Pretend, pretend, pretend. That's what they were selling in the '80s."

This was anathema to the young woman who had spent so much time in areas of the arts where talent trumped all. From directing theater and being on the faculty of many theater departments, she was accustomed to having a voice and a modicum of respect. In contrast, Hollywood "sucked." She saw other women in the business move ahead using seduction, and admits that her reaction to all the transactional expectations was to "become more of a bulldozer and just already have my shields up." Did her reactivity get in her way? Without a doubt, and she says that she could have been more understanding that these were the rules already in place.

It wasn't just Gates. As women, most of us were told the same thing. I remember the "Who do you think you are?" talks I would get from agents and managers when I simply wanted to be treated with respect. I was told I would have to wait and see if I got powerful enough in the business to earn that kind of respect. It certainly gave me an understanding for the women who used any means necessary to climb the Hollywood ladder. The times it didn't pan out for those women were when the promised transaction wasn't honored. There is no HR for that situation.

McFadden turned down the role of Dr. Crusher several times, thinking she didn't understand the world of television or the world of sci-fi. "I still don't," she told me. "How you develop a character over seasons and stuff. I wish I'd had a mentor; I desperately wanted a mentor." Many women were still in the mindset that to help a woman in the same field would be to help *her* secure the job in place of you.

UNEQUAL OPPORTUNITIES

Gates talked to me about something that, looking back, I think was taken for granted at the time. Once she accepted the role on TNG, she never felt that she had the same access to the producers that the male actors did. "I can't just flop on the couch, put my feet up, like a guy can, and chat. It would be seen as a sexual come-on of some sort, and so it inhibits your behavior."

Even though I was married to Alexander Siddig for years, I never knew he hung out in Rick Berman's office during shooting until he told me of a time when Terry Farrell was brought in when he happened to be there. She was inspected in her costume and told to lose five pounds. Siddig was mortified to have witnessed it. I never even thought hanging out in the bosses' office was an option, and nor did many women I spoke to. Whether it would have been encouraged or not, as women at that time, we were over-trained to stay in our lane. It would take *Star Trek: Voyager's* women to break that rule. That lack of access meant that Gates didn't lobby for her character or for her career.

She made the formal request to direct during the first season, and was told "absolutely not," even though she had substantial experience directing in theater. Her one show, "Genesis," is considered a success, but she was never asked to direct other iterations of the show. Although Gates was probably the most experienced director going in, her male co-stars ended up directing more episodes. Patrick Stewart directed five episodes; Jonathan Frakes directed eight and went on to direct the movies and other shows in the franchise; LeVar Burton directed two and went on to direct *Star Trek: Deep Space Nine* and *Voyager*; Michael Dorn directed DS9 and an episode of *Star Trek: Enterprise*.

In the end, Gates built a theater in Atwater Village in Los Angeles to give herself the chance to direct. However, she made a point to tell me that she "had a fabulous time working on *Picard*. There was less bias in things, and maybe [that] included me. I felt listened to in a way I had never felt listened to on TNG." She credits this change not only to including more women on staff, but also to the reality that it's a different moment in our culture, one with more awareness of the destructive drip that bias can be.

But in that first season on TNG, her enthusiasm to "change the world" got her in trouble. When she saw potential sexism or racism in the first season's scripts, she spoke up. She loved that her role on the show was a single mother who was the chief medical officer, a commander who could take over the ship. But she chafed at the "bays" the characters were kept in, and the competitive relationship women actors were placed in at the time. Only one woman would be bestowed with the "Sexy One" crown, and if that wasn't you, your opportunities shifted a few rungs down the hierarchical ladder.

She also tried to communicate her feelings to production that women, in fact, have deep conversations with their sons, and that this wasn't sufficiently reflected in the scripts. One of the male characters would get that scene, and although Gates acknowledged the importance of showing strong male mentorship for young men, to fail to demonstrate a single mother's strong influence on her son is a mistake by omission. What a missed opportunity to not do more with that mother-son aspect, and to not have the doctor mentor other young women. We would have to wait for *Voyager* to see that particular story unfold.

To my mind, her character was a healer, but because she was also a mother, she often was slipped into the "caretaker" archetype. Women caretake their young when they are totally dependent and shift to a mentoring role for the rest of the child's life. Caretaking can infantilize, while mentoring teaches you how to grow yourself. Gates herself mentors and loves to see how it transforms people. Mentoring, which it turns out she actually did in a huge virtual way over the many years the show has aired, was one thing she would have wanted to include in her character, had she been able to give input.

Without that ability, McFadden felt that she was relegated to a narrow spectrum of what she could actually bring to the character. Like many of the cast members, male and female, she found the first season particularly frustrating. Most episodes featured Dr. Crusher delivering medical technobabble. Even if the Writer's Bible said she was the captain's equal, it often didn't play out that way. In "The Battle," she tells Picard,

> She loved that her role on the show was a single mother who was the chief medical officer, a commander who could take over the ship. But she chafed at the "bays" the characters were kept in.

"I'm the only person aboard this ship that can give you an order," and tells him to go to sickbay. I cheered the authority, but the next line is Riker informing the captain the Ferengi are on the line. The captain says, "Sorry, Doctor, duty calls," and leaves. Crusher is left having to make a little "Oh, well" gesture with her head. That way, it's cute and understandable that he brushes aside her orders, and she can remain likeable—all important for TV stars in the 1980s.

In the scenes between Crusher and Picard, and in many other episodes, I'm struck by the full range of emotions the captain navigates, from humor to anger to frustration. Crusher, on the other hand, seems to exist to make him feel better and remains reasonable and kind in all circumstances, giving medications to him first and explaining what they were afterward, the way you might do with a small child. Even when he is borderline rude by asking her if she is accustomed to getting her own way (because she is treating him), her answer is gentle. I can imagine what McCoy's reaction to Kirk would have been in the same situation, and you can as well. Those characters were always two humans allowed their full range of emotions, which of course served to make their relationship more relatable. To be fair, I think the gruff doctor and the adventuresome captain were easy for people to recognize as typical military men who already had a frequency they related on. There were far fewer examples of women in the workplace.

Star Trek's writers were trying to stay the course with Roddenberry's vision for the future and advance social issues. Did they always get it right back in the Eighties and Nineties? Was it only the two women leads who lacked complex characters with rich histories? No, Geordi and to a certain extent Worf get shortchanged as well. But, at the end of the day, this was a production company trying to tell stories, and make them entertaining. It was inevitable that threads of attention to certain social issues got dropped. Particularly in those early years, the show was often written by veterans of the 1960s and of predominantly male cop shows. It seems that they couldn't help falling back on the female archetypes that had filled TV for decades: the wife, the siren, the girlfriend, the annoying mother.

I wonder if being established at the beginning as a love interest for the captain put her immediately into the 1980s box of "Nice Girl Next Door," because the "Sexy" box was already filled by Sirtis. That is a dreaded Eighties/Nineties box, because it means that in the future you may be the designated wife and so should be nurturing, sensible, and sexy, but not so sexy that there will be fights over you.

In the "Nice Girl Next Door" box, you are there for the male in the story. You're not there to live out your own adventure, but to show the audience how the hero feels when he's hurt, let them see when he's scared, when he feels any kind of vulnerability. And in order to do that without confusing an audience as to who their focus should be on, you are herded to a nice, reasonable, two-dimensional place.

This is complicated territory. With hindsight, it's easy to criticize *Star Trek* for what it didn't do. But the leap it made by making the chief medical officer a woman was a huge, impactful step. At the time, Gates didn't understand what decades of experience would teach her: Dr. Beverly Crusher would inspire generations of people, especially women, to pursue careers in medicine and science. She showed that traditionally female strengths such as caring, kindness, and reasonableness were valued and could get you to the point where you were in charge of a major department on a starship, or a hospital.

She also had the courage to stand by her ethics when it was called for. Even if *Star Trek* defaulted at times to a dated

sensibility about women, Dr. Crusher would blow the minds of a lot of thirteen-year-old girls and make a huge impact on their lives. Major Mel Baars O'Malley, a chaplain in the US Army, recently called upon her favorite character to help her pass the rigorous Army Physical Fitness Test. Getting promoted means taking it again, and at forty, with two small children and a hectic life, the physically fit O'Malley had her doubts about passing some strength tests. "Do it for Beverly," said her internal thirteen-year-old, and the mantra got her through.

At the end of the first season, an announcement was made that McFadden was leaving the show to pursue other opportunities, but she says the truth was she was deemed trouble by season two's executive producer, Maurice Hurley, and was fired. Gates says she received thousands of letters of support from the audience. Her popularity no doubt had an effect on the decision to bring her back. Hurley left the show, and Rick Berman became an executive producer. He and Patrick Stewart wasted no time in convincing her to return for season three. The actor who had taken over the role of the doctor, Diana Muldaur as Dr. Katherine Pulaski, left. It would seem that casting Muldaur simply didn't work, even though she was Roddenberry's choice. She had guest-starred on the original series and brought a plainspoken gruffness I imagine reminded him of McCoy, but she didn't take to the show and the show didn't take to her.

With Dr. Crusher back in season three, her character started to gain some dimension but, to my mind, still seems

ABOVE: Gates was known for her intelligence, and she is a very thoughtful actress who isn't afraid to express opinions.

OPEN A CHANNEL: THE WOMEN OF *STAR TREK*

to develop other characters' stories more than her own. The first episode of the season centers on Ensign Crusher's experiment to evolve nanites, two of which get loose and are able to reproduce, becoming a conscious collective entity that threatens to destroy the ship. Dr. Crusher is worried that her seventeen-year-old son isn't having enough fun, and talks to Picard about Wesley being the only officer aboard who has his mother along too. For Beverly, there is the 1980s trope of a stereotypical overbearing mother, worried and slightly bewildered by their offspring, wanting him to be a normal seventeen-year-old and then worried when he is. She seems conscious of the fact that being on board with your mother can be embarrassing, but then tracks him down on the intercom when she doesn't find him in his room.

Today, the scene in which Wesley snaps at his mother might be probed a little deeper to understand both of their feelings, but it was good to see him trust her with the revelation that he made a mistake. Although it is implied, missing for me was the scene in which mother and son work on it together. Screen time equals priorities. *Star Trek* is brilliant at showing behavior that can be modeled, and single mothers with sons and the issues both face is worthy of a deeper dive. In Eighties culture, it stayed, as a friend of mine said at the time, "Light, bright, and trite."

But Beverly does start to develop some defining characteristics that add complexity. One theme of her character is her courage to stand by her ethical beliefs. She stands up for the collective consciousness of the nanites, speaking for their right to life. Later in the season, in "The High Ground," Crusher is kidnapped by a terrorist, Kyril Finn, on a planet where the *U.S.S. Enterprise*-D is delivering medical supplies. I noticed a tone shift in this episode written by Melinda Snodgrass, with Michael Piller now co-executive producer. Other than Troi, dressed as a fairy princess, giving Wesley the news that his mother has been kidnapped—completely distracting from the harrowing news—I found it a good episode for women. It allows Crusher to show her ethics, her dedication to healing no matter who it is, and to have a heroic moment. So, the good news: It features one of our women characters, she is proven brave and idealistic, and we get a great guest star. Kerrie Keane as Devos, the planet's head of security, is a fully developed character. We are allowed to understand her focus on stopping the terrorists and what she has witnessed to make her determined to end them. There is a passion and intelligence that underlines the struggle to move forward with impossible choices when choices must be made. She has scenes with Riker that don't have one drop of sexual tension; they are equals, and she has more important things on her mind. She even saves Picard in the final scene by shooting Finn, although she is reprimanded by Riker: "You didn't have to kill him." But even here, she is given the dignity of comprehending the gray area of her decision. She understands she just created a martyr for the terrorists' cause.

The not-so-good news is that we really don't gain more insight into Dr. Crusher, or the emotional complexities she went through as a kind of prisoner of war. One of the difficulties of having standalone episodes is the effect on character development. Crusher couldn't have a confusing arc of recovery from trauma over several shows that may not be viewed sequentially, so the whole idea of consequences and recovery seemed to be ignored. But I think that was partially a reflection of the times, as well. Therapy was gaining a foothold in society, but I remember that admitting to using a therapist carried a social stigma. After all, in the 1980s, "hysteria" had only just been taken off the books as a medical condition for women. The writers may have thought showing emotional consequences for their doctor might depict weakness. It's possible that Crusher was herded into the same territory that returning World War II soldiers were in: Get back to work and get on with it.

But Crusher has her heroic moment, too. She works with a child in an earlier scene to ease the suffering of the ill. After Devos kills Finn, the child raises his gun to kill her. Crusher tells him, "No more killing," and he eventually drops it to his side and is taken into custody. Devos sees the child as the next incarnation of Finn, meaning that the fighting will

OPPOSITE: Gates on location filming "The Survivors" shortly after she returned to the series in the third season.

never stop. Although Devos was able to be the cowboy and kill the bad guy in this sequence, it's actually Crusher who might stop the violent loop by offering the child a simple alternative to the reaction to avenge.

NO ANGER

Being idealistic made Crusher vulnerable, and her goals to help outweigh her instincts for self-preservation, which, by the way, ends up causing deaths for other crew mates during her kidnapping. Picard is eventually kidnapped as well, but he has a scene in which he is enraged by being kidnapped and stripped of agency. In the scene, he seems to wonder, along with the audience, how she cannot be feeling the same. In contrast, Crusher follows the terrorists' orders when she is taken and doesn't look to escape. Her concern is for the sick she finds there, and about the future danger of the dimensional shifting they are using to avoid detection. We are told that she feels fear, but there is really no exploration of it. This weight for Crusher to be helper and healer flattens, I think, the truth of being human. Courage is most interesting when we are informed of its costs.

Although she has philosophical arguments with him over presumably many days, when Finn is killed, there is no indication of what it means for Crusher; she is just seen checking if he's dead. We don't know what she felt, if anything at all. I can't help thinking that if the roles had been reversed and Picard had spent days with a terrorist, there would have been a filmed moment to understand what the death meant to him. In these relational moments, a complex human is brought to life. When Crusher is reunited with her son, she realizes she is holding him too long when Picard orders him back to duty, and she has lighthearted "whoops" look on her face. It's a big moment, but it's played as a nod to anyone who's had an overbearing mother. It is such a contrast to Picard's fully realized rage in previous scenes that it made me wonder: What is so scary about a woman having a big emotion?

Season four's "Remember Me" was a bottle show with Gates as the main character. Intended to save money by limiting the cast, it is a real chance to get inside Dr. Crusher's mind and reveals her intelligence, trust in herself, and self-control. Trapped within a static warp bubble of her son's making, she creates her own reality before she is rescued by Wesley and a mysterious alien called the Traveler.

Because she was thinking about the emotional cost of losing loved ones when the bubble formed, this is the basis for her version of the *Enterprise* and her reality. One by one, the crew members disappear, each time being only remembered by her. Before she dares to go toward the thing that frightens her instead of resisting it (nice metaphysical points for that), we can see just how much she trusts herself, and how much she believes she is trusted by her crew mates. Against the odds, she doesn't devolve into thinking she has lost her mind. Her mind's version of Picard doesn't, either, telling her, "Your word has always been good enough for me." Her version of Counselor Troi is supportive and compassionate, and they have a sensitive, warm conversation that has nothing to do with men. Tellingly, when she tries to describe the now-disappeared Troi to Picard, she says, "Deanna Troi, your ship's counselor, half Betazoid, loves chocolate; the arrival of her mother makes you shudder!" Even Crusher didn't have more personal details about the counselor.

Crusher's scientific mind refuses to succumb to the panic of limited time left as the bubble starts to collapse and finds the portal to escape to reality. She does a wonderful job of holding attention throughout the show, and keeping the balance between thinking she might be going mad but knowing that giving in to that thought will accomplish nothing. Crusher is smart, relentless, and very human in this episode. When she hugs Picard and her son in the end, there was no sitcom feel to the scene. She wasn't "The Girlfriend" or "The Mother," she was Beverly Crusher, who had helped save herself by going toward what she feared.

Gates found out she was pregnant during filming for this episode. She told me that she had asked to have her pregnancy written in to avoid hiding it through limited filming, desks, and carrying things, as was customary on TV back then. Unfortunately, she found out they were

allowing another actor to play her pregnancy on DS9, and they couldn't have two *Star Trek* women pregnant at the same time. That other actor was me. She spent the rest of the season hiding her belly in limited scenes. In all the time I've known her, she had never told me my pregnancy had so affected her work. Like women writers at the time who fought for the "woman's slot," pregnant women had a slot, too, and I had beaten her to it.

Jeri Taylor was a producer on the show by this time, and understood that there was an opportunity to change how women in the audience saw themselves by how the women of *Trek* were represented. Writer Lisa Klink credits Taylor with teaching her on *Voyager* how a head writer can make a writers' room both safe and creative. I believe their effect on the show is evident in this season, but not only with the

inclusion of strong women guest stars such as Michelle Forbes as Ensign Ro and Denise Crosby as Tasha Yar's daughter Sela. The portrayal of Dr. Crusher also definitely improves as the writing leans into her intelligence, strong moral sense, and the ability to take command.

In "A Matter of Time," Crusher is onto the con man, Rasmussen, and deftly turns down his advances while remaining in complete control. She is there to witness his undoing at the end, as well. On first glance, it may seem unimportant who is included to witness the denouement of the episode, without lines to say, but being present means the character's

ABOVE: Roddenberry sold Gates on the role of Dr. Crusher by telling her she would be one of the most senior and powerful people on the ship.

opinion on the action matters. Having Crusher there, even though she wasn't in much of the episode, meant her opinion of this man counted.

"Cause and Effect" is another episode that demonstrates Dr. Crusher's ability to analyze and remain scientific through confounding events. In the episode in which we see the *Enterprise* blow up, over and over, we learn that the ship is caught in a time loop, and Crusher is the one to first recognize the repeating events are more than just déjà vu. She has a natural scene with Picard in which they exchange ideas as equals and he heeds her take on things. Her smile at the end is warm and sweet, and there is no sense of having to be in the "Girlfriend" box.

Her capability and ethics are also clear in "Ethics" and "I, Borg." In the first, she demonstrates how a doctor's emotional involvement with a patient can make the ethical question of when and how to do research involving patients clear. When Worf's spine is crushed, she resists the spine specialist's desire to test risky new research that would restore his body, but might also kill him. His Klingon belief system demands he commit suicide rather than live with a disability. I was thrilled to see that the specialist, Dr. Toby Russell, is played by a woman. She is quick to show Crusher professional respect when she first comes aboard, and the two are equals in terms of intelligence and ability. Dr. Russell loses a patient because she is more interested in proving her research than saving people in the here and now, and Crusher forbids her to practice medicine on the ship. When Worf agrees to try the surgery that might kill him, the doctors work together to save his life. The scenes of surgery are

so well played, I found myself wanting a doctor like Crusher myself.

She has an effective scene with Dr. Russell in which she lays out the dangers of keeping one's eye on the laurels of new discoveries rather than lives, and it is an example of two women with different approaches showing disagreement right alongside dignity and professional decorum. In this episode, our doctor is focused, capable, and has authority. I can see why so many women have told me this character was their inspiration to go into science and medicine.

The first episode of season seven lists Jeri Taylor as executive producer, Merri Howard as line producer, and Wendy Neuss as producer, as well. We are firmly in the 1990s, with more women in charge behind the scenes, and it's reflected in the show.

With a story by Jeri Taylor, "Descent, Part II" has Dr. Crusher commanding a skeleton crew aboard the *Enterprise*, and she proves herself to be an excellent captain. The doctor is self-assured, capable, and all business as she makes rapid-fire decisions to rescue the away teams and fight an attacking Borg vessel.

The tensions caused by the increase of women in the workplace at the time are reflected in an exchange that had been atypical of the dynamics between Starfleet officers in this episode. An ensign of only six weeks takes command of the technical station during the Borg attack, and seems grateful that Crusher doesn't simply dismiss her. When Lt. Barry, back from the away team, replaces her, Crusher says the ensign is needed at the science station.

In coming up with solutions to save the ship, it is

obvious that the lieutenant is uncomfortable with an ensign contributing to the conversation, and attempts to shut her down. There is tension in their exchanges, as first the lieutenant and then the ensign have the stuff to save the *Enterprise*. The scenes show a realistic resistance some men felt to newcomers who they saw as interlopers who don't deserve their positions. It also demonstrates the value of both, and the camaraderie possible when shared objectives are met by collaboration.

As far as love goes, "love is love is love" is not true for Beverly Crusher in season four's "The Host." When she falls in love with a handsome Trill, she is unable to accept the symbiont in a different body. She struggles to accept him in the body of someone she sees as her brother, Will Riker, and rejects him when he is placed in the body of a female host.

What made this difficult for me is the scene in which the doctor remains with the pulsing slug that's waiting for a host. She seems happy to accept that the slug holds the entity that she loves. She can love a slug, but not a woman? Picard is allowed more complexity: You see him suffer, knowing there is someone else she loves other than him, but he tells her he supports her in every way he can, and follows through.

The beauty salon scene in which Troi teases the relationship details out of Crusher seems to be stereotypical. However, Troi later tells Crusher to not miss the opportunity for devotion, no matter what it looks like. While, of course, people will make a variety of life choices based on what is right for them, *Star Trek* has built into it the responsibility of being more than just a TV program. We come to expect challenges to the status quo in these stories. This has grown over the years as the content creators see just how much it is used as inspiration, fodder for debate, and the delivery system for incremental acceptance of new ideas. Sometimes, especially for the early shows as we look back, this is a heavy weight. Crusher's 1990s choice may not stand up to what many today would think of as progressive, but at the end of the day, it was her choice to make. And she made it.

A lot has been said about "Sub Rosa," the episode involving a ghost lover who romances generations of women in Crusher's family. Sometimes an episode jumps the shark,

and it seems McFadden got stuck as the lead in it. That said, the Scottish feel of the show suited her, and she gamely made love to air. It felt like a romance novel and a pretty one, just odd for *Trek*. Brannon Braga told me romance always felt somewhat awkward to write for the show, and this one is awkward to watch.

CRUSHER'S CHOICE

"Attached" is much more interesting. After seven years, Picard and Dr. Crusher look likely to end one of the popular tropes of TV at that time: the "will they or won't they" question when a man and woman work together and have sparks fly. The answer is "not now," and the one to decide that is Crusher. I liked that she has agency in this relationship. That's admirable, but—like with so many episodes—I felt I was supposed to be more interested in how this rejection feels for Picard than how it feels for both of them. The camera holds on his tortured, unhappy face when she walks out. Maybe Crusher is meant to be an enigma, but too many times, in emotional scenes with Picard, it feels like we are meant to see with his eyes alone.

When Beverly returns in *Star Trek: Picard*, you can see how the times have moved on. Despite having Picard's child, she has rejected him and set out on her own path. When he complains, she points out that he always put ship and duty first, stating that this wasn't enough for her. For me, and I think for Gates, we finally get to see the Dr. Crusher that was promised to us in the beginning. And it is quite thrilling.

When the ship is fighting the Borg, she takes command of the tactical station and manually plots an impressive attack that takes out the weapons that are about to destroy the *Enterprise*. When the rest of the crew raise an impressed eyebrow, she responds that "a lot has happened in the last twenty years." How true.

OPPOSITE: Gates was an experienced theater director but didn't get her chance to helm an episode of TNG until the seventh season.

Marina Sirtis as

COUNSELOR TROI

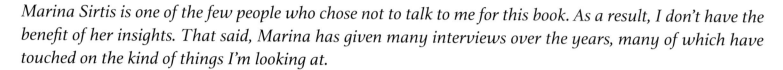

Marina Sirtis is one of the few people who chose not to talk to me for this book. As a result, I don't have the benefit of her insights. That said, Marina has given many interviews over the years, many of which have touched on the kind of things I'm looking at.

In 1987, Sirtis was a determined young English woman who, despite her parents' objections, had studied at the Guildhall School of Music and Drama, joined the Connaught Theatre, done some British TV shows and several movies, and was now trying her luck in Hollywood at thirty-one. Unless you've lived it, it's almost impossible to imagine how difficult coming to Los Angeles like that is.

Hollywood is a hard place to feel connected in the first place. It's geographically spread out, making it difficult to form friendships in a culture that requires a car for even the smallest outing. Since then, small communities have cropped up. Back then, there were very few. Just bumping into someone to casually talk to was virtually impossible; taking a walk down the streets of Los Angeles would have made people wonder about you.

I arrived in the Eighties, too, and sometimes the only people I saw were the women I was competing with for a job. It was rare, but not impossible, to find a friendly face in those waiting rooms of casting offices. I noticed that the times I was up for a character role, the women were more friendly. The roles were always smaller, too. The big roles, with big stakes, were cast with beautiful women, and those rooms could be as dangerous as a jungle. There were women who would use psychological warfare by trying to diminish the rest of the room's confidence, speaking loudly about their last role or their tight relationship with the casting director. Sometimes a withering look at how I had dressed would cause a nervous

system reaction that would hijack the brain I so desperately needed to audition with. Of course, you either let it get to you, or you put on some armor to protect yourself.

Now, I would recognize the game, but then, the competition took energy to manage, and it reinforced the idea that there wasn't enough for all of us. This wasn't an easy place to find women's friendship and support.

Six months into her stay, Sirtis had maxed-out credit cards and had an expiring visa. She got the call to audition for the ship's chief of security, Tasha Yar, with Denise Crosby trying out for the Counselor Troi role. After three auditions, the powers that be decided Sirtis should try for Troi and Crosby for Yar. Three more auditions got them each the jobs. By the time she was under contract, Sirtis would have been made to understand the stakes involved and the lottery she had won: years of work in a show with built-in fans, with money enough to pay off the credit cards, and a lot more. It was hers to lose. Job insecurity, especially in the tumultuous first year—when she was written out of four episodes— must have felt like an ever-present cloud.

But what was this role? Years later, Sirtis herself asked: "What did we know about Troi? We know she worked out. And she had a mother." Troi was half-Betazoid, an empathic humanoid race useful for their telepathic abilities. Early memos describe her as a hypersexual hermaphrodite with four breasts. Thankfully, writer Dorothy Fontana talked Roddenberry out of this idea. At other points, they considered

giving her an enlarged cranium. They tossed around the idea that because she was telepathic, she wouldn't have been able to speak without the aid of technology. In the end, black pupilless eyes were the only physical manifestation of her Betazoid genes.

Like so many things in the early days of *Star Trek: The Next Generation*, the concept for Troi was ambitious. You can see the origins of the character in memos about a new science officer, and later a "con officer" who always presented the captain with alternative ways of looking at things. The Writer's Bible describes her as vitally important, "a master of Human and Alien Psychology, also Starfleet-trained as a bridge officer." The plan was for her to be a regular part of the away teams. She is seated next to the Captain, a place of importance that was influenced by the growth of women in the workplace at the time.

NEW TERRITORY

Troi's role as a therapist was a new development for *Star Trek*, too. Therapy was big in the 1980s, and its representation in the show makes sense. However, Brannon Braga told me he found the actual job of a therapist for people who have reached the crew's level of perfection strange and difficult to write. So was her telepathy. They couldn't make her too powerful; if she knew exactly what their opponents were thinking, the story would be over too quickly. More often than not, she has a vague sense of someone's motives that, frankly, most of us could tell by simply looking at them. "He's hiding something, captain" has limited use when that could always be surmised from the actor's performance. But difficult to write for or not, her position as a counselor had a big impact on the audience. As I was writing this book, countless women came forward and told me that Troi's calmness, kindness, and confidence inspired them to become therapists themselves. Counselor Troi is a large stone thrown into the global lake, whose positive ripple effect continues to this day.

I've learned that writers look for aspects of a character that will generate story ideas. Because Troi's professional life didn't seem to be as fertile a territory as Roddenberry had hoped, and there was very little personal history established for them to mine, it took a while for the writers to figure out what to do with her. Difficult to write; even more difficult to play.

In those early days, there was a lot of turnover in the writing staff, and somewhere along the line, Troi turned into a more traditional character. She was put into the "Sexy" box and given the traditional female virtues of being caring, kind, and insightful. Wonderful qualities, but at issue is her lack of history, agency, goals, dreams, and complexities. Without those, her character strengths become assets for others rather than part of a more complex character.

In "Encounter at Farpoint," Troi is emotional and often in tears, feeling the feelings of others but seemingly emotionally blank herself. In "The Naked Now," we get to see what some cocktails would reveal about the ship's counselor. The men have various reactions to the infection: Wesley Crusher wants to take over the ship, and Geordi La Forge has deep questions about his eyesight, but the women all want some action with their crew mates. Roddenberry is obviously in charge here. I recall his comment from the original series of a few women on board being able to service all the men, and this seems to revisit that fantasy. Predictably, Troi feels huge attraction for Riker. Although every other infected character makes it to sickbay or ambulates themselves to where they wish to go, she is swept up into his arms and carried off, at once reminding me of how little girls were raised on a diet of princess tales and also how infantilizing it is to be carried off unnecessarily by a man. The net effect of this moment, it seems to me, is not so much to add to the complexity of the woman as it is to improve the optics of the man: Now he appears strong, heroic, a good protector.

It's an example of Troi serving others, and all too often that's how women were presented at the time. The romance of the moment may have appealed to girls watching the show—a familiar trope they had been taught they could aspire to. Come for romance, stay for a bit of science and ethical concepts, which really isn't a bad deal and might have been highly effective for both sexes.

Perhaps because they struggled to get a handle on her character, the writers often defaulted to giving her romantic storylines. Season one's "Haven" is a good example of how Troi helps us understand other characters, without revealing much of her own emotions, conflicts, and dreams. We learn that according to Betazoid tradition, she has been promised to a man since childhood, a human doctor named Steven Miller. When his family turns up to start the marriage process, she reacts with tears, crying, "No, no, no." This felt like

OPPOSITE: Marina said her first outfit made her look like a "cosmic cheerleader," but at least it was a Starfleet uniform.

ABOVE: Deanna's relationship with her mother wouldn't have been out of place in a Sixties sitcom.

she has no agency, with her automatically becoming a victim of whatever is going to happen. But that is the last discernible emotional reaction from Troi I could see on the subject. She behaves like an obedient Betazoid, a "good girl." After talking to Riker about his feelings, she goes to talk to Steven Miller about his. There is a woman he has dreamed of since childhood, and it's not the counselor. Again, although she is calmly going through with this marriage, I understand nothing of how this affects her. Is she hurt? Jealous? It seems she is understanding, because she admits she has feelings for Riker as well as an acceptance of her husband to be. As she later tells a visibly upset Riker, she is able to hold more than one person in her heart.

MALE PERSPECTIVE

But I get to understand nothing of what this means to her, other than her uttering the words. Betazoid marriages were done in the nude. If only we had been given some insights as to the emotional truths of the story from Troi's perspective, the nakedness could have referred to revealing the character, rather than just being a titillating concept that goes nowhere. Of course, when it comes to it, she doesn't have to marry the handsome doctor, who it turns out is telepathically bonded to a blonde with an impressive midriff.

When Miller says goodbye to Troi while standing next to his dream girl, Troi wishes them both well, says a small quiet goodbye, and looks down. In the last scene of the episode, we hear how happy Picard is to have his advisor still aboard ship, but the counselor is mute—the only reaction to her story arc a quick smile between Commander Riker and herself.

Looking back, I think that's how television often was. It was focused from the men's point of view. It wasn't exclusive to *Star Trek*. What is beginning to change is increased cultural awareness from the top of the industry and the presence of women in the writers' room and elsewhere. But until women were included at every echelon, change would be limited to what the powers that be would allow. I spoke

to so many of the women writers, bursting with sci-fi love and a wish to see themselves represented in the adventure. But just like in the space program, where there were plenty of talented women ready to be trained astronauts, until the ex-military officers who ran NASA gave them opportunity, no change could happen. But change happened in TNG when Jeri Taylor arrived as co-executive producer alongside Rick Berman and Michael Piller.

Looking back on it, Sirtis has said that she wishes she had come up with more ideas for her character to help enrich it, as she saw other actors do, notably Brent Spiner. The image that comes to me when I think of this disparity is seeing people feeling safe enough to stretch out to rest in a park and wondering why you yourself couldn't have enjoyed doing the same, forgetting that you were the one sitting next to the hive of antagonizing bees at the time. But neither Gates McFadden, Terry Farrell, nor I, all leading ladies at the time, felt we had that ability to contribute to our characters. I think sometimes women become so accustomed to the cultural undertow that they wonder how it was that they didn't have the energy or the opportunity to do more. In the 1980s, most actresses were so worried about their looks (which we were led to believe were why we had been cast in the first place) that it became a primary focus.

Troi, who the Bible describes as "exotically beautiful," was put in the role of the "Sexy One." Most TV shows offer up beautiful people in the hope that we'll keep coming back, because we enjoy looking at them. But for an actress, being stuck in the "Beautiful" box brought a lot of pressure. If you are there because of the way you look, then you'd better look good.

In a BBC Online interview, Sirtis was harsh about her looks. "It was just a question of how the heck do we make her look half decent?" she said about herself. Quite slim by most people's standards, she was told to immediately lose five pounds—a really problematic demand for someone with an eating disorder.

She said the reason she wasn't in the uniform the other crew members wore was that with the extra weight she carried, it was determined that she couldn't pull off the look.

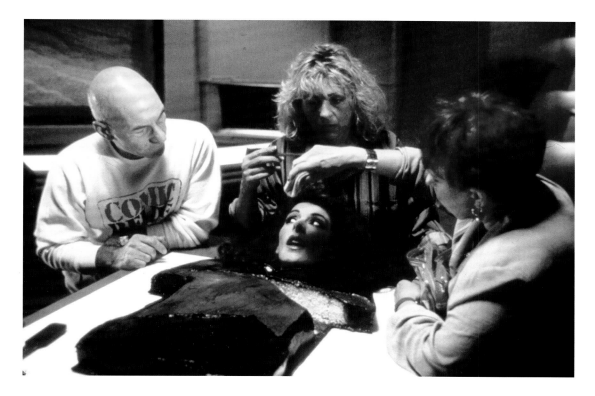

Thus, the skant was born. A short tunic extremely reminiscent of the minis worn by the 1960s *Star Trek* women, it was outfitted with knee-high boots. We see Troi, and briefly Tasha, as well as male and female background players, sporting them in the first season.

Roddenberry had brought William Ware Theiss with him from the original series, and the designer tried to imagine a future in which women and men wore something unisex, but still sexy. To justify showing the male audience some leg, the producers put the male crew members in the skant as well. But whereas in the 1960s, the miniskirt was the choice of the actors and denoted to them empowerment and freedom, it just didn't play twenty years later. Ultimately, with her big Eighties hair and Jane Fonda-like headband, Sirtis saw Troi's original costume as a "cosmic cheerleader"—not a good look then, and certainly dated decades later. It was rapidly phased out. But her rank pips disappear with her miniskirt, and she is dressed in a series of low-cut dresses and fitted jumpsuits for the early seasons of the show.

Taking Troi out of a Starfleet uniform had unfortunate consequences for the character. All too rapidly, the writers forgot that she was a fully trained Starfleet officer, who should have been able to hold her own in a fight and know the ship's systems inside out. In Mark A. Altman and Edward Gross's oral history *The Fifty Year Mission: The Next 25 Years*, Sirtis said that once her wardrobe was sexualized, "I became decorative, like a potted palm."

In articles and interviews, her cleavage, which was typically on display, very often gets mentioned by fans and by Sirtis herself as an issue. In more than one interview, she says that the message sent by the costume was that a woman can't have breasts and a brain, because she didn't have a brain until she was given a uniform in season six.

So, the first season can't have been easy. The character Sirtis was playing must have seemed different to the one she had auditioned for, and I'd guess that as an actor she could feel that the writers were struggling to work out what to do with Troi.

In Hollywood, having gotten a job is only the beginning. As Sirtis put it, it's still a "boys' town," and women are more likely to get fired than men. Particularly in an ensemble cast, you're always worried that you could be let go and sent back

to the endless round of cattle calls, only this time with the stigma of having been seen to fail.

In the 1980s, the system clearly told you that how you looked was vitally important, and almost every actress worried about her appearance. That's not all: As a woman, you worried that you could be let go if you were too demanding. The (mostly) unspoken message is: Make a fuss and we'll get someone else. There's always another beautiful girl waiting to take your place. Where Gates fought within the system, only to get fired after the first season, and Denise simply walked away, Sirtis stayed and worked within it.

In my experience, that takes a toll. The daily contraction to accommodate others' perceptions of how you should look, feel, and behave can take emotional and energetic space in your head that you could be using for other things. It can become habitual. You can become so familiar with what is expected that you start providing it automatically.

Having a regular job meant Sirtis was no longer alone in Hollywood. She says that the cast became her lifelong friends, and the Roddenberrys became her surrogate parents, even inviting her to spend holidays with them. Having Majel Barrett-Roddenberry play her mother, Lwaxana, must have further encouraged the friendship. In many interviews, Sirtis aligns herself firmly with Roddenberry, going as far as saying what she knew he would and wouldn't like in the shows following his death.

Despite her close friendship with the Roddenberrys, Sirtis was clearly worried that her position was in danger. She remembers hearing rumblings that it was in jeopardy that first year. Adding to the insecurity, Troi was written out of four shows in the first season. When she asked Majel if there was indeed a possibility of her being let go, Majel told her that Roddenberry felt (as difficult as this is to fathom) that there were too many women on the show.

Early in her tenure with the show, Barrett-Roddenberry invited her to take part in a *Star Trek* convention. This would have been the fans' first introduction to one of the new cast members, and Sirtis made connections there to do more. She remembers that she became popular with the fans at the events, and credits this with helping her keep her job. It's one of the examples of how the *Star Trek* audience is hugely influential in what happens in the franchise.

To Sirtis's mind, Denise Crosby's decision to leave also helped to protect Troi. She has said, "Denise quitting saved my job." By the end of the first season, the decision was made to fire Gates McFadden, and the game of thrones left Sirtis as the only original female series regular contracted to start season two.

VICTIM

In rewatching episodes, I was struck by how many times Troi's body or brain is used against her will. Most of the writers I spoke with mentioned the difficulty of telling stories without the drama-boosting interpersonal conflict. For his new *Star Trek*, Roddenberry had created a mandate that humans had evolved to a point where conflict could only come from the aliens they encountered, and even then the Prime Directive had rules of engagement. The original *Trek* had many instances in which McCoy got hotheaded, Kirk got angry, and Spock disagreed. Picard also seems to slip by this rule, and is often annoyed at Worf and Tasha Yar, and has peccadilloes such as not liking children.

Finding a way to use a woman character who was under the idealized human concept, without slipping into a soapy romance of the week, must have been challenging. At the time, it must have felt necessary to take away what is most valuable to a character to understand how they would behave. Michael Piller said you can't kill a leading character, so you kill the guest star they are in love with. For Troi, it seems they often chose her agency and emotional sovereignty as the things to take away. For women, these are undoubtedly valuable possessions. Now, with the benefit of hindsight, I can look at episodes such as "The Child," "Violations," and "The Price" and see the missed opportunity for exploring what assault, sexual and otherwise, leaves in the bodies and minds of those affected.

In season two's opener, "The Child," Troi is impregnated by an alien energy that wishes to experience being born and living a life as a physical being. The scene of impregnation struck me very much as a rape. The pin of light representing the life form slowly, sensually creeps up her sleeping figure, but Troi feels the presence as unwanted and wakes in a disturbed state.

The men start a discussion among themselves, while Troi looks down as if shamed, as to whether the child should be aborted or not. Thankfully, Troi makes her own decision concerning her body, to keep the child. It's also her choice for Data to help her in the birth. She bears the child, and in a matter of days, it is the size of an eight-year-old. When the entity realizes that it is endangering the crew because its radiation speeds the growth of plague samples the *U.S.S. Enterprise*-D is carrying, it sacrifices its body to save the ship. What ensues is a tearful scene of Troi not wanting her child to die, ending with her acceptance of why he must. When the crew gathers for the final scene on the deck, Troi cheerfully joins them and laughs at the good-natured ribbing Wesley Crusher receives for his decision to follow his own dreams and stay aboard the *Enterprise*. His B storyline to ask to stay on board is what the time is used for. We end with a happy crew. What? The experience left Troi feeling nothing? This strikes me as a wealth of possibilities for mining the character left unexamined. Making the birth be without trauma or pain reinforces the idea to me that there was no harm, no foul to Troi, so we can all just go happily forward as before.

While some may view this as a story about abortion, I see it as a missed opportunity to do what *Star Trek* does best: offer the thoughtful 30,000-foot view of issues that humans deal with in the present day: assault, permission, sovereignty of one's own body, and the aftereffects of loss. But unlike *Star Trek*'s best episodes, it falls short because it doesn't go deeply into the moral issues or consider the consequences of the story. The character arcs that had been showrunner Maurice Hurley's goal when he took over the show didn't appear to include Troi.

Generally, I find that things improve for Troi as the series progresses. In "Loud as a Whisper," she saves the day by inspiring the broken negotiator Reva to turn his disadvantage to an advantage. In season three's "The Offspring," she passionately argues with Picard for Data's right to create a child.

"The Price" offers some upgrades to the counselor's agency, even if Troi is given another romance. A half-Betazoid male named Devinoni Ral visits the *Enterprise*

OPPOSITE: Troi was tempted by a love affair with Devinoni Ral, but shows resolve when she discovers he is manipulating people.

ABOVE: Like so many female characters, Troi provided a love interest. Her affair with Riker would eventually end in marriage, but was ignored for much of the series.

during negotiations for a wormhole. The two are immediately attracted to one another, but it's hard to watch their initial love scenes without wondering how Troi could turn a blind eye to this character's creepy inappropriateness. When she admits that she had been thinking of him all day, he replies, "Then you must have had a good day." What? He then picks her up in his arms and carries her to bed. (What is it about men picking the counselor up?)

Once Troi realizes he is using his mind-reading abilities to his advantage, she uses that Betazoid honesty to expose him to the negotiators and the rest of the crew. Finally, Troi takes action to cause a shift in the story, regardless of her feelings. The fact that the wormhole is quickly revealed to be worthless steals a little of that thunder. But Troi is allowed the last line of the episode, and it was one that I'm sure women responded to, and still respond to, when they are treated as solely existing for the benefit of others.

Ral says that exposing him has made him take a hard look at himself, and he doesn't like what he sees. He wants to be better, and he asks Troi to come with him and be his conscience. She answers, "I already have a job as counselor," rejecting what would be a one-sided relationship.

PSYCHIC VICTIM

Season five's "Violations" has a teleplay written by Jeri Taylor and Pamela Gray, and a mind-reading Ullian with daddy issues named Jev. He forces Riker, Troi, and Dr. Crusher to relive traumatic moments in their lives, while inserting himself within the memory. With Troi, there is the added dimension of attraction he feels for her, so the memory he probes is a romantic one. We see, in her memory, Deanna on the floor while Riker gets on top of her, and she is saying, "Don't, we can't, not when we are serving on the same ship." Suddenly, it is the Ullian Jev on top of her, obviously raping her. There is an overhead shot of Troi lying in her pink nightgown, unconscious, hot chocolate spilled on her abdomen like blood, in a coma that will last several days. It is a shocking image, but the rest of the

writing in the episode seems to walk this strange line in not calling it rape.

There is a scene at the top of the show in which the Ullian father offers to read Dr. Crusher's mind and is reminded that in their culture, a mind probe is not allowed without permission. The father trivializes this and charmingly says, "But sometimes, with a beautiful woman, I cannot help myself." Dr. Crusher laughs at this and leaves the room with him. Of course, this is a plot point to remember for later when the son places blame on his father for the unwanted mind probes, but to me it also points to something else. When someone pushes an agenda that is not welcome, women are encouraged not to make a fuss: Be a diplomat, don't make it awkward. This would be true in the story and also, back then, on set. For an actor to say, "I wouldn't laugh at this," could result in a slowdown of work.

Also, at the time, sensitivity concerning a woman's issue could elicit groans or worse with a mostly male crew. I found Worf's line, "Klingons do not allow themselves to be… probed," which is said for smiles, quite troublesome because it frames rape as something you allow or don't allow. If you're raped, that means you allowed it? Of course, I know that is not the intent, but with the benefit of time, we can see how lines like these, watched over and over and with much affection, could be confusing for young people—including young men who are fans of Worf and could have suffered rape—without a discussion of where we were in this time's culture.

Also dated is the fact that it was acceptable to have Troi relive the trauma again, to see who the guilty party was. And if we hadn't seen enough, we get a third installment of her rape, this time with the guilty party in the room. Troi yells a fierce "No!" and fights him off with some pretty good moves, but her doors open and Worf, Geordi, and Data are there to finish him off. If it were filmed today, I have no doubt Troi would have been the one to handle it herself.

These shows are so iconic that I think it serves a purpose to look back, with affection and understanding that it was a different time, to discuss what has changed in our understanding of the issues at hand. That way, what we can add to the experience is context of where we have come from so that the shows continue to inspire and entertain and maybe provide a small history lesson as well.

At this point in the seasons, the show is beautiful to behold: The lighting, sets, special effects, and acting are good reasons for the phenomenal hit it was. The writing and guest stars also shine.

Finally, in the sixth season's "Chain of Command," Troi gets her Starfleet uniform back and, for the first time, it came with pants. Jeri Taylor, who was now running the writing staff and therefore deciding what stories *Star Trek* would tell, set out to give more attention to the female characters. In the previous season's "Disaster," Troi had seemed like an untrained civilian with very little understanding of the ship's systems, at least compared to another woman— Ensign Ro—who really does have her shit together. Taylor and the writing staff were determined to put that right, so Troi not only got a uniform but was also promoted to commander.

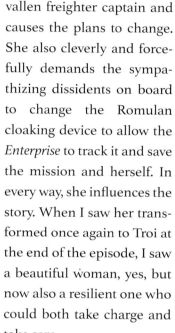

She herself has said this on many occasions, but here I quote BBC Online: "I got all my brains back...I was allowed to do things that I hadn't been allowed to do for five or six years. I went on away teams. I was in charge of a staff. I had my pips back. I had phasers. I was absolutely thrilled."

It's late in the game, but Troi starts to be given much more to do and the opportunity to break out of the limitations that are all too often imposed on beautiful women. Sometimes in sci-fi, back in the day, the best way to accomplish that was with a lot of alien makeup.

In season six's "Face of the Enemy," the counselor is kidnapped and surgically altered to help Romulan dissidents get a sympathizing government official to safety. She takes on the identity of a Romulan Tal Shiar major called Rakal and is forced to playact the part in order to save her own life and that of the official. The story is full of danger for Troi. She is on the Romulan ship *Khazara*, with a sharp Romulan commander in charge, played by Carolyn Seymour. With new alien parameters for behavior, Sirtis takes on Romulan harsh edges, and we see her ability to take command and play mental chess.

Even her Betazoid telepathy has real traction here, as she senses the lie from the Corvallen freighter captain and causes the plans to change. She also cleverly and forcefully demands the sympathizing dissidents on board to change the Romulan cloaking device to allow the *Enterprise* to track it and save the mission and herself. In every way, she influences the story. When I saw her transformed once again to Troi at the end of the episode, I saw a beautiful woman, yes, but now also a resilient one who could both take charge and take care.

Unlike most of the characters on TNG, Troi has significant relationships with other people. However, the love affair with Riker, and the attempt at one with Worf, never revealed much about her. You can sense a wariness about really pursuing them. Going through the early memos, there's a fascinating idea that could have made the relationship with Riker very different. The writers thought about making Troi and Riker into a couple but keeping it secret from the rest of the crew—like Frank Furillo and Joyce Davenport on *Hill Street*

Blues. Presumably, the episodes would have ended with them sharing their thoughts on what had gone before. But the idea was dropped. Character development takes time and is best accomplished on a serialized show. Practically, not making them a couple also meant that they were both free to have relationships with guest stars—relationships open to more conflict than one between Starfleet officers at this point in time and leading to more interesting goodbyes.

Thankfully, Troi has another defining relationship. She is almost the only person with a family that we see more than once. Every season, bar one, features a visit from her mother, Lwaxana. Like most things, it becomes more sophisticated as the seasons progress. In "Haven," "Manhunt," and "Ménage à Troi," they are like boxers in a ring. In one corner, we have the stereotypical overbearing mother who just wants to see her daughter married. In the other corner, Deanna Troi, constantly hurt, embarrassed, and angered by her mother's outrageous and un-Starfleet-like behavior. They come to the middle and have scenes that seem as prescribed as a fixed fight. Because it is one of the few representations in the show of two women in a relationship, I would have loved to have seen more than mere comic relief. However, let me just note that their relationship existed, which is the only reason I could even have the opportunity to complain about it.

But then, finally, in season seven, there is "Dark Page," written by Hilary J. Bader. It starts with Lwaxana looking for a husband for Troi, and Troi being annoyed and embarrassed. Boxers to their corners. But when Lwaxana falls ill and is discovered to have retreated to her Betazoid meta-conscious mind because her psyche is collapsing, Troi is allowed to show what she is made of. At huge risk to herself, and meeting enormous resistance from Lwaxana, she vows to help her mother by entering her consciousness. Throughout the episode, she is compassionate, strong, and determined. She brings her mother back from a coma-like state and shows skill as a therapist in speaking to her mother's trauma of losing a daughter when Troi was an infant. Interestingly, Troi is dressed in a gown for the early scene in which she is hawked by her mother as a potential wife. For the rest of the episode, she is in a Starfleet uniform. As Sirtis has said, the Starfleet uniform seems to elevate the character wearing it.

On a *Mission Log* podcast recorded in 2012, Sirtis was surprised at first that she had so many women fans, because she was "the sex symbol of the show." This presupposes that women wouldn't identify with her or root for her as such. Certainly, in 1980s Hollywood, the woman with the most sex appeal was the woman to beat. But the fact that she had so many women supporting her indicates that the audience was maybe shifting faster than Hollywood was.

COMPASSIONATE INSPIRATION

When I spoke to audience members who were fans of Troi, they gave very specific reasons why she was their favorite character. Being compassionate and reasonable made her seem like an ideal mother figure to people from chaotic homes. For some, it was an ideal that defined what they wanted in a partner. For others, finding someone in *Trek* who represented who they were led to self-acceptance and a feeling of worth. After all, beautiful, sexy women watch *Trek*, too. It would have also been instructional for little girls in what men find attractive. Rightly or wrongly, it was deemed desirable to be a demure woman unafraid to show her curves, and young women would have met with success if they followed Troi's example. The issue is only if this is the sole example of desirability to a wildly diverse audience.

Many women told me it gave them permission to be feminine in the workplace, and added romance that they wanted included with their dose of science. It also elevated the profession of therapist to make it a job women would consider to be in their wheelhouse. So many women in various countries became therapists because of Deanna Troi that it's impossible to know just what kind of change in the world this *Star Trek* character really made. With our current understanding, Troi may have been a missed opportunity to ask questions that women back in the day were wanting answers to. Those questions are undoubtedly being discussed in the rooms where the women who took a leaf out of Troi's book are treating their patients today.

OPPOSITE: When Troi finally got her Starfleet uniform back, the writers started to focus on her intelligence and professionalism.

RIGHT: Like many actresses, Marina was valued for her beauty and her traditionally feminine qualities, and these became defining elements of Troi's character.

Majel Barrett-Roddenberry as

LWAXANA TROI

When Gene Roddenberry started work on Star Trek: The Next Generation, he saw the opportunity to employ his wife again. This time, he told her, no acting was required. He described the role to her as the "Aunty Mame" of the Galaxy. This, he said, was a character with flair and a heart of gold, very close to Barrett-Roddenberry herself. Majel Barrett-Roddenberry first appears as Lwaxana Troi, the mother of Deanna, in the episode "Haven."

From the beginning, Lwaxana represents something that was very rare on modern *Star Trek:* an almost purely comic character. It appears that Roddenberry brought some 1960s prejudices about older women with him for this part, and many of the jokes about Lwaxana are based on her gender.

Dressed as what reads like a Western space madam, Lwaxana is the stereotypical nightmare mother: loud, embarrassing, and primarily interested in marrying off her daughter. Her sexuality is played for laughs by making her overly aggressive and indiscriminate, with the men of the *Enterprise* comically avoiding her. I very much doubt that the writers would have gone for the same gag if Lwaxana was a young woman.

She is also the image of the nontechnical older woman. In "Half a Life," where she plays opposite the great David Ogden Stiers, she asks at a console about a button, "What does this little one do?" She also rolls over people's agency, setting up a picnic like "everyone's mother" while the crew are working, saying, "Now, now, now, if you don't eat you'll get sick."

The Sixties idea of a woman's identity is all over the line "I am a woman dressing for a man," the explanation she gives her daughter for fussing so long with her gowns. Troi tells her mother, "You're insatiable"—certainly a fear some people carry about women's sexuality. Where a man might be called sexy, a woman is called rapacious. It's hard not to

look at the image of Picard cringing at Lwaxana's advances and feel that older women are being schooled in how not to behave. That Lwaxana is over the top in every way just forces that conclusion.

On the positive side, Lwaxana is a useful disruptor. She acts as a mouthpiece for some audience members who would question why the crew operates as it does, and also adds friction to a show where almost everybody else is incredibly evolved and never argues.

The basis for "Half a Life" is a look at the purposefulness of the elderly in society. In it, Stiers's character, Timicin, is obligated by his world's customs to commit suicide upon turning sixty. Lwaxana and Timicin fall quickly in love, and share a moving scene in which she argues for his life. Lwaxana rages and cries and almost stamps her foot to get her views across, while Timicin patiently but passionately explains his position. Childlike characteristics are wonderful in a scene, but it comes off as more of a parent-child relationship to me, rather than an argument between equals.

Other characters call Lwaxana strong and powerful in a good way, but she doesn't have the opportunity to demonstrate this until the end, when Lwaxana is given a chance to grow. She accepts his decision to return to his world, and goes with him to bear witness to his death, a custom for loved ones on his planet.

In "Ménage à Troi," she again appears as the stereotypical mother, concerned that Deanna "find yourself the right man." She martyrs herself for the sake of her daughter and Number One, playing a sexual assault from a Ferengi for laughs. It's possible, of course, to get too earnest about situations characters find themselves in, but with my eyes trained on the treatment of this character, I felt uncomfortable. Replace it with a younger woman in the Ferengi's bed being held against her will, and there would be a sense of tension and danger. It looked as though, because she was an older, annoying woman, she was somehow not worth taking seriously. During negotiations for her return, even Deanna smiles at the humor of it all.

Was it the writing, the box the character was placed in, or the actor herself that stereotyped the only female elder connected to our heroes? I don't know. Just when you think Lwaxana is "only" a one-note comic character, *Star Trek* does what it does best and shows us that there is more going on.

When she arrives on *Deep Space Nine*, she is still lascivious and chases Odo in a way that would be considered harassment today. But she has a series of scenes while stuck in a turbolift with Odo that are poignant. She allows herself to focus on him, showing understanding for his shame at being unable to hold his shape any longer, and makes herself vulnerable so that he may feel safe with her. Removing her wig and offering it to him was a beautiful moment. It seemed to me a gift from the writers that

showed connection, compassion, and depth: all the things Lwaxana rarely got to exhibit, and all the things that come with age.

I sighed at the beginning of her final TNG appearance in "Dark Page." Once again, Lwaxana seems preoccupied with finding her daughter a husband. The tenor quickly changes, though, when Lwaxana is diagnosed with a collapsed psyche and she retreats to her Betazoid meta-conscious mind. In a coma-like state and mentally unreachable, her daughter takes the risk of entering her mother's memories and discovers the pain that has always been there. An older sister of Troi's who she never knew existed, Kestra, tragically died while on a family picnic. Barrett-Roddenberry plays the traumatic scenes with a depth I couldn't have guessed by watching her performances in other episodes of the show. The character is finally given more, and she does the most with it. It was written by Hilary J. Bader and treats the subject matter of loss, therapeutic help, and moving on quite deftly.

Lwaxana returned to her annoying "Space Karen" ways in subsequent shows, but these truthful scenes added a complexity to her character. Once I saw that part of Lwaxana, I saw lines such as "All the men I've known have needed to be shaped and manipulated and molded" in a different way. Yes, the writers are telling a truth of why men are often scared of older, experienced women. But after seeing her depth, I gave her the benefit of the doubt that maybe, really, she had needed to take some control.

THE BORG QUEEN

When I met Alice in London, I felt as if I was interviewing someone who had just drifted out of an eighteenth-century painting: Hair to the middle of her back, wearing velvet jewel-toned clothes, and speaking with a plummy English accent, she struck me as the epitome of the kind of actress I idolized as a teenager. She also happens to be as open and kind as she is impressive.

Although she is aware of how the business can treat women, she was mostly untouched by harassment or any other bias other than the lack of parity with men in terms of salary. "I guess I must have been aware of biases, but I just decided to ignore them and put my best foot forward."

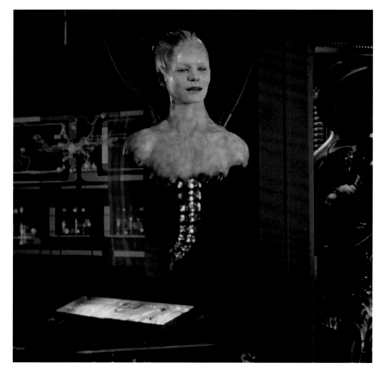

Like many women I interviewed, she attributed the fact that she hadn't suffered sexual harassment not to luck or human decency, but to the fact that she "must be like the Ice Queen." If you assume that men show appreciation through unprofessional and sexual behavior, the only one to blame is a body or personality that somehow isn't sufficiently desirable. This thought seems to lie at an unconscious level for many women so that, victimized or not, we are all affected by it in one negative way or another.

Although she has had a highly successful career, what *Star Trek* did for Alice that other jobs didn't was allow her to play the kind of role usually reserved for men. The Borg Queen gave her an opportunity of "not being contained by stereotypes and narrow parameters of behavior. You can live large; you can make bold choices." But there are still reflections of the sexual politics of the time. Having a full-spectrum character means having a backstory, and that was something that the Borg Queen didn't have. Alice said, "No one could tell me who or where she came from."

Another sign of 1990s thinking is that she uses her sexuality as a weapon to come between two males, Picard and Data, and "only her destruction can restore the 'natural order of the patriarchal world'" (*She: Gothic Reverberations* in Star Trek: First Contact by Linda Dryden, Napier

University, Edinburgh). She is not only poisoned by Data, but also then has her spine broken by Picard. The thing that made her a threat, her sexual power, is transformed into hideousness—not so different from deaths in fairy tales of old crones or sexy, evil stepmothers.

The Borg Queen was dressed in a costume that wouldn't have looked out of place on a Versace runway in 1996, the year *Star Trek: First Contact* was released. According to an article in *INDIE* magazine ("Why Is BDSM Still Being Borrowed for Cultural Cachet?" by Rachel Wilson), appropriation of bondage gave a dark edge to fashion at the time. I remember owning pants with unexplainable leather loops and wearing leather cuffs myself. Ms. Wilson points out that BDSM allows both sexes to play with their gender and experience a fuller spectrum of sexuality. In fashion, it allowed me to announce that I didn't necessarily conform to what the culture expected of me. In a reaction to the expectation to be "good" and to conform to what a mother in her forties was expected to look and act like, I dressed slightly "bad." Neither choice of dress actually told my story. But for a woman villain to look like a dominatrix gives a sexy, it-hurts-so-good feeling to the part. In fact, Alice said some of the fans "are enormously conflicted, because they find her attractive, and somehow she shouldn't be." This, too, is a function of storytelling: a chance to explore all of one's human responses.

She didn't come to live in Hollywood until her thirties, which she believes saved her from being eaten by the machine. The machine, of course, is the culture of Hollywood, which since the 1920s has been dominated by men who in many cases lost sight of decency in their pursuit of money and power. Search the internet for "victims of Hollywood" and there are more than 200 million entries. Alice feels that because she had a strong identity before reaching Hollywood, she avoided the lure of conforming in order to succeed. Alice has escaped the dreaded ageism that exists in the business. Believing that turning forty would mark the end of her career, she notes that "I have continued to work, and I am so far past forty at this point it's not worth thinking about."

OPPOSITE: The Borg Queen's entrance is one of the most memorable scenes in *Star Trek*.

TOP: The Queen combined elements of BDSM with *Alien*.

ABOVE: The Queen's creepy sexuality made her a real threat to Picard, who is very much TNG's patriarch.

ENTER NANA

Hollywood in the 1990s

This is where I come in. Star Trek: Deep Space Nine *launched in 1992. After a rocky start,* The Next Generation *had become a big success, and Paramount Studios decided to commission a second* Star Trek *show. By then, things had changed at Paramount. Gene Roddenberry died before DS9 launched, and the veteran producers he'd brought with him from the 1960s had all retired or left the show.* Deep Space Nine's *creators were from a different generation. Things had changed for women, too. The culture was moving quickly as more and more women entered the workforce.*

There are subtle and not-so-subtle differences to the ways that women experienced the Nineties. Some climbed the corporate ladder and felt their success showed other women it could be done. Many of those women reasoned that to succeed they needed to make sacrifices for their careers, and lacked empathy for other women who may not share the same strengths. Some had such specialized knowledge that they couldn't be ignored, like quite a few of the astrophysicists I spoke to. They got the jobs but then had to develop double competency to meet the challenge of working with men who weren't used to sharing their workplace with women. Some got tired of the fight and found other ways to make a life for themselves. Single mothers, women with low economic status, women of color, or a combination of all three had the strongest cultural currents working against them and had the least hope of succeeding.

A few women climbed the success ladder and pulled other women along with them, but there was still a feeling that it was a game of musical chairs. As Laura Behr, physicist, ballet dancer, choreographer, and wife of Ira Steven Behr told me, a lot of women wasted energy seeing each other as the reason they couldn't win. In fact, when the music stopped and women rushed for a seat at the table, the real issue was the inequity in the number of chairs available for women.

It's important to understand that the women of the 1990s had grown up in a different age. There was a slow drip of daily experience through the Seventies and Eighties that led to how I experienced life. I made little cultural adaptations through the years when met with biases. They were such small adaptations that I didn't think they could possibly matter, but they led me to accept this pattern of reshaping myself to get ahead and get along.

There was also a backlash to the strides women were making by many influential people. We didn't call them influencers then, but influence the culture they did. One of them was David Letterman. What he said and how he said it would flow all over the audience with the message that his way of reading the moment was the way the cool people looked at life. Watching it now, I see how women guests were mostly unable to fight against his confirmation bias that women were there as sexual objects and fodder for jokes about them as opposed to with them. Nell Scovell was a writer on his show who wrote an article that called the star out for sexist behavior behind the scenes, which included sexual relations with staff and advancing male writers over female ones. Letterman read it years after it was published and immediately apologized. As part of the apology, he said that, at the time, he was simply unaware that how he behaved was a problem. Men are caught in the cultural amber of our times as well, of course, until they choose to educate themselves.

When I look back with my more enlightened, present-day lens, it's hard for me to imagine that I sat in front of the TV laughing at the jokes at Monica Lewinsky's expense. I also bought the media's judgment of Anita Hill, who in 1991 heroically went to trial accusing Supreme Court Justice Clarence Thomas of sexual harassment. Again, my reaction at the time stuns me. If I didn't quite believe that this was a case of a woman scorned, I didn't completely dismiss it either. In 1994, journalist David Brock wrote a book about Hill, arguing that there was no reason to believe her. He famously called her "a little bit nutty and a little bit slutty." In the early 2000s, he wrote another book wanting to set history right, and claimed that he had lied in his previous book to protect Thomas.

The news media had moved to a twenty-four-hour format, and fallen women were its favorite subject. News about women out of control was entertainment. Is it what we wanted, or what the news media found profitable, easy, and in their political lane? As Allison Yarrow says in her book *90s Bitch: Media, Culture, and the Failed Promise of Gender Equality*, "women internalized the language" of the era: "Sluts, whores, trash, prudes, erotomaniacs, sycophants, idiots, frauds, emasculators, nutcrackers and succubi." Women were solidly in the workforce now, and some people weren't happy about it.

The third wave of feminism in the '90s was becoming more of a grassroots movement. It was dedicated to many social issues and shared information through various means, including the internet. But this new movement included so many issues and such disparate groups that it didn't have the focus to balance the constant outpouring of sexist media coverage.

Still, there were lots of shows and movies celebrating feminism and the power, even the superpowers, of women: TV shows such as *Ally McBeal*, *Murphy Brown*, *Moesha*; Dana Scully in *The X-Files*; *Xena: Warrior Princess*; and movies such as *Nikita*, *Terminator 2*, and many more. There were examples of women in music, such as Madonna and Queen Latifah, who empowered women to own their sexuality by example. In politics, Ruth Bader Ginsburg was effecting change in the Supreme Court. Madeleine Albright became the first woman US secretary of state. Mae Jemison, a NASA astronaut inspired by none other than Nichelle Nichols, became the first woman of color to go to space, in 1992. There was much to celebrate.

And yet, singer Kathleen Hanna said that her reason for forming Bikini Kill, a feminist punk rock band in the Nineties that dealt with hard-hitting subject matter for women, was to prevent young women from believing feminism had disappeared.

For every powerful example of womanhood at the time, there seemed to be a punishment from the patriarchy for any woman who stepped too far out of line. It's a split reality I could see in myself. I bellowed feminist anthems such as Helen Reddy's "I Am Woman" and Gloria Gaynor's "I Will Survive" at the top of my lungs, and believed I could have it all. At the same time, I understood that the world didn't really work that way. Why had I adopted a learned help-lessness mode of believing that "it's just the way things are," instead of questioning why it had to be like that? I got there a drop at a time.

Once I had left the halls of my decidedly feminist school, the culture of New York City in the 1970s took over my education and taught me the realities of being female at the time. As author Jess Zimmerman has said, it's just one comment, one small denigration, one biased opinion to swallow. It's just one drop, but one, after the other, after the other, after the other, can change your trajectory, your focus, even who you think you are.

Here are some of the drops that built to a wave big enough to erode my sense of self: a doctor who didn't catch my endometriosis when I was a young teen and told my parents the extreme pain I felt must be the psychosomatic result of my discomfort with the idea of being a woman. To help the pain that would have me screaming two days out of every month, I should "put my feet up." I thought, "What's wrong with me?"

The group of boys in New York who surrounded me at a stoplight and, without saying a word, put their hands everywhere on me, silently leaving when the light changed. My response was to freeze until they moved on and question the way I had chosen to dress that day. Being out with a boyfriend with a large group of men and women and having him put a finger over my mouth when I contributed my thoughts to a lively discussion. I was younger than most of them and hadn't registered till then that it was a discussion that only the men at the table were participating in. My thought was, "A new social rule to incorporate—pay attention!"

The drinks after rehearsals or the industry parties I skipped because I only had subway fare to get home and anything could happen to a young woman in the 1970s in those tunnels. There was a huge benefit to those who attended and met the people in production; with so many

actors, familiar faces would be brought in for roles first. But better to be safe than to get yourself in trouble.

The man who yelled, "Smile, you're not pretty if you don't smile!" from a car as I crossed 86th Street when I was fourteen. Note to self: You better smile no matter what you may be feeling at the moment. Being on alert on a set or a show if someone was showing interest in me, as it could lead to complications that would affect my work and my job—another thing to manage and take my energy.

Cutting off bits of my personality that seemed to be "too much" for the men I was auditioning for. Don't be too smart, soften your eyes, sexualize yourself to be the kind of woman who a man wants to fuck because that gets you the job. No matter your talent, more important is that elusive fuckability that we were told, over and over, gets you in the door. The boyfriend who told me if anyone came up to me and asked for my autograph in his presence again (I was on a soap opera at the time), he would leave me. He subsequently got on a soap opera as well, but giving autographs in my presence wasn't questioned—by either of us. Back then, this didn't feel like outrageous behavior, but a natural attempt for him to be the dominant one in the relationship. It wasn't the only time this happened in relationships, and I would take it on as my responsibility to manage a man's ego and make myself smaller, in order to be loved.

These drops are manageable and part of life, I always told myself, mostly because to start to protest or question could lead to trouble or outright danger. Scream when the boys surrounded me? I knew better. They were preteens to teens in age, and I was in my twenties. There was a reason

> Why had I adopted a learned helplessness mode of believing that "it's just the way things are," instead of questioning why it had to be like that?

OPPOSITE: My first makeup tests for Kira. Ironically, being an alien gave Kira license to access the full range of human experiences.

they felt entitled to do that in the middle of a sunny spring afternoon. Even though they were young, they were many, and any reaction from me could have made it much, much worse. No one stopped their day to help. It was a reminder of my vulnerability in the streets that made me ask myself, "Did I really need to go out?" for years after.

Believing you were powerless to change the reality, the answer was to get on with life and accept that it's up to you to stay vigilant. But as I write, I have looked back on my life and started to see all these drops that took my energy, ate into my focus, and made my immediate world smaller. I'm able to see it for what it was: a cultural norm that worked against women, and women of color much more so. In the business, the boxes they were allowed to inhabit were few and most of them insulting—especially degrading when that's what you are asked to play over and over. I understand that if my experience in the business was on a graph with other women's from good to bad, mine would be very close to good.

In 1992, TV was still considered the outlet for less serious actors: If you wanted to be a real actor, you did movies.

ABOVE: I loved the fact that Kira wasn't afraid to confront Sisko.

OPPOSITE: When I first saw the script, I thought Kira could have been a man. It was rare for female characters to be given such strong views and senior positions.

But when I was twenty, a film director with a sadistic streak shouted insults at me through a bullhorn. We were setting lights for a shot, and he wanted me to act as my own stand-in. We were in the middle of a heat wave in Brooklyn, and as I stood stock still for over an hour, sweat pouring down my armpits, the director circled me at close range, shouting about my stupidity and incompetence. The worst part for me at the time was that it was in front of an enormous crew, other actors, and people watching a film being made. The screaming seemed to go on the whole day. My role was called "Girl at the End." What could I have done with my few lines that warranted this? One of the assistant directors slid up to me at one point during this, and in hushed tones said that this director was known for picking a victim on his movie sets, and that he was sorry that this time it was me.

THE COST OF THE JOB

Months later, when they called me to add my voice to the soundtrack, which I was contractually obligated to do, I refused. If the director was going to be there, I wouldn't go. I had no idea of how the world worked. The casting director told my agent that she would blackball me in the movie industry if I didn't show up, no matter what had been done by the director, who, by the way, was a friend of hers. My agency shamed me with how stupid, sensitive, and naive I was being. I became frightened my powerful agent at ICM would drop me. It was made clear to me that I had no rights here—I was young, female, and I wanted to be an actor and have a career. In other words, I was expendable and had a passion to be a part of something. Wanting something in the business makes you vulnerable. The gatekeepers told me there would be a hundred young women just as qualified standing in line to be where I was. So, I went. He was there, but it was thankfully uneventful. After the looping session, as I walked home to my parents' apartment, a limo started following me slowly down the street. The window rolled down, and the director shouted to me that he wanted to talk to me about something—would I join him for dinner? It felt

like vindication: Standing up for myself had been the right thing after all. I thought he must be impressed with not only my acting but who I was as a person. There might even be an apology. Maybe it had all been a test! There were quite a few people who handled the details of this meeting at his hotel, and not one indicated it was anything other than the possible start of my "real" career. After I arrived, we stayed in his room for only a few minutes, and on our way out the door to have dinner, he sexually assaulted me. In an awkward flurry, I fought off his hands and he stopped, with a smile on his face. I still, amazingly, followed him to dinner, where he told me he would make an offer. Here it was—I was going to have a major role in a film! I remember it was a very fancy restaurant in the hotel, and as he laid out the very old plot that I would be his mistress and he would make me a star, I left my body at some point and watched myself as I first finished dessert, and then got up and walked out. I don't remember, but I'm sure I was

careful not to hurt his feelings. I felt shame for thinking I was being taken seriously; I felt shame for being naive; I felt shame telling my parents it wasn't a big movie role, but a proposition. I also felt trapped. If movie directors ran movies, and casting directors, agents, and studio personnel turned the other way when a girl was involved, movies weren't for me. I would have a career, I decided, in TV. Directors didn't have godlike power on TV, and jobs were quick and then over. No months or years of being trapped with someone more powerful than you. And if you did get a series, you rose hierarchically in importance—not as easy to mess with. Well, that was what my twenty-year-old self believed. I avoided auditioning for films, which disgusted my agents. I made a long-term decision based on making a cultural adaptation. If I could get hurt in the ocean, I would limit my swimming to the lakes.

But TV had its own sharks to look out for. One leading man whom I shared multiple love scenes with wouldn't stop

once the cameras stopped and was constantly propositioning me. When talking to the actor didn't work, I told the executive producer it was becoming such a problem that I wanted fewer bed scenes with the actor. He told me I obviously wasn't happy working there, and I was kindly released from my contract. I later found out that the actor and the producer were good friends. Another leading man stuck his tongue down my throat in a kissing scene—to the point of gagging me—and leered about it to the crew. But at this point, the message had become clear: You are on your own, and there are plenty of people who will do what you won't to have a career. I wanted the career but not the rest of it, so I determined I would bob and weave, play the game just enough to get jobs, but not let it go further. I avoided going to parties or social events where things could get sticky and unclear. My persona became businesslike on set. I changed my natural enjoyment of the camaraderie of the work and became a loner. My mother begged me to not let the business take away her sweet daughter. I told her it was the only way to survive it.

By the time the 1990s were happening, I was sure I understood the rules of this particular game. Mold yourself to the shape that pleased the people who were hiring, keep your expectations low, and if anything untoward happened, it was your fault. Resist the rules, and there are a lot more women just like you willing to do what you won't. This was the cultural amber that set around me to make me a fossil of my time and allowed me to find the male comics on TV hilarious when they skewered women such as Monica Lewinsky. She hadn't played the game right. That's what she got, and what I'd get, too, if I wasn't careful. Comedy is often hilarious when the subject matter is your own Achilles' heel.

In sharing this, I recognize how often my nervous system took over, how often I gave in to victimization and made myself and my life smaller. When I have shared this with other women in the business, once in a while I was told I had been stupid. I should have known. Don't go to a hotel room to meet a director. And yet, over and over in these interviews I have been told this scenario happened to others as well.

I think that harsh judgment is harmful. That a woman is "stupid" for getting in a bad situation throws out so many women's experiences and reinforces some things that may have gotten them there in the first place, like shame, feeling worthless, the nervous system's freeze response. Shame shuts you away by yourself and stops connection and growth. Worthlessness makes you pick the same negative people or circumstances because you believe that's all you deserve. If a woman is sexually harassed or raped, the only answer that seems to free her from judgment is that she fought or ran. A woman I spoke to for this book whispered to me that she was raped decades ago, but she always blamed herself and never spoke about it to anyone. She had frozen and therefore believed she had allowed it. But she was subsequently taught that freezing is an ancient and real nervous system response designed to keep you alive. It will hijack the part of your brain that can strategize and come up with a plan. Now in her late eighties, she is finally able to drop her guilt and speak truthfully about her experience.

SELF-PRESERVATION

I think some women who offer judgment, instead of holding another's experience with care, do so for a couple of reasons—both of them self-preservational. When I told a very close friend that I had been kidnapped by two men, she said she just couldn't have me in her life anymore. The way I saw it then, and now, is that she needed to believe I had behaved in some bad, reckless way to have that happen to me. This would be a thought she could hold like a mental talisman to keep her safe. It wasn't a random, horrible act. I had somehow asked for it; therefore, it couldn't happen to her. To hold on to this viewpoint, she couldn't be a part of my post-traumatic process or she might lose her talisman. This is only my supposition about her behavior, but it makes sense to me. The other response (although there are many others, these are two I have personally experienced) is one I had had myself with Monica Lewinsky. "She didn't play the game right." At issue, of course, is the fact that the game rules

aren't published, they keep changing, and if young women don't have mentors in the business, sometimes you wouldn't even know the "rules" existed. When you are learning on the fly, it's easier to make mistakes. It also releases men from any accountability. To think that "men just aren't capable of better" is an insulting bias against them.

Some of the rules have shifted in a positive direction recently, but as we know, there's still far to go. Instead of judging, let's open channels of discussion, with an understanding that some people have life experiences that naturally lead them to deal with hardships in ways that at first may seem inexplicable. So, let's be curious instead of judgmental and listen to what happened. Let's keep the channels open, so that as long as the game has rules, we can share them with transparency, and women can then choose to play by them, or not. And let's not judge them, whichever way they choose.

How did I begin to be aware of the unconscious cultural accommodations that were continuing to shape me? When you are caught in the bubble of how you believe things have to be, it's difficult to discern the truth of any situation. But that seventeen-year-old I had been, the one who believed that as a woman I could have agency to build my place in the world, was still inside me. She would pop out rebelliously from time to time, sometimes in frivolous ways, and sometimes in impactful ways just in time to save me. This was the part of me who found an open door in the shape of a TV character, and she rushed through it as fast as she could.

STAR TREK: DEEP SPACE NINE

Work on Star Trek: Deep Space Nine *began in 1991. It was less than five years since Gene Roddenberry had created* The Next Generation, *but a lot had changed. Roddenberry knew about the series, but he died before the real work began, so for the first time ever, he wouldn't leave his fingerprints on the characters. Instead, the show would be created by Rick Berman and Michael Piller. Both men were in their forties and considerably younger than Roddenberry. They had been shaped by a different era and had been in their twenties when feminism exploded. From the beginning, they proposed a show in which women were in positions of power.*

The series seems almost countercultural in its boldness. The writers wanted to do things that TNG hadn't. The new show included a person of color as the commander and Number One on the call sheet, a multicultural setting that didn't go anywhere but boldly into interpersonal relationships, and strong women leads who didn't follow the status quo. There were also several large roles for women guest stars of a diverse enough nature that representation was better covered than in most TV shows at the time.

NEW ERA

But DS9's creators were still products of their time. When they created the show, female characters who broke out of the traditional roles were still considered a novelty—something that was worth talking about because it was unusual—and Hollywood was definitely still Hollywood. There was no question that the studio really cared what a woman looked like, and even if we were making tentative steps, women were still being pigeonholed. Before DS9, I was still going up for the same kind of roles I had been five years earlier.

Still, things were just beginning to change. There were lots of shows and movies celebrating feminism and the power of women. On TV, *Murphy Brown* was a big deal.

In the movies, Sarah Connor was reinvented as an almost unstoppable force who could take on a Terminator, and Jodie Foster gave one of her most memorable and brave performances in *The Silence of the Lambs*. There were examples of women in music too, such as Madonna and Queen Latifah, who empowered women to own their sexuality by example.

Once Berman and Piller had created the show, they handed the reins over to Ira Steven Behr. Over the next seven years, he would shape the characters we played. The number of women was increasing in the workspace, but there was still a feeling that it was a game of musical chairs. As Laura Behr, physicist, ballet dancer, choreographer, and wife of Ira, told me, a lot of women wasted time and energy seeing each other as the reason they couldn't win. In fact, when the music stopped and women rushed for a seat at the table, the real issue was the inequity in the number of chairs women were allowed to sit down on.

Deep Space Nine would have the most male writing staff of all the shows. Every now and again, a woman would contribute a script as a freelancer, but in its seven years, not one member of the writing staff was a woman. We didn't have many female directors, either. Of 173 episodes, only seven were directed by women.

If women were going to make progress—and we did—we would depend on the kindness—and perspective—of men.

Nana Visitor as
MAJOR KIRA

I was a mother of a three-month-old baby when I got the pages to audition for a character on a sci-fi show called Star Trek: Deep Space Nine. *The last job I had done was a guest star on a sitcom called* Empty Nest, *for which I had bound my five-month-pregnant stomach. I was the breadwinner of the family and needed to get back to work as soon as possible. We were in debt because I couldn't work the last few months of my pregnancy, and although it was the last thing my body or emotions wanted, I needed a job.*

This show, *Deep Space Nine*, had some points against it. In those days, sci-fi was where actors went when their careers were dying. But I was thirty-five years old—it was now or never. My managers were already concerned that my use-by date was expiring. Another negative was that the show was in syndication, which meant it wasn't the big payday or national attention you got on a network show. It was definitely not looked at as winning the Actor's Lotto.

And yet, the constant stream of girlfriend, wife, mother, dead girlfriend, evil girlfriend, and victim roles I was getting were always in service to another character, without agency or depth of their own. Major Kira was so empowered in the scenes sent to me that I called my managers to ask if they had made a mistake and submitted me for a man's role. It was no mistake. For once, I dared to take the chance to audition with the full spectrum of unique attributes that made up me.

It was a man, by the way, who guided me to take that chance. My longtime acting teacher and my brother, Ian Tucker, was the champion and mentor to my seventeen-year-old self, the part of me that wanted to be the keeper of this character more than anything. He gave me the courage, and the tools. I didn't make myself smaller, or fuckable, or even likable. And I got the job.

Major Kira was the most human character I've ever been asked to play, and of course, she was Bajoran. But this was the beauty and freedom at the time of playing an alien in *Star Trek*. The usual acceptable lanes for a female actor to stay in didn't apply.

The two-part pilot sets up a main character, Major Kira, who is not tied to Roddenberry's rules about perfectly evolved people. He had envisioned a future in which his Starfleet people had lost the need for conflict and fighting. Several of the writers told me this made them work hard to find drama or growth, and they had often had to turn to alien guest stars to make sparks happen.

Because the main characters of DS9 didn't always agree, it explored what it took to establish trust and respect in a multicultural society. The alien first officer, Major Kira, was allowed to disagree, show her displeasure for the presence of Starfleet, speak her distrust of the foreign minister of Bajor, and roughly correct the insulting view of her world by the young doctor with stars in his eyes. This made for conflict, which brought an immediacy to understanding all the characters' points of view, and forced an intimacy between them because no one had the emotional luxury to simply fly off to other worlds, never to be seen again. It was essential that eventually they figured out how to cooperate.

The role of Major Kira was originally written as Ro Laren, a Bajoran lieutenant in Starfleet. Ro had a rich backstory as well, and the excellence of Michelle Forbes's acting

in *Star Trek: The Next Generation* gave Patrick Stewart a fire-starter for many of the scenes they were in together. Clear eyed and equal to everyone she spoke with, there was nothing performative about her character.

Major Kira, originally a small role, was elevated to first officer because Forbes chose a movie career instead of getting locked into a yearslong series. I am grateful she did, giving me the opportunity to embody Kira. Even though the producers sent me VHS copies of all her shows, I didn't see her episodes until years later, mostly because I worried about copying a performance instead of creating one. Seeing her performance

now, it's no wonder they wanted to star her in the next iteration of *Star Trek*. She boosted the energy and women of TNG, and without her, the writers may not have realized what an asset an alien with a complex history could be.

Ira Behr recently shared with me that he remembers the moment Michael Piller came to his office and apologetically told him DS9 wouldn't ever be THE *Star Trek* show—that honor would be passed from TNG directly to *Star Trek: Voyager*. *Voyager* had to be the face of *Star Trek*, positioned as it was as the flagship show of the brand-new Viacom Network. Ira added that the lack of fan love DS9 was receiving made the decision an easy one. He waited until Piller left to silently cheer. We would fly under the radar of any studio executives who might micromanage everything from storylines to casting to women's hairstyles. Left with fewer cooks in the kitchen, we were much freer to take creative chances.

Kira had the full scope of emotions, a complicated past (gold for an actor as well as writers), goals and dreams, appetites, sexual and otherwise, and my goodness, yes—agency. Her goals for her people and her personal ethics took precedence over being liked by the new society she found herself in. She had spiritual beliefs she practiced even when no one else was around. There wasn't anything about the writing that was gendered, and I felt free to bring my particular brand of humanness to the part. It was with a mixture of disbelief, joy, and worry I might be fired at any moment, that I delivered my performance.

There were people who thought I was going too far. I remember Marina Sirtis coming to our makeup trailer and telling me my performance was wrong because I was trying to have a man's strength as opposed to a woman's. My immediate internal reaction was my go-to: What's wrong with me? But that seventeen-year-old in me made me stick rebelliously by my interpretation. At the time, I saw this as an attack from Sirtis. Now understanding what she had experienced in the early years of her show, I see it as perhaps a warning and an attempt to protect me.

Sirtis wasn't the only one who thought Kira's attitude in the first year was giving off PMS vibes or male energy. Laura Behr read the early scripts to see how the women's characters were developing, and felt that Kira didn't show the full spectrum of emotions that women are capable of. She thought it was telling that the major was written by a man, because they are more likely to cover uncomfortable emotions with anger than a woman is. She told Ira that instead of thinking "male" or "female," he should write "human."

She also noted that, as the show progressed, he learned to write the full-spectrum woman. I saw a full-spectrum woman from the beginning, but one who had been destabilized by huge trauma. Marina needn't have worried; our show had producers and writers who weren't from the 1960s, as TNG had done in the early years, and we weren't under the close scrutiny they had been.

That show had been a chemistry experiment, mixing Roddenberry and his associates from the original with new writers and Paramount executives trying to get a new concept for syndication off the ground. Now Roddenberry had passed, and Berman and Piller had proven themselves with TNG. I couldn't know it at the time, but my character wasn't going to get dropped or compromised. Not that I didn't get notes and attention to my appearance.

I can count the times I was in Rick Berman's office on one hand, and they were usually about approval for hair or makeup. Candy, our hair supervisor in the early years, took the golf cart trip with me from the makeup trailer to Berman to get my look approved. "Doesn't she look beautiful?" she asked him as I stood there for inspection. "We don't need her to be beautiful," he answered. To my 1990s mind, this made me believe I wasn't in the "Sexy" box and was therefore expendable. (What's more important than being desirable and a potential mate for the men of the series? That means a place in the hierarchy and dependable work.)

THE GIFT OF KIRA

I still didn't understand what a gift that statement would prove to be, the freedom it would give me. Nor did I understand that my character would be fleshed out to the point where no one cared about whether she pleased other people.

I remember another call from Berman asking me to stop walking the halls of the Promenade like John Wayne. I loved my ability to stride along the way that was natural to me in my flat, practical boots, but the note was enough for me to realize that of course there were still limits to how far I could go in allowing myself to be comfortably me.

Eventually, I was called to meet with Ira (someone else was present, but I can't remember who) and asked for ideas about how to soften my performance. It was clear to me that Ira was responsible for the large acting space I was given to play in. Michael Piller had told me Behr was the true keeper of my character.

I understood this meeting was in response to the studio having qualms, or to the audience disliking my strident behavior, or the writers wanting me to start to have an arc.

Maybe it was all three. To be clear, I have heard that, from *Voyager* on, *Star Trek* actors have occasional meetings to talk to producers and writers about their character's arc. We had nothing like this. If you were brought into the offices and you were a woman, something was wrong.

I didn't have a name for it then, but my angry behavior was based on my understanding of post-traumatic stress disorder (PTSD), a term used since 1980. I once heard a Navy SEAL say that post-traumatic stress isn't a disorder, but proof that you had a human response to inhuman treatment, and since then, I refer to it as PTS as well. I had no idea that in a few years, I would myself suffer with it, and its effects would last for over twenty years.

MAKING ADJUSTMENTS

What I did know from firsthand experience when I got to DS9 were the effects of war. I had an aunt named Suzanne Charisse who had been a French Resistance heroine in World War II. We visited her and my uncle in England when I was around fourteen years old. I'll never forget meeting this astounding woman whose mental wounds were so severe that it was impossible to interact with her normally. She spoke in a constant monotonic, angry stream that repeated her traumatic war experience over and over as if it had happened in the present, even as she served us lunch.

No one else in the family had the opportunity to speak much, and her husband looked at her through it all with a mixture of agony and deep respect. Remembering my aunt, I drew the conclusion that anger would be the only safe emotion for Major Kira to exhibit after the trauma of Cardassian rule.

I had been expecting this meeting since I started the show; in the early 1990s, women who drew outside the lines were usually yanked back, one way or another. I wasn't cast

as a villain, in which case the "Bitch" persona would be acceptable. I was a lead in a series whose character wasn't looking to make friends, not your typical 1990s woman. At the time, being yanked back into the lane of acceptable behavior meant "feminize yourself and fast" to me, and it rankled me that I might be forced back to that dull and performative place.

What I didn't know was that the writers would give my character a graceful arc as she gradually recovered from the damage done to her during the occupation of Bajor. I assumed that there was a box waiting for me to crawl into so I could be more acceptable to an audience who sometimes called me "butch" or "bitch" when I met them at conventions. That didn't happen too often, and they were balanced with women who seemed to gain room in their own lives from a character who had so few cultural encumbrances. I found that I had quite a number of lesbian audience members who liked Major Kira. I was surprised to find that some of them wanted me to align in my own life with their expectations of me. "Are you gay?" I was asked more than once. I would answer no, and more than once the answer came back along the lines of "Oh, you are. You just don't know it yet."

My identity, the one I inhabited thanks to Kira, was most natural for me. But in the 1990s, most women were still there to be performative and to act for the benefit of others rather than themselves. And even some people who lived outside the dominant culture were confused when they saw a character who wasn't like that and lived in a less binary reality.

It is a testament to how we have grown as a society that I no longer feel internal confusion or a need to explain myself. It's a balanced and safe place I have found. I now give my support to those people who live outside the lines of "normal" because I know how much self-doubt and worry about fitting in filled my brain, robbing me of energy and focus for other pursuits.

> I was a lead in a series whose character wasn't looking to make friends, not your typical 1990s woman.

When I had that meeting, I remembered Berman's comments about my striding the Promenade. I immediately thought that putting me in heels would end that problem, forcing me to walk with a sway in my hips and smaller steps. Heels make me aware of my whole body because there is such a difference in how your body has to move.

A new costume caused self-consciousness, too. This one was skintight as opposed to the all-business corduroy two-piece I had started with, and it emphasized the gel breast enhancers I was issued from the beginning. Primarily for women who have had mastectomies, they look like raw chicken cutlets and fit into a bra much larger than your own size. I was given two pairs to wear at once, and told there wasn't a choice about wearing them. This was still sci-fi, I

was still a woman, and terrorist or freedom fighter (I could choose my moniker), but I was going to have large breasts either way. This was one aesthetic that had been decided from the top, whether you were expected to fill the "Sexy" box or not.

But I was the one to feminize my look with heels and a sleeker costume, and I suggested it for what I believed was the self-preservation of my character. If I was getting negative feedback, which I was, I needed to fly further under

ABOVE: Early on there was concern that Kira was too strident. The first thought was to alter her appearance, so I gained a tighter costume and high-heeled boots.

the radar. If my aunt could parachute behind enemy lines, I could certainly disguise myself as a woman slowing herself down with heels to make herself more easily caught by a man pursuing her. What really mattered, I reasoned, was what she did once caught. In my mind, it would never be what the man was hoping for.

The other grace given to all the characters in DS9 was serialization, which meant we broke away from the stand-alone, episodic style of the previous two shows, and it allowed us to slowly build character arcs. The writers gave Kira intimate, emotional connections with the people who inhabited her world.

The excellence of the actors I worked with, from Avery Brooks and my dear René Auberjonois to a multitude of stellar guest stars, made going to the depths the part required thrilling. Each show that centered on these relationships helped to explain where Major Kira had come from, even as it hinted at what she might evolve into.

ABOVE: Kira had several love affairs, but they were always serious, and I never felt they trivialized her.

OPPOSITE: Refreshingly, the "sex" scene with Odo was entirely about Kira's pleasure.

HEROIC LEAD

The director of photography (DP) Marvin Rush, and later Jonathan West, supported the character by giving her many close-ups. Rush explained to me early on that he gave my character "hero shots," which for him meant shots framed from below, looking up and tight to the face. This was usually reserved for male actors at the time. The effect it had was to let the audience know you are one of the people they should be rooting for. It wasn't as pretty as the typical frame for a woman, but it let you see the emotions and intentions the actor was projecting, as well as the strengths (and flaws) in the face. Very often, it was Major Kira's face that was the last shot of the scene, allowing you to see her thoughts on what had just transpired.

The close-ups seemed to be equally distributed among the cast. I had seen in TNG that the close-up was mostly reserved for Picard, allowing us to align ourselves with him primarily. On DS9, there seemed to be an effort to understand everyone's point of view—even if they conflicted.

In terms of guest stars, there were many: all of them epic actors. Each of them served to build out the story of the Bajorans, a spiritual people who had been oppressed by a dominant race. Camille Saviola as Kai Opaka is the first spiritual leader of Bajor we meet. Her performance made it easy to feel the connection Kira had to her faith. Brian Keith as a stubborn old Bajoran farmer in "Progress" let us examine society's choices and what they cost us. In this episode, Kira has to choose between an older man she has deep compassion for and her duty to her job. Sisko takes on a mentorship role as he helps her see just how difficult building a new and fairer world can be, especially when it requires tearing down the old and more familiar one.

EVOLVING CHARACTER

The process she goes through matures Major Kira, and because the show was serialized, it was a change you could see in subsequent shows. Written by Peter Allan Fields, as so many strong Kira episodes were, it got the tone and banter of a bond between a young woman and old man just right.

Another script of his, "Duet," is my favorite episode of all. It examines the relationship between Kira and a Cardassian she believes is a famous war criminal. In the end, she understands the truth of this man broken by the occupation of Bajor as much as she was, and truly mourns a Cardassian's death. At the beginning of the show, she is prejudiced against this man simply because he has a Cardassian face. By the end, she understands the mistakes that are made by making lazy, quick assumptions based on confirmation bias: judging a situation by seeing through the lens of what you already believe.

Working opposite an Academy Award winner is something you dream about as an actor. The actual experience, I imagine, can sometimes be a disappointment, but Louise Fletcher was everything I could have hoped for. Down to earth and kind, she not once made me feel that acting with me on a sci-fi show was anything but joyful. She was a true actor, there for the work. I felt like I was playing tennis with a far better player, and I stretched to try to reach her abilities.

Interestingly, her character was created because Avery Brooks was cast as the series lead. In the original bible for the series, Sisko was conceived as a young man needing mentoring. Kai Opaka was going to be his Bajoran spiritual guide, who would help him become the Emissary of the Prophets.

Ira told me that when the writers saw Avery, the part of Kai Opaka became unnecessary. He was so poised and

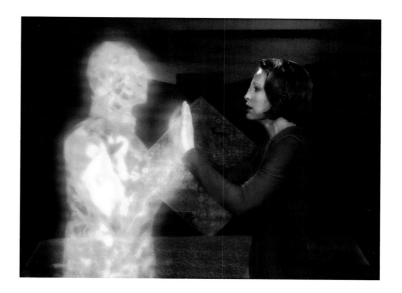

powerful already that he didn't need a mentor. In order to tie him to Bajor, the writers would need a daunting archenemy. Enter Louise Fletcher as Kai Winn. She added political intrigue to the spirituality, once again showing life in shades of gray. Sisko had a worthy opponent, and the Kai forced Kira to not only acquire political savvy but also maturity and emotional control that she kept to the end.

Serialization allowed for a love life, as well. As Brannon Braga told me, building a relationship between characters takes time, and it was almost impossible on TNG because the episodes were designed to be seen as standalone episodes. Major Kira had a few love interests on the show: a fellow freedom fighter named Shakaar, played by Duncan Regehr; a Vedek named Bareil, played by Philip Anglim; and Thomas Riker, played, of course, by Jonathan Frakes.

Taking a peek into chat rooms can be a terrifying experience, but I wanted to see what was being said about the fact that Kira had a few lovers before she committed to a relationship with Odo. In the 1990s, women were still largely held to a different standard than men. The reactions ran the gamut from feeling she had loose morals to that she had every right to satisfy herself sexually.

The only thing that bothered me about her lovers was the fact that it seemed to me that there was a male perspective about what kind of man would attract Kira. Shakaar and Bareil were both powerfully positioned, typically good-looking men. Although I mourned the fact at the time that the Odo/Kira relationship was going to fall into the 1990s trope of friends-with-sexual-tension, I loved that Kira chose a person and not a type in the end.

With a serialized show, we were able to build the relationship in a believable way, until the audience just wanted to see us finally together. Our connection was based on trust and mutual admiration, and when it was broken, it was painful. In season two's "Necessary Evil," Odo discovers that during the occupation, Kira had killed a Cardassian collaborator and hid the fact from him, fearing his judgment. At the end of the episode, she asks him if he will ever trust her again. There is no answer from him. It's a moment that made me understand the gray ethical area my character lived in, and again it was not a TV moment that would have been possible without serialization. Trust lost would take time to recover.

Odo seemed to accept the whole person Kira was, failings and all, and recognized her struggles to grow.

To me being a shape-shifter is a beautiful metaphor for loving someone over time; you can't expect that the person you see today will be the same person you will be with in ten years' time. In that way, I think most people who continue to evolve are shape-shifters. Kira couldn't fully understand his life experience, but respected and honored him.

Kira was ready to go all in on a relationship that required accepting and loving the full being, and not having preconceived expectations of what that should look like. His need to spend some time in a liquid state echoes what I know of living with someone who is disabled or has a chronic illness. In "Chimera," she understands that his need to be a part of the shape-shifter's Great Link may take him away from her. That he decides to stay is his decision alone. It was clear that these were two individuals who chose, over and over, to be together in spite of their differences.

When Odo becomes a mist and envelops Kira to give her an approximation of what it feels like for Changelings to link, it is the ultimate act of "love is love is love" to me. It certainly wasn't what a love scene would have looked like between the major and a hunk. It was nontraditional, intimate, and a gift to Kira.

In the finale of the show, Kira's gift to Odo is that she has true mature love for him. Instead of seeing his decision to rejoin the Great Link as abandonment, she supports him. With total love, she releases him to the next part of his journey, respecting his sense of duty and purpose.

Our show does well on the Bechdel Test, a test conceived by writer Alison Bechdel that looks at how often women have conversations with other women on TV shows and movies. In order to pass it, the women need to have names and not be speaking about a man. When I asked writer Jane Espenson about it, she said, "I think it's amazing because the whole point is she set this really low bar and then said, look how few things pass it. We should set a much higher test. Let's have women drive the story. Let's have women be as complicated as men. They don't have to be stronger, better people than men; I think that's a trap. But have them be as complicated as men. Never feel like you've got too many women or people of color in your story. There's no such thing as too many. We've had a lot of—so many—decades of stories without them."

Jadzia Dax and Kira have a true, trusting friendship. In their scenes together, there is humor, affection, and advice given and taken on way more than men. There wasn't a doubt in my mind that they supported one another, were not in competition, and celebrated one another's achievements and personal happiness. That, to me back then in the 1990s Hollywood culture, was true science fiction.

After two years, I was excited by the opportunities Kira offered me, but still wary about how much rope I was being given. I couldn't believe that I wouldn't still be yanked back into line. But the signs were good. I was somehow keeping my head above water with the long working hours and the realities of being a newly single mother of a small boy. But playing Kira took an emotional toll.

The way I approached the work would have suited the stage better than a seven-year television run. In the theater, the boundaries between the stage and your actual life are much clearer, and are set up with protocols and rituals. I hadn't found a way yet that protected my nervous system and was still truthful storytelling, and I chose good storytelling over mental health. I would spend days of work in a dark place, where thoughts about ethical dilemmas, loss, and the horrors of occupation were constantly being dropped into my head and were the reality my body believed.

Michael Piller's observation that you mine a character's makeup by taking away things they value to see how they react comes to mind. In my work life, I would lose friends, trust, and very often I would lose sovereignty over my body. Kidnapped, tied to tables, eaten by a rock, they were storylines that forced Kira to confront her fears and her truths. All of it, traumatic. My body got so used to being in fight or flight, it seemed to be my default state.

OPPOSITE: When I got pregnant, I genuinely thought I could be sacked, but with a little help from Laura Behr, the writers found a way of writing it into the scripts.

ABOVE: I love the fact that Kira has a questionable past: Was she a freedom fighter or a terrorist? There are no easy answers.

Rape is a story that is told about women so often that it is a familiar trope. But it isn't just a storytelling device, it is also a reflection of what too often happens in real life. While Kira was moving through an arc of recovery as she dealt with post-traumatic stress, I was taken down during the third season of our show by my own trauma, which took me way longer than seven years to emerge from. The rape I recovered from eventually. The moral injury took more than twenty years to heal.

By season three, I had bought a modest house in Benedict Canyon that had, thrillingly, been previously owned by Harrison Ford. It was postage stamp sized but had beautiful woodwork throughout that the seller told me was done by Ford himself. He had converted the garage to a workspace, so I parked my Mama-Proud minivan in front. I was divorced from my first husband, and had found a wonderfully kind older man to be nanny to my son. My Rottweiler and German shepherd completed our little family unit.

Late one work night, bleary eyed from the long hours, I traveled on an empty Sunset Boulevard toward home. I noticed headlights behind me, the only other car besides me on the road, but they didn't seem to be making an effort to keep up, so I relaxed. But there they were again, and they took the turn with me on Benedict Canyon, and then, alarmingly, on to my tiny road.

As I slowed by my house, now on alert, they drove past me, further up the hill. "See?" I told myself. "Always so

OPEN A CHANNEL: THE WOMEN OF *STAR TREK*

scared. They're neighbors going home. Maybe they're on a TV show too and just getting home."

As I opened the door of my minivan, there was a nine-millimeter at my head. The two men had turned off their engine and rolled down the hill. I pushed past them and ran as they shouted they would shoot and then they did. I froze and they had me. Thrown up against their car several times, I told them I hadn't looked them in the face and wouldn't, so I could never ID them. They pushed me down into the passenger leg space of the front seat of their car, and although I knew this meant it would probably end badly for me, we were blessedly driving away from where my two-year-old son was sleeping.

One drove this car, which I later learned was stolen, and one drove mine. They had the same R&B station on that I had been listening to on the drive home, and I could smell beer and pastrami. The rest of the night came in continuous flashes to me for the next twenty years. Standing with them. Getting money at the ATM. Not enough for them. They're angry. Back in the car. This is happening. This is happening. This is happening. Stay here. Stay thinking. We stop.

Being thrown down on the ground in a small park in the foothills of Beverly Hills, hands tied behind my back, on my knees, face in the bushes. I saw peaceful-looking houses yards away and wondered how no one could hear this.

They are by the car, arguing about where to dump the body. My body. Maybe outside Vegas again? Their voices are raised. How does no one hear this? I start to shake so severely with fear that I am jumping off the ground I'm kneeling on. I tell myself that at any moment, I will feel the gunshot in my head. I tell myself, "Okay, if you are leaving this Earth, don't do it with these two men in your head. Leave them where they are, don't let them be a part of your last moments."

I forced calm through my body, and stopped shaking. And waited. The rape was bad, but it wasn't a gunshot. Back in the car, I start talking. Of the two men, the one driving me at this point seemed more human, and I talk fast about my life, my work, my baby. I didn't beg, I spoke as if we were friends.

They wanted me to lead them back to the house. One of them kept demanding it, and I said I didn't know where we were anymore—my eyes were down. Maybe this way—no that way? I don't know! This went on for a while until the man driving my minivan cut us off and switched places with the driver. I started to talk to him, as I had the other man, looking down so I wouldn't see his face, speaking fast, until he told me to shut up. "I'm the one with the power 'cause I'm the one with the gun." He cocked it and put it to the left side of my head.

I can still, all these years later, all the psychological treatment later, I can still feel it there. He drove with one hand, the other keeping the gun to my head, and told me to take them to the house. This moment destroyed me for so many years to come. More than the rape, leading these men to where my baby slept caused a moral injury that didn't allow for safety, or comfort, hope, or joy. These emotions lived in me subterraneanly, and to glimpse them at all, I would have to talk myself through a human experience. "If I was a normal woman, I would be feeling joy right now." I could feel around an emotion, but not be in it.

Because of my self-preservational act of doing what they wanted and leading them home, I called myself a "bad mother," "instinct-less woman," and much worse. I believed I should have gotten shot before I took them to my son. We walked up the steps, and as the dogs barked, they said they would shoot them if they attacked. I assured them they wouldn't, and indeed my sweet dogs were happy to see us.

My nanny came out of his bedroom to see if I was okay, saw them, screamed, and started running for the back door. In my peripheral vision, head still down, I saw the one with the gun raise it to shoot. I yelled to my nanny to stop running, they won't hurt us, they want stuff. They hog-tied us both.

This kind soul who cared for my son like a family member was crying and begging, which worried me because I thought that it would eventually anger the men. One stayed downstairs with us, eating cookies I had baked earlier, playing with the dogs, while in the other hand he held the gun on us.

The other, more dangerous man was upstairs. Through the baby monitor that sat on the kitchen counter, I heard him in my son's room. Somehow, my boy stayed quiet, as I prayed that somehow he would. As part of treatment, twenty years later, I wrote in many different forms about "what happened." Emotionally, what I was feeling at that moment, hog-tied and gagged, as the man destroyed my home around my sleeping son, is best done cryptically. I don't want to use more words.

> *Pow*
> *power transformers explode in my brain*
> *Boom: panic*
> *Boom: prayer*
> *Boom: RAGE I'm in sync with this stink and think*
> *Dogs, different dogs if we live through this hell not to*
> *play with you but to spay you then you'll be prey too*
> *and—I see. Now I'm lost too.*

The man eventually came downstairs demanding the "real stuff." He had my jewelry box, which held the topaz earrings my parents had given me, an Elsa Peretti small diamond on a short chain from an ex, and my wedding rings. The rest was costume. He threatened to bring my child downstairs, to force me to give him the safe containing the valuable jewelry he believed I had.

This got me talking as fast and as earnestly as I could. I told him I would find a way to get him something valuable, somehow; I would send the money, anything, but there was nothing in the house more than what he found already.

This caused them to hurt me violently again, I guess to make the evening worth their trouble, and then pick me up by the ropes tying my ankles and hands together to throw me face-down on the sofa. One of them quickly covered my head with a pillow. I was sure they did this to save themselves from having to look at me when they shot me. I braced for it. Nothing. It was dawn and they had left.

I managed to get out of my ties, helped my nanny to do the same, got my son, and ran to the neighbors to call the police. After that night, the rage descended somewhere deep inside like my other emotions. The only emotion I could dependably feel was fear. Like white noise under everything in good times, like gunfire by my ear in bad times.

I left the house with my child and never saw it again. My brother took on the details of my life for months to come. My two-year-old and I lived in hotels, and eventually an apartment Paramount helped me find.

They found the men and asked me to ID them. They had done this to a number of women in the space of days, and the police told me they were also suspects in a murder in Las Vegas they wouldn't be prosecuted for. I agreed to come down to the police station, with my brother Ian by my side, and wondered how I could possibly help because I had never seen them. But I had heard them, and it was with a kind of grim satisfaction that I had each man in the lineup repeat, "I'm the one with the power 'cause I'm the one with the gun." I correctly identified them, and the case went to trial.

I was encouraged not to testify by others in the business; being on a TV show and being known as the "actress who was raped," I was told, would ruin me. I didn't see a choice and I testified against them, as did several other women. On the day of the trial, as I was repeating the details of what had happened in the witness stand, I saw a writer with the *Enquirer* taking notes. So, I thought, everyone was right and now I would be finished. But when the article appeared, it was a small blurb that gave no details of what I had had to recount in graphic detail. I was so grateful.

The men were each given multiple life sentences, not just for the rapes they had committed—that was a lesser offense. But because they had committed the crime of kidnapping, they were in jail for years and years. When they were given a chance to speak, the vicious one said that he had heard all these women testifying about how this had changed their lives. He said, "How come no one is thinking about how this is changing mine?"

I was given Xanax by the hospital to cope and was back to work soon after. I remember I was so emotionally dysregulated that the first man I saw on set, our kind, sweet, supportive DP, Jonathan West, terrified me and caused me to become so frightened I thought I would pass out. For months, my brother became a fixture on set, sitting off in a chair, quietly reading a paperback. Some angels appeared for me when I needed them, and he was one of them. No one

OPPOSITE: Kira was always a warrior and got to fight, but over the years, she started to heal from the damage that was done to her psyche by the occupation of Bajor.

spoke about what had happened, and that worked for me because I automatically started functioning with a fractured self who still knew Kira and knew how to work.

NO GLAMOR

One of the first episodes back for me was "Heart of Stone," a show I still haven't seen. One of the few times my rage surfaced during this time was at our director Alex Singer, who really didn't deserve it. It was a long day of being frozen inside a rock, which was hugely uncomfortable to begin with. As it tightens around me, the script directions say something along the lines of "Kira is in agony."

Being a man of the times and knowing full well that beauty counts for female leads, Alex told me he was going to do another take for me because in the last one, my painful expression had caused me to look "grotesque." I remember screaming at him, "That's what violence does! I won't do it another way." Sexualizing or glamorizing a woman's pain is something I have been aware of ever since.

As Kira was becoming trusting and more open, my life shrunk to what felt safe enough to feel or do, and that was a very small room to live in. Around twenty years later, I found myself in the office of a psychologist, Dr. Gabrielle Chiaramonte, who specialized in helping soldiers with post-traumatic stress. Although it isn't effective for everyone, she combined exposure therapy with Jon Kabat-Zinn's Mindfulness Based Stress Reduction, and I was eventually free of the crushing fear and guilt. I understood what I was experiencing was simply a result of chemical reactions happening in my body. Trauma can become like a file on a computer that just won't close. Learning that we build synapses in our brain, actual pathways with our thoughts, made me aware of thinking better, more truthful thoughts about myself. By going over and over the events of that night, they became my story, my experience, and not simply something that was done to me that would pop back to Technicolor life in my head when I least expected it.

There is such a thing as post-traumatic growth, and I feel that is what happened for me. I became more compassionate toward myself and others, and more aware of being purposeful in my life. Looking out toward other people became more important than focusing inward.

Speaking of my trauma is a way to tell others who have had trauma in their lives that there was real hope and that there is healing. When I told my doctor I was a broken person, she told me about *Kintsugi*, the Japanese art of mending broken pottery with gold, and the Leonard Cohen lyrics "There is a crack in everything, that's how the light gets in." Seeing this as an opportunity to cultivate deep parts of myself changed me.

It's recently been determined that post-traumatic growth can be shared. I was at a convention in Raleigh, West Virginia, when a sweet-faced soldier came up to me, and told me she was a chaplain. She heard many stories of trauma from soldiers needing help. She gave them what she could, but being a soldier is a transient business, and she would see someone in the depths of despair and then never again, as she or they were transferred elsewhere.

Listening to Gates McFadden's podcast, where I told my story, gave her hope and comfort that some of the people she counseled could find their way to heal. Out of character for me, I asked to take her picture. Days later, I realized I wanted to include her in this book. A tweet posting her picture and asking for help in finding her was successful almost instantly. In interviewing her, not only was I impressed with the depth, intelligence, and strength of this human, but that the actors on *Star Trek* are capable of still positively affecting people years after the series is done, both through the role they play in the series and their own experience. In a world where so many of us are transient, actors who have been present in people's lives since they were young continue to offer "hope, courage, and the fact that we are not alone," according to that chaplain, Major Mel Baars O'Malley.

But before this healing, I had to get on with a life where there was "before it happened" and "after it happened." I had a baby with actor Alexander Siddig, who played Dr. Bashir. Being a working woman with two children was the dream of having it all, but the reality was more like a house of mirrors: I never was where I thought I should be.

Having an infant when I started the show, I felt the split many women feel. When I was with my child, I believed I was stealing time from learning the next day's dialogue. When I was at work, I felt not only responsible for organizing

RIGHT: My scenes with Odo were a highlight, and I miss René enormously.

OPPOSITE: Kira evolved in seven years as she overcame post-traumatic stress and became more thoughtful.

everything concerning my baby's day, but also heavy guilt for not being there. Friends who were mothers too, and some who weren't, would ask me how I did it. They could never leave a child to be raised by someone else. I would wildly wonder what the answer could be. As the breadwinner, I needed to bring money in to raise a child. I had never held another job other than acting.

One day at work, I was called in at 5 a.m. to be in the first scene. For one reason or another, the day was switched, and I would now work at the end of the day, which could be more than twelve hours away. My son had been running a high fever and was still an infant at the time. I asked the AD, who was a woman, if I could go home for an hour to check on my child. She said, "You should have thought of things like that before you took this job," and refused. I felt hot shame for stepping out of line.

DOING IT ALL

I decided that if anyone was going to suffer for the fact that I was a working mother, it wouldn't be my baby and it wouldn't be my job; it would be me. I was naive enough to believe that a philosophy that basically ground me physically and mentally down could be good for anyone. I got used to being mama in my trailer with my son to switching on the walk over to the set to Major Kira.

I slept very little, sometimes getting home after 1 a.m., I would learn the next day's lines, sleep three hours, and get up in time to fix breakfast for my son. I always thought that falling asleep at the wheel was a foolish thing: If you felt sleepy, wouldn't you just pull over? What I didn't realize is that you simply lose consciousness. I did it on the road coming home, luckily waking as my car went slightly off the road. I remember more than once losing consciousness while playing with my son.

A.H. (after it happened), I was fractured into work mode, which was my functional self, and being a mother. Because I so mistrusted and detested myself in this role, I would ask myself, "What would an actual good mother do?" And I

would do that. The trauma, from the time my son was two, left me guessing at how to behave. I believed my instincts were no good. Getting pregnant again, I worried for my children having a mother like this, and I worried that now I would have made my professional fear real. I would be fired. The response that came back from our producers, once we told them I was pregnant, was very different. Not only would they not fire me, but they also wrote it into the show.

Ira's wife, Laura, came up with the idea of a shuttlecraft accident. Keiko O'Brien, Dr. Bashir, and Kira would be traveling together, and to save the fetus Keiko was carrying, Bashir would operate to move the baby to Major Kira. Brilliant. I could continue to work, there was fodder for storylines around Kira, Keiko, and Miles O'Brien, and I didn't

have to hide the pregnancy. Bob Blackman even designed a costume that was comfortable and practical.

It was funny to me that a shuttlecraft accident was the tool used to save me. Every year, I would try, as every actor did, to renegotiate a better deal. Every year, it was the same response from the studio lawyers. There would be a shuttlecraft accident, and Major Kira would be dead if I continued to ask for more. This time, a shuttlecraft accident worked in my favor.

Kira continued to evolve in the remaining years. She experienced a mature, loving relationship with Odo, and she overcame her unconscious bias enough that she could work with her enemies, the Cardassians, during the Dominion Wars. I can see the dignity with which she started to approach life. The warrior spirit was always there, but it seemed to me that she gained the wisdom of when to use it and understood the value of a calm, strong presence in the face of adversity. I could see strength, but also vulnerability and the joy her personal connections brought her. Just as I had acted a syndrome that I hadn't personally experienced at the beginning of the series, my own post-traumatic stress forced me to approximate what it would be like to possess a groundedness I didn't have in my own life, in order to show Kira's growth. It wouldn't be her seven-year timeline, but I would find that Kira's evolution—in the end of her arc that was written and conceived of by writers—to be very close to my own. Life is strange sometimes.

I **DIDN'T JUST PLAY KIRA.** I also played her exact opposite in the Mirror Universe. The Intendant was a self-indulgent narcissist who either kissed or killed (and sometimes both) someone in each of the five episodes she appeared in. The sadistic ruler of Terok Nor, she was in league with the Cardassians, owned slaves, and thought nothing of torture and execution.

Her costume was like a precursor to Seven of Nine's iconic metallic skin. It looked vaguely like a dominatrix's getup, which may have seemed sexy onscreen, but in reality was anything but. We discovered that the thin rubber it was made from showed sweat as a dark spreading stain. During a heatwave in Los Angeles, the darkness grew in all the wrong places. A giant electric fan was brought into the soundstage, and between takes, I would stand like a starfish in front of it to keep my costume one color.

When I walked and talked at the same time, I knew I would be spending time in the looping studio because the costume squeaked with every step. The headpiece was made from something that was as hard as metal, and which had the unfortunately comical effect of raising up off my forehead if someone placed their hand on the back of my head to kiss me.

Playing an inversion of Kira helped define her even more for me, as I was forced to build a spectrum, with Kira on one end and the Intendant on the other. This made me consciously more aware of where Kira lay on this spread.

ABOVE: The series ends with Kira taking control of the station. It was an incredible journey and one of the defining experiences of my life.

Terry Farrell as

JADZIA DAX

As a young woman, I read fashion magazines religiously. Helen Gurley Brown's Cosmopolitan *was a bible for how to behave in order to get the life you wanted. "Times are different!" the magazine trumpeted. Women didn't have to wait for marriage for sex or fulfillment. You could have it all as a single woman. But in the end, I found it to be a very limiting look at female empowerment.*

It was under the guise of sexual freedom, but actually taught a performative way to secure your priorities. Articles advised on the various ways to get and keep a man, including losing weight, plastic surgery, and how to please him in the bedroom.

If the hoops to jump through were exhausting, well, it was just part of the price to be paid. It was a handbook on how to work successfully in a patriarchy. I read it fervently every single month. Being a glamorous cover girl seemed to me at the time—the 1970s—the ultimate way to achieve this worthy goal.

When I was cast as Kira, I knew about Terry Farrell the model. I loved her full-lipped, perfect-eyebrow look, and I wasn't alone. She graced the covers of magazines through the Eighties, including *Cosmo*. I remember Alexander Siddig eagerly making predictions about her when we learned they had finally, after an exhaustive search, hired her for the role of Jadzia Dax. We were in the makeup trailer between scenes, and Sid enthused that the combination of science officer with magazine-cover looks would take the sci-fi world by storm.

My heart, now shaped by the culture to believe that there was only room for one successful woman in a room, sank. Yes, it made sense to me. I was getting to play a role that I could only dream of: strong, with a backstory and full agency, but it would be completely overshadowed by a *Cosmo*-girl science officer.

Rick Berman has always been very clear that the producers wanted a "beautiful woman" to play the role, and that meant the casting was slow. Dax was the last series regular to be cast, and Terry only arrived after the rest of us had started filming.

At the time, no one questioned why a new TV show felt the need to cast a beautiful woman. It was understood that lots of people tuned in to look at attractive people and that men who might not care about the story would stay to look at a pretty face. It wasn't considered at the time, but there were women who enjoyed that, too.

As I struggled with finding a box to put myself in, always coveting the powerful "Beautiful" box, Terry was firmly placed in it, but experienced it as a cage: hard to escape from and hard to be seen through.

It took almost thirty years for me to understand the cultural wounds she brought with her to the job. I made the assumption many women, especially young girls, make: being pretty equals ultimate power. In some cases, it certainly gives you a leg up, but it's not a pass from feeling objectified or used. In fact, it can do just the opposite. For the young girl who just wanted to be seen, it ended up making her feel invisible a lot of the time.

When Terry still lived in L.A., we would take regular walks in the hills above the city, and we went on one for this book. She is self-aware, and realizes her life is privileged. As a White, successful woman, she was toward the top of the pyramid for women's opportunities in the world of the 1990s. Talking about the cultural currents that worked against her made both of us think about how much harder it was for women of color during the Nineties, who had to deal with soul-crushing treatment at a level I can't imagine.

On our way up a steep hill, Terry said she could feel herself going invisible. "I'm going safe behind this invisible bubble." Knowing what we were going to talk about, she was preparing herself with a tool she had used since childhood. To avoid punishment, shame, or the risk of being a disappointment, Terry would make herself small.

As a girl, Farrell also bought into the cultural fairy tale that if she were pretty, she would be loved. And if she was good—which meant doing what people wanted of her—she would be loved. "I would be accepted, and I'd have friends and a family, and everything would be great and—pretty girls get things."

But Terry was sure she didn't fit into the "Lucky Pretty Girl" box. The person she saw was too skinny, too tall, with hair cut too short. She's seen herself that way for most of

ABOVE: Early episodes focused on Dax as an object of desire, but at that point, the idea was that she was almost celibate.

OPPOSITE: Dax was the station's science officer and was meant to be incredibly old and wise. This is an incredibly difficult thing for an actor to play because it doesn't give you anything obvious to actually do.

her life, even after she became a cover girl. With a home life that didn't include, according to Terry, an education big in self-love or self-respect, she wasn't at all prepared to move by herself to New York City. But, she was signed by the Elite modeling agency at seventeen and believed she would finally be seen, accepted, and loved and all because she was being formally inducted into the "Beautiful" box.

THE COST OF BEAUTY

Being a model proved to be a double message: You are valuable but also expendable. It's a profession that makes a very clear connection between physical beauty and worth. Now that she was in the professional arena, things that are often a normal part of being seventeen became problems for the people hiring her: Minor things, such as a breakout on her face, could cause more work for others, and shame for her.

It was acceptable to decide in front of her if she was the "right" kind of beautiful, or even tear her apart, feature by feature. She struggled with the endless judgment of an appearance she couldn't control—having blue eyes and brown hair weren't simply traits, but something to be judged. There was the assumption that her thoughts and feelings didn't matter; it was just her profit-making exterior that made her valuable.

The modeling world was filled with men who wouldn't have counted themselves as predators back then, as sleeping with young models was all so acceptable in the business. "A lot of it was scary. Sometimes, I ran. There were a couple of times I literally left because I felt uncomfortable, because I was asked to take my clothes off, because I felt outnumbered. And I was by myself." She never told her agent what happened, because "that was our culture, right?" That meant that all she had on her side was the amassed knowledge of a seventeen-year-old in one of the toughest cities in the world. The answer seemed clear: Do what you could to keep yourself safe but still remain in the business. But stray too far from the lanes you are told to stay in, protest your treatment, and well...the same old message: There are a hundred young women behind you ready to take your place.

There's a certain irony in the fact that Terry Farrell could be seen everywhere on magazine covers and street posters, and that fact made her feel all the more invisible. It seemed to her that many men wanted her to be the static, one-dimensional cover girl, and not the living, breathing person in front of them. She competed with these images as much as any woman who wanted to look just like her would have. "You're not seeing me. You don't care about me. You care about the brown-haired girl that's on the cover of *Italian Vogue* this week...that's the girlfriend you want on your arm."

Terry's goals included being "a part of a community." When an agent suggested she go into acting, "every door opened, and I went through it." She became a regular in the series *Paper Dolls*, and was in the film *Back to School* with Rodney Dangerfield. She guest-starred in several TV shows and studied acting with the legendary teacher Stella Adler. And that led to her audition for *Star Trek*.

Terry remembers Michael Piller and Rick Berman telling her that Jadzia Dax was a cross between Grace Kelly and Yoda. Wow! That's an acting challenge. Terry took the note to mean "a quiet...majesty. This elegant, strong woman." The character was conceived as a combination of the humanoid Trill species and a symbiont, a wormlike creature that sits inside its host's abdomen after surgical insertion. The symbiont had lived seven lifetimes before being joined to Jadzia.

From the beginning, it was obvious that Dax was going to raise questions about gender. The Trill have their origins in the TNG episode "The Host," where Dr. Crusher finds that when the physical gender of her lover changes, she cannot bring herself to continue the relationship.

Dax was both man and woman. Here was a character who had experienced life as both genders, so it made perfect sense that "she" wouldn't conform to stereotypical versions of either. But in 1992, it wasn't clear how any of that would play out.

When an actor auditions for a role, they try to find the qualities the producers are looking for in the two or three scenes used in the audition process. You don't have the opportunity to understand the full scope of the work that could be in front of you if the show goes to series. Basically, you say yes to a job and hope for the best. At twenty-eight years old, Farrell was faced with embodying someone with seven lifetimes' worth of experience.

A lovely young woman who has three hundred years of experience is a wonderful concept on paper, but Michael Piller admitted that there was confusion about how to develop Jadzia once they were in production. The casting of the other characters played a part, too. Ira Behr told me that Avery Brooks was far more confident and commanding than the Commander Sisko that Piller and Berman had originally envisaged. He didn't need Dax as a mentor.

This wobble in bringing the character to life, combined with the amount of technobabble the science officer was given to recite, made for a rough start for Terry. It's hard to memorize material that isn't grounded in familiar words and doesn't connect to emotions or relationships.

In the earliest episodes, the struggle to find Jadzia's character is easy to spot. In shows featuring her, Dax appears on screen very little. Terry told me that this is the period of time

when she was told she was in danger of getting fired and the production hired her an acting coach. Talking to her, I realized that for much of her life Terry had been told that she was only there because she was beautiful. The message she was given was that no one assumed she had any other qualities. In fact, worse than that, they assumed she didn't.

One of the most anxious situations you can put a human in is rejection by their community. From inside the "Beauty" box, Farrell already felt unseen. The late casting of her character led her to feel like a teenager joining the school year halfway through, when everyone else has already joined cliques and formed bonds. Knowing her job was on the line and having an on-set coach would make her feel like her worst imaginings were true: She wasn't up to the task and not one of the "real" actors.

In truth, the acting coach told her she didn't need acting lessons at all, just someone to run lines with. The catch-22 with remembering lines is that once you've lost confidence in your ability to do it, your nervous system takes over to lock you out of the part of your brain that will help you the most.

But who was the Jadzia Dax of the first season? In those early days, there were a lot of scenes that involve people lusting after her. Quark and Bashir both compete for her attention. The way it's played, it's clear that both characters are motivated by that perfect Terry Farrell figure, rather than her brilliant mind. This is typical of the way beautiful women are often presented on TV.

But there is something else going on. A lot of emphasis is placed on the wisdom that seven lifetimes should give you. In those early episodes, Dax is meant to be serene and wise. The men may lust after her, but she calmly brushes it off. Interestingly, the bible makes some references to Dax's sex life, or lack of it. It says that the old, mature Curzon part of her has no need for such things, but occasionally the youthful Jadzia's impulses would take over. That's an idea that the writers would ultimately flip on its head.

The episode "Dax" starts to delve into the difficulty of having a blended consciousness that is hundreds of years old, housed inside a young body.

In the end of the episode, she has a conversation with a lover of Curzon Dax, Enina, played by Fionnula Flanagan. There is a tension to the scene that comes from Jadzia having awareness of Curzon's love for this woman, and Enina sensing the person she loved at least partially existing in this new body.

COMPLEX CHARACTER

The episode includes very little screen time for Terry, but the character development is good news. For the audience, this was a character firmly outside the acceptable cultural lane for women at the time. That meant people who felt uncomfortable in their skin, or dealt with a neurodivergent brain, or dealt with gender identity issues, or simply didn't fit into their communities in ways they were expected to, had an avatar they could experience the story through. That Jadzia struggled with her multiple consciousnesses normalized the struggles they themselves encountered. Watching her navigate as a brilliant science officer gave them hope. This representation would give so many people a chance to believe that, in the future, they could be who they were, in the field of their choice, and still find acceptance and even love.

Season two's "Invasive Procedures" is another episode that centers on Dax but has very little of Terry in it. When another Trill comes aboard the space station to steal the Dax symbiont, the doctor is forced to perform the transfer that will most likely end Jadzia's life. Although most of the action happens around her, Terry, simply a Trill once the symbiont is removed, gives a heartbreaking depiction of the crushing loneliness of losing part of yourself. You understand the loss through her acting of only a few sentences. Both these shows point to the writers being at a little bit of a loss as to how to leverage the actor they had so that her character could be activated to tell her own story.

A three-hundred-year-old, Spock-like character for Sisko to confide in and maybe have a confused attraction for? Sounds like a good idea. The backstory had the last host, Curzon Dax, as a mentor to Sisko. Throughout the show, Sisko refers to Jadzia as "old man." But sometimes what looks good in the bible just doesn't come to life onscreen. What they finally found after a season of searching, with Piller once again giving Ira Behr credit, was a kick-ass woman ready for adventure who had the voices of all those lives going on in her head. Terry was up for it, and added vibrancy and a sense of humor once she was freed from the passive adjectives of "beautiful and wise."

That process of redefining Dax begins in season two. In "Playing God," instead of a character that looks young and beautiful and sounds wise, they gave Jadzia things that she does. We build who we are by what we do, and I saw Dax come to life in this story. From passive beauty to conflicted entity trying to find the balance in herself, her character is expanded just like the proto-universe in the storyline.

A young, naive Trill comes to the station to have Jadzia Dax be his field docent, who will ultimately recommend him to be joined, or not. He expects to find someone closer to the difficult Curzon Dax he heard stories about. Jadzia remembers Curzon as her own field docent, one who rejected her, and wants to be as different in her approach to the job as she can.

Throughout the episode, we see her mentoring, and being mentored by Sisko, to eventually find herself in the last line, "I'm not Curzon." Every scene of this show seems to be an opportunity to see the character in terms of an accumulation of life experience, as opposed to simply more information held in a brain.

We start to see a version of Dax that is uninhibited, and certainly not constrained by the rules that were typically applied to women. The first scene finds her playing Tongo with a group of Ferengi, winning and leaving the game when she wishes to, despite Quark's protests. When the young Trill first finds her in her quarters, a well-built male alien answers the door while Dax gets out of the shower. Wonderfully, it is because he is her wrestling coach and not her lover. Maybe he is both, but there is no judgment or conclusion about her that we or the Trill are asked to assume. This is her life she is opening the door to, and how she lives it. It's the kind of life that would have been available to Captain Kirk but not to many women at the time—at least on TV. She plays chess with Sisko, pilots a runabout through the wormhole, heartily sings in Klingon with the Klingon cook, "hates to be appropriate," and collects forgotten composers.

OPPOSITE: Dax became more interesting when she revealed other sides of her personality.

ABOVE: Dax was always meant to be beautiful, so the Trill makeup was redesigned as a tattoo that showed off Terry's model looks.

We hear that Jadzia used to be brilliant but something of a wallflower. Being joined brought so many interests, so much to be curious about. There is technobabble for her to say, a lot of it, but it supports our understanding of her as a science officer. It's also supported by her active interest and work on discovering the truth of the material that hitched a ride on the exterior of the runabout. Discovering the proto-universe is Dax's achievement, and she is thoughtful about any action taken to destroy it. She is daring in her quest to get it back to its proper side of the wormhole.

This show effectively takes a character with attributes that are subjective and prone to judgment, and turns her into one with many, many actions that point to several lives well lived, with a youthful body

ready to experience more. It gives her the agency that was too often denied to women and gives her the appetites, intelligence, and enthusiasm that were too often reserved for male characters. I asked Ira if this was about trying to redress an imbalance in the way women were represented. His response was that it was about making her a fully rounded "human" being. To my mind, that says something about the culture we were raised in, which told us that women were limited and that the full human experience was only for men. The genius of *Star Trek* is that by making Dax an alien who had past lives as a man, it was a simple step to give her those qualities.

With this new understanding of Dax, "Rejoined" took the character and used it to really push at society's taboos about love. Trills are forbidden to have relationships with former lovers of the symbiont. A science team comes to the station, and among them is Lenara Kahn, played by Susanna Thompson. She is a former wife of Curzon, who Dax discovers still has strong feelings for him, and she feels Curzon's devotion to her. It's a love story about second chances.

It also included one of the first kisses between women on TV. The kiss is passionate and truthful, as is the entire episode. That the taboo of the Trill culture is as harsh as many people's treatment of homosexuality on Earth is hard to ignore as a typical *Star Trek* allegory. That you simply experience two people who love each other is a testament to how good everyone involved in making this story was at their job. I have been told by lesbians and trans individuals alike that this kiss made them feel seen in the world and hopeful that if this was on TV, acceptance couldn't be that far down the road.

Of course, it was not shown on the first run in many parts of the country, with some parents objecting to their children being exposed to homosexuality from a trusted franchise. In the *Star Trek: Deep Space Nine Companion*, producer Steve Oster recounts overhearing a P.A. take a call from a man complaining about his children seeing two women kissing. The P.A. asked the man if he would be okay with his children watching one woman shoot at the other. He was.

In "Blood Oath," Dax is given even more characteristics that had traditionally been reserved for men. When three Klingons show up at the station, we learn that the diplomat Curzon had made a blood oath to help them find and kill a man, known as the Albino, who had killed their three young sons. One of them was godson to Curzon Dax, and Jadzia

ABOVE: "Rejoined" is one of *Star Trek*'s most important episodes. When Dax reunites with a former female lover, their genders are completely irrelevant.

OPPOSITE: Dax was redefined as a fun-loving character who had an affinity for Klingons.

must untangle where her moral duty to these men lies. With their love of fighting and drinking, the Klingons fulfill plenty of male stereotypes, but Dax fits in right alongside them, with no question given to her gender.

There is a scene with Kira that meets all the Bechdel Test requirements and more as Jadzia asks Kira what it's like to kill. It's a scene without any tells of the gender of who is talking, and deals with ethics, obligations, and compassionate understanding of what it takes to follow your own moral code. Wielding a *bat'leth*, Dax convinces the men she is as capable as Curzon of going on the mission, strategizes the attack with them, and helps them meet honor, even in death.

There is a beautiful performance from Terry in the last scene, where she faces Sisko, who had told her he would question her allegiance to Starfleet if she took part in this vengeful act. She had defied his wishes and is uncertain of her reception back at her post. She takes her place at the science officer's post anyway. The trauma of the experience, as well as Kira's words, that every killing steals a piece of oneself, seem to play on her face. Gender isn't an issue. The ethical dilemma is simply human.

With Dax now an expert in all things Klingon, it seemed natural to pair her with Worf, and that gave the writers the opportunity to play with a romance between two fierce and well-matched individuals. In "Looking for Par'Mach in All the Wrong Places," a beautiful Klingon is romanced by Quark with aid (a lot of aid) from Worf, who is falling for her himself. Worf misses the relationship that has been right under his nose, until Dax points it out to him with a *bat'leth*.

Because *Par'Mach* for Klingons translates to "love," with more aggressive overtones, Dax and Worf become lovers and end up in the infirmary, along with Quark and the Klingon, Grilka.

In this love story, the woman is the one who pursues the man, and the one to set the timing for any future plans. Dax reacts to the other woman without jealousy, but simple curiosity for what makes her so appealing to Worf, and never demonstrates a need to denigrate her in order to elevate herself. Why would she, with the experience of over three hundred years to draw on? The writers and Terry were able to model a new way for women to behave in the 1990s, where more than one woman at a time can find *Par'Mach*.

Terry told me that playing Dax helped her to stand up for herself during the negotiations for a seventh season. She gained confidence in her abilities, and changed her brain by dropping the empowered thoughts and words of Jadzia Dax into it for six years.

To give you some context, when we'd joined the series, we'd all signed on for six years. Now the studio wanted to emulate *Star Trek: The Next Generation* and take the show into a seventh and final year. That meant offering the actors new contracts. The rest of us signed on, but Terry didn't.

On our walk in the hills, she told me all she had wanted was a chance to negotiate, to not be told an automatic ultimatum of "sign the contract or your character dies." She wanted to be able to do the last year on her own terms, with what felt healthy for her at the time. She wanted to become recurring, like so many of our guest stars were, with the opportunity to take other jobs if they came up. The studio turned her down flat.

Of course, producers are always worried about setting precedents—"give this to one actor, and they will all want it" thinking. Terry looked at fellow castmate Colm Meaney

RIGHT: Dax in full Klingon regalia. The writers reinvented her as another warrior, who was more than capable of holding her own in a fight.

OPPOSITE: When Terry decided to leave the series, the writers killed off Jadzia Dax. As a result, there was no way back for her.

OPEN A CHANNEL: THE WOMEN OF *STAR TREK*

at the time and saw that from the beginning of our show, he was granted an arrangement where he was let out to do other work.

Of course, Colm had signed on to *Deep Space Nine* after years on TNG, and had a burgeoning movie career. The producers probably figured they needed the continuity of the character to bring familiarity to their new show, and were prepared to make some concessions to bring the busy actor to DS9. While this is a realization that comes to me with over thirty years of hindsight, nobody was offering explanations to us at the time. Talking to Ira (who knew nothing about the negotiations with Terry), I also realized how difficult it is for the writers when they don't know if a particular character will be available to write for. With all the other balls the creators have to keep up in the air to make a show, they didn't want to add wondering about availability of another lead character.

Were other actors given different treatment? Yes. Was this a moment where an actor felt strongly enough to refuse a take-it-or-leave-it offer, even though that meant leaving the show when she would rather have stayed? Yes. Were things said that shouldn't have been to Terry by production? I know so.

Just as Terry joined late, she left early, believing that sticking to her principles was the road to not getting sucked under by the harsher realities of show business. The character struggled with learning what living an ethical life could mean throughout the show, and Terry had to live with being summarily killed by Gul Dukat with very little meaning to the death.

This may just be the actor's perspective, but I've noticed that when actors ask to leave, their characters are rarely sent off somewhere they could easily return from. In fact, they're often killed. I remember doing a show that I regretfully couldn't continue with because I was raising two little boys by myself. I was killed in a way that my character's DNA could never be recovered, and the literal overkill felt like punishment. There's no chance for a guest appearance if that happens.

Of course, for Trills, things can be a little more complicated. Because of the sci-fi nature of the character, they could

kill Jadzia but keep Dax, and that's exactly what happened.

Cutting off the extra year from Jadzia's life doesn't change the fact that because Terry was given a job and a chance to work through a rocky start, she and the writers turned Dax into a breakthrough character who became an icon. Dax is appreciated by people such as astronaut Samantha Cristoforetti and content creator Bryan Fuller. He told me he saw Dax as one of the most important noncoded queer characters in television. Her ability to accept not only her male, female, and nonbinary identities but also her humanity made her a character that was accessible to a large spectrum of the population.

The producers were absolutely determined to hire a beautiful woman to play Jadzia Dax, and what they gave us turned out to be a character free from the baggage that so often came with the "Beautiful" box.

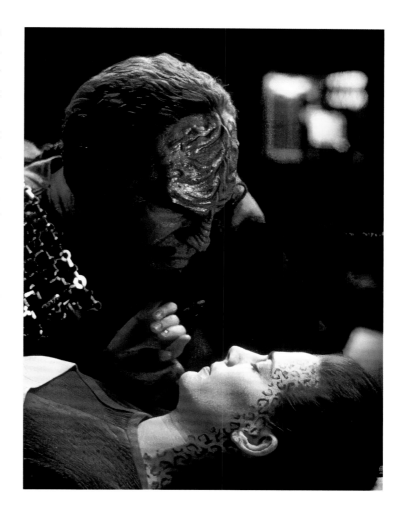

Nicole de Boer as
EZRI DAX

Nicole was a busy actor in Toronto when writer/producer Hans Beimler asked her to audition for the role of Ezri Dax. He had worked with her years before and vowed he would someday put her in Star Trek *makeup. When the production team looked for an actor who could replace Terry Farrell, he immediately asked De Boer to put herself on tape.*

According to the backstory to set up the character, Ezri was the only Trill aboard the shuttlecraft transporting Dax when the symbiont began to fail. (Those shuttlecraft were damn useful.) The only way to save the worm containing the memories of eight lifetimes was to join it to an unprepared Trill. Instead of years of training and preparation for joining, Ezri Dax got a quick speech from the doctor on the transport. She also got no way out of her predicament, because removing the symbiont would now kill it.

Years later, Michael Piller said that he wished the character of Jadzia Dax had started with this premise. Beginning from a place that acknowledges the youth of the actor is an interesting starting point and gives her somewhere to go. It also gave the character immense vulnerability, which would make it easier for the audience to accept the new character that would be seen as the beloved Jadzia's replacement.

Being a counselor was the perfect job for someone with over three hundred years of life experience and would give her a chance to interact with a whole variety of people on the station—and who among us didn't need a little therapy? The audience could infuse her with their own memories of Jadzia without expecting her to be the same. Where Jadzia was fearless, Klingon-loving, and ready to take on all challengers for a game of Tongo, Ezri was not certain until she checked under the covers each morning whether she was male or female. She was concerned about her reception

from the rest of the crew on the station, and was prone to space sickness.

In the second episode of *Deep Space Nine*'s seventh season, "Shadows and Symbols," Ezri arrives with Sisko and Jake and walks onto the Promenade for the first time, with a sense of wonder and familiarity that is surprising to her. She turns to look at the rest of the crew, who have gathered to welcome the captain home and are surprised to see a new Dax. They look back at her with curiosity and a bit of confusion. Nicole de Boer looks radiant and ready to take on the challenge. The rest of us look battle-worn but connected through the shared experience of six years. To infuse her character with vulnerability and a little uncertainty informed a natural way for all of us to treat not only the character but the actor.

It's hard to say if a memory transfer, from actor to actor, would have helped or hindered Nicole's experience on the last year of the show. Coming to work and leaving work in darkness, dealing with dark subjects, and sensing subtle tensions without knowing details about where or how they originated led to a confused feeling for the twenty-eight-year-old actor when she was on set.

There were strange rules to learn, too. She tells of asking Craft Service, the arm of production that provides food and drink on sets, if they had the makings for a tuna sandwich, a normal request for most productions. She was pulled into the

craft truck and asked worriedly if she could please just eat the sandwich in the truck, so as not to be seen by others on the set. Curious behavior, she thought. But this was just an indication that you're working on a syndicated series now: Don't ask for special food orders. Do what we all did and eat what's set out on the table. But she was working on the legendary Paramount lot, in Hollywood, playing a major role on a sci-fi show she considered the biggest she had ever been on. Make no mistake: This was a very exciting time for De Boer.

From the start of her career, Nicole was put squarely in the "Young Cute Girl" box. Because she looked youthful for her age, she was consistently cast in younger roles, and she remembers changing the timbre of her voice so that it sounded more like the voice of a sixteen-year-old. What bothered her was that her own voice hadn't been that high at sixteen, but being an actor sometimes means conforming to other people's expectations rather than the actual truth—especially then.

THE BEST FRIEND

The mold the business put her into made her believe she wasn't leading-lady material. In the 1990s, the assumption was still that women only had romances and were the focus of stories if they met certain criteria. If they didn't, they were the sidekick and got to reflect the experience back to its owner, the female lead.

Nicole told me that because her face was round and she wasn't stick thin when she started out, the roles she got weren't romantic leads but the "best friend of the popular girl." She started acting as a child, so "you don't question so much...what the directors do or what people say, because they're all grown-ups and you're a kid. So that unfortunately stuck with me as I got older."

Nicole seems free of a lot of the cultural adaptations that Terry and I had made after years in Hollywood. Working first in Canada may have had something to do with it, as did her upbringing. She was raised by a single working mother and ever-present grandparents. Her grandmother was her primary parent, she said, and taught her that "if you want things done, do them yourself." She was taught by her mother to love men, but not to be surprised if they disappointed you. According to her family, being resilient wasn't just a necessity but a natural-born gift that all women possessed.

When I asked her what she had been like as a child, she spoke of already being an actor in a Canadian theater company called Stage Center Productions. She did all the plays with age-appropriate parts, and she loved it. When there were no parts for her, she worked backstage and loved that too. The theater was family and community for the girl whose father was absent, and she went from being a shy child to a confident and engaged one. Her experience onstage led to screen opportunities, and she worked in films and series such as *The Kids in the Hall*, a slew of TV movies, and a few sci-fi shows, such as *The Outer Limits*.

She favored sci-fi: Not only did she love the genre as entertainment, but she was also attracted to science. Technobabble fell off her tongue because she understood the meaning of it, and finally she wasn't playing someone's girlfriend or the lead girl's friend, but had roles that required pluck and intelligence.

Nicole didn't experience any of the sexual harassment that her friends told her horror stories about. Like many women I interviewed, she chalked it up to not being the cultural romantic ideal of the 1990s. It was a reality that being that certain brand of physical desirability gave women power. It was also annoying or scary when attention was unwanted. But even when it was annoying, male attention was a sign that you still were in the game.

I remember going to auditions in New York as a very young woman. It was impossible not to walk past a construction crew, whichever way I went, and one day I heard something unusual as I passed: total silence. I was so used to catcalls and indecent proposals that I assumed that I looked bad, and my chances for the job I was auditioning for must be very slim. Did all women take on this baggage that was handed to us to carry? No. Did we all have one way of dealing with it? No. Did I realize at the time that the silence, which would become something I became used to in my fifties, would mean a kind of freedom to redefine myself for myself? Not until much later.

When a woman casting director told De Boer she didn't get a role because she had "zero sexual energy," she thanked her for the feedback and, like so many women in the business, accepted a totally subjective opinion of a three-minute audition as an unchangeable fact. She reminded me it was a woman who had said it, but women casting directors had bosses to please, and the bosses believed they knew what the audience wanted.

Once you are given the outline of your limitations, being put in any kind of box feels like a gift—a way for you to fit in. Nicole had worked with Hans Beimler previously, and he brought her in to audition for Ezri. It seemed that the producers were looking for an actor with cute girl energy. "Did it feel like a box? I guess. It's all boxes, but it's a box I felt fine about being in. I felt it spoke to my wheelhouse and my strengths at the time. And I loved the character."

On the day of her screen test, Jeri Ryan happened to walk by in her Seven of Nine costume, and Nicole felt her confidence drain. If that was what they wanted on *Star Trek*, she reasoned, she had no chance at this job. Thankfully, she was wrong. Different box to fill.

It's a sign of how much *Star Trek* was growing up that even though Nicole wasn't a six-foot-tall cover girl like Terry

Farrell or Jeri Ryan, half of the male characters on the station were instantly attracted to her. In that seventh season, the cute girl was the romantic lead. Quark was smitten immediately and delusional in thinking he had a chance, Jake found her attractive, Worf had unresolved feelings, and Bashir was the one with whom a flirtation grew into a committed relationship.

Odo, Kira, Bashir, and Ezri became couples who hung together. Alexander Siddig has said that he never saw the possibility of his character becoming romantically involved

OPPOSITE: Nicole was in the unusual position of playing a character who was new but had a history with the established cast. Having learned from Jadzia, the writers made this Dax much more uncertain and confused.

ABOVE: Although Ezri was young and feminine, the writers quickly gave her a traditionally masculine storyline where she was tracking a serial killer.

with Jadzia, as she was so extraordinarily powerful and wouldn't have a need for him. Ezri, on the other hand, was physically small and vulnerable, and gave Bashir the chance to feel important in her life.

Ezri and Nicole had the benefit of a writing staff that had found its feet and had firmly stepped away from what were now old-fashioned ideas about women. Ira Behr told me he wasn't pushing agendas but was always looking for what was human, whether the character was male, female, or something else. Despite resistance from the studio, DS9 also benefited from a willingness to tell serialized stories. That allowed the characters to become much more nuanced and complex—often things that were particularly denied to female characters.

It doesn't take more than a few shows before we see that Ezri is good at her job. Using her own experience of anxiety

to form a bond, she compassionately and patiently works with Garak on his crippling panic attacks. It wasn't just a one-and-done scene, either. The show does a good job of showing how nonlinear progression can be for people struggling with mental health.

In "The Siege of AR-558," we see Ezri's confusion at remembering battles her other lifetimes lived through, but still being unprepared for it herself. Seeing the courage with which the young Trill faced the realities and losses of war added hugely to the overall message of the episode. Again, we see an enormously human experience, not limited to either men or women.

Episodes in which Ezri talks about pronoun confusion and not knowing what gender she happened to be when she wakes up in the morning seem like they were written in the

last five years, not almost thirty years ago. It's no wonder the LBTQIA+ community has found representation in this iteration of Dax as well. The fact that Ira saw it only as human is an interesting fact in itself.

The queer and trans communities can use the character as an avatar or as an indication that they indeed have a place in the future. People who had anxiety fitting into their world or their body are able to project themselves onto the character and feel included in the social conversation. Giving a character a full-spectrum life allowed viewers who looked like her, or struggled like her, or worked in her field to imagine themselves having the full spectrum of the human experience, too. That is what good storytelling can do.

If Nicole were to go back in time and change one thing for herself, she says she would have more confidence. One reason she was anxious to work on *Star Trek* was because the usual rules for women in the "Cute Girl" box did not apply to alien species in the future; she experienced romance with Dr. Bashir, was a scientist, and had personal struggles she examined and addressed. *Star Trek* allows aliens to be the leads of their own stories. Since most of us feel like aliens at one point or another in our lives, this is a very hopeful message.

OPPOSITE: I have a very clear memory of filming the scene where the Intendant kissed the Mirror version of Ezri because suddenly the set was full of people who weren't normally there.

ABOVE: A lot of the last season was about Ezri learning who she was after bonding with the Dax symbiont. It ends with her and Bashir becoming a couple, something that is very much her choice.

Penny Johnson Jerald as

KASSIDY YATES

Ira Behr told me that Kassidy Yates is one of the women he is proudest of having written. Kassidy helped us see another side of Benjamin Sisko, but she wasn't a character who existed only for the male lead's sake. There was a sense that her life went on, even when the character was off camera. All-importantly, she was his equal. Captain Sisko was impenetrable and powerful with his colleagues. With his son Jake, he was a loving, strong parent. With Kassidy, he had to share the power. He was knocked off-balance, and we could see his vulnerability, doubts, fears, and accountability for mistakes he made. It was a very equal relationship between two evolved humans.

When Penny Johnson Jerald was offered the role of Kassidy in *Deep Space Nine*, she wasn't into sci-fi and would have turned it down, if not for her husband/manager. Gralin Jerald is a *Trek* fan and told her in no uncertain terms, "You are going to do this." The third-season episode "Family Business" introduces the freighter captain Kassidy Yates as a love interest for Sisko. Jake thinks it's time his father has some companionship, and encourages them to meet. Once they find they share a love for the little-known archaic game of baseball, their relationship begins. In the years that follow, they present the audience with a modern ideal of a healthy relationship. Kassidy isn't there as an appendage of Ben's, and her independence is clear: She would love to be with him but makes her own decisions in life.

In "Indiscretion," she tells Ben she is considering taking a job working for the Bajorans, delivering cargo to their colonies. When Dax suggests Kassidy move to quarters at Deep Space 9, she sees the sense, but Sisko sees commitment he isn't sure he's ready for. After she holds his feet to the fire and insists he is honest about his fears, he tells her he lost his wife because of his job, and worries what danger he might put her in if they are together. She coolly replies, "Why not let me worry about that?" Thinking she needs his approval, Ben tells her to take the job. But she already has: "Did you think I'd give up a great opportunity just because you got cold feet?" She is his equal, with an emotional intelligence a couple of steps ahead of his. The rapport between them is palpable onscreen.

Penny is every bit as impressive as Kassidy. She has a self-confidence and an unwillingness to bow to the limitations that society has tried to impose on her. She was six years old when the riots in the late 1960s made her family move from the inner city to a predominantly White neighborhood where she remembers her family being labeled "those damn Johnsons." Her self-possession never wavers as she tells me she recalls people throwing things at her mixed-race mother in the streets around their new home. She found a safe place in the art of pretending. "Truth be told," she said, "my grandmother's the best actress that ever existed because she could just pretend. You just wouldn't know it."

I remember meeting her on the set of DS9. Self-possessed, confident, she had a sharp sense of humor and an even sharper sense of how to read a set and fit into it. I assumed it was because she was a graduate of the prestigious Juilliard School and had massive acting experience. She credits the latter with the former, saying that the name of the school allowed people in the business to assume she had enough of a foundation to navigate a set and all it entails. That gets you in the door, but Penny has an ability to tell the truth on camera, which led to longevity in the business and roles in shows such as *The Larry Sanders Show*, *24*, *Castle*, and *The Orville*.

What gave her the confidence to shoot for Juilliard was a woman named Sally Feinstein. I include this because it demonstrates the difference strong mentorship can make. Sally was on the board of the Park School in Baltimore when she saw the sixteen-year-old Penny in an improvisational circus eating fire. (Yes, eating fire.) She insisted Penny attend the school, and made it possible financially.

Sally was a true mentor, and the support wasn't just monetary, but also emotional as she pushed her to do her best all the way to senior year, when Sally passed away. It may have been the experience of having support from a "woman who could not just see your talent, but also see your soul" that gave Penny the confidence not to listen when she was told that Juilliard would be overreaching. Penny saw the current was against her, and swam harder.

Even though the neighborhood the family of eight lived in was racist, it wasn't the culture of her family. "I didn't

know what my skin color meant because my parents never taught that to us. Their friends were both White and Black. So I had White uncles and Black uncles and not necessarily biological ones, growing up."

Pursuing acting taught her that there was a difference, because now she had to go up for Black roles. "And so you have that against you. And then you're freaking female.

OPPOSITE: Kassidy and Sisko's marriage was one of equals. She is a captain in her own right and not under his command.

ABOVE: Kassidy represents the life Sisko dreams of, and he plans to build them both a house on Bajor.

Because if I were a male, I'd be turning it out. I would actually be behind the camera so much more than I'm in front of the camera, but it was a man's world coming in."

When I asked Penny if she'd encountered sexual harassment on set, she said it "dehumanizes the person so they cannot be free to be totally who they are." She had a father who was a boxer and brothers she knew would come to her defense. Growing up with them made her feel that "physically I am a good fighter." But also, she told me, there was a part of her that felt able to take on the male ego.

As a young actor, she was asked to deliver a script to a man playing her father, and he answered the door to her naked. She told him to get dressed, and proceeded into the house to read through their scenes. When he let the robe he

ABOVE: Penny was cast because she could more than hold her own against Avery Brooks's Sisko, which is no mean feat.

OPPOSITE: DS9 was one of the few shows in the 1990s that showed a Black family, but Penny still felt there was a nervousness about showing intimacy between a Black man and a Black woman.

put on fall open, he said "Oops...I didn't mean to shock you," and she got out of the house. This was one of a few examples where Penny was put in a sexual position she didn't wish to be in. Instead of a collaborative afternoon spent on getting the scenes grounded, it was a setup that would force her to make a series of mental chess moves to ensure her safety. That's a lot of energy stolen from a young woman who had to use so much to get to where she was.

She believes it's up to women to understand their power and to set boundaries to protect themselves, but she also looks to her husband, Gralin, as her protector. There have been times Gralin has intervened with other men who have harassed Penny, and she likes it that way.

When asked what it was like to join DS9, Penny spoke of the strictures of the scripts, where every word was treated with an air of solemnity. She said that Avery, as a Black man, leading the tone of the show, impressed her. Under his largess, she was able to "do what I wanted to do, as long as it serviced the show."

One thing she wanted but didn't get on DS9 was a truthful, emotional, and physical love scene between two Black lovers. Not "screwing or something like that, but an opportunity to be something so beautiful." LeVar Burton was directing an episode in which all three thought the moment was now, when the word came down from the offices that it was not. "And we weren't on BET and we weren't doing pornography. We wanted to do that gentle, wonderful, beautiful thing. Just to say, 'Guess what? In the future, you will finally see us just like you. We actually do this, too.'" She feels that we had skipped a step as a culture. Gays and biracial couples seem ubiquitous now on TV to her, but not that romantic, intimate love scene she wished for between two Black people in love. "I would still like to see that because I believe that still, people are affected by what they're seeing in the future, and then it warrants you to accept that more."

The women who come up to her at conventions to share the effect she has had mention her authority, strength, commitment to her beliefs, and ability to love through it all. Not to mention she carried the powerful position of "captain."

Kassidy also played a role in breaking down one of society's unhealthy stereotypes. She was the good stepmother. With so many blended families today, it's important for people to have positive role models. Women in a stepmother capacity would tell her, "You were just so open. And you weren't overpowering, you didn't try to become Jake's mother. You existed as a family, and he saw the love his father was now having." That opened doors for people's perception of the classic evil stepmother role to shift. The evil stepmother trope is threatened by the other wife and the existing children, and makes life hell for everyone. Kassidy showed respect for not only Jake's mother but for the father-son relationship as well. Annoyed with Sisko in "Indiscretion," she tells him that Jake must have gotten his smarts from his mother. It keeps Jennifer Sisko in the conversation and demonstrates the dignity of recognizing a former relationship and not reacting with jealousy.

In season five's "Rapture," Sisko's visions from The Prophets put him in physical danger. With Sisko unwilling to have the surgery he needs because it will stop the visions of Bajor's future, Jake is left with a life-and-death decision. He decides to go against his father's wishes and gives Bashir permission to go ahead with surgery. When he comes out of surgery, Sisko is frantic about having lost his connection to The Prophets. Kassidy calmly but firmly puts his son's hand together with his, and reminds him what connection he hasn't lost.

It's clear that Penny brought every bit of grit, charm, and willingness to meet all challenges she learned in her own life to help create the freighter captain who had agency and a life with and beyond the man she married. Her strength, when she learns that she may not see the father of her unborn child "for a year, or maybe yesterday," let me know she would keep her promise to wait for him. But she wouldn't be waiting in stasis.

Rosalind Chao as
KEIKO O'BRIEN

The studio had wanted a beauty queen for the role of Keiko, and Rosalind Chao is grateful that the team of Rick Berman and Gene Roddenberry fought against it, not only casting her, but also giving her stories to tell on The Next Generation *that felt interesting to play.*

The fact is, the studio was going for the "Beauty" box, and in the 1990s, believe it or not, Rosalind wouldn't have fit inside it. As an Asian-American woman, she was often cast as the best friend of the Caucasian star. I asked her how she deals with bias in her life, and she told me she doesn't mind taking the time and effort to educate, because she finds that prejudice usually stems from ignorance, which in turn usually stems from lack of exposure to different cultures.

Her character, Keiko, was a Starfleet botanist who married Miles O'Brien. Although the character lacked development, she had a job at the arboretum and played clarinet in a woodwind quintet. She was sent back to childhood in "Rascals," examined memories in "Violations," and had Worf as a birthing coach for daughter Molly in "Disaster."

TNG's producers had tried to sign her to a contract to make her a series regular, but Chao had formed a line in the sand about her work/life balance. Her parents were owners

of a restaurant when she was young, and she basically grew up at their workplace. It wasn't what she would call a "normal" childhood, and she wanted to give her own children a very different experience. In order to do that, she chose not to take series-regular roles or extended location jobs. When the O'Briens were moved to DS9, she held firm on this stance.

"I still remember Rick Berman phoning me to make sure I realized what I was giving up by not signing on with Colm as a regular on DS9," she says. "I was pregnant with my oldest and about to film *The Joy Luck Club*. I knew that if I took on a regular role at that time, my children would not have the childhood I had hoped for. That is not everyone's ideal, and it truly was a gamble."

The dilemma of how to combine motherhood with a career is something that many women actors confront. Like several other *Star Trek* actors, I chose to try to do both—to have it all. I can honestly say that it was hard, and I was never

RIGHT: The O'Briens' marriage was shown in a pretty realistic way. Keiko was supportive but had strong opinions and her own needs.

OPPOSITE: The writers struggled to find storylines for Keiko, and there was a tendency to show her in her role as wife and mother.

PAGE 141: Keiko was brought over from TNG, where we had seen her and O'Brien get married.

sure I was doing the right thing. In my experience, the 1980s and '90s TV shows didn't make any effort to accommodate children, and people were forced to choose between family and career. Rosalind made the other choice and, as a result, passed on more than one good role.

"I missed out on quite a few career-changing opportunities while my kids were home, and perhaps would have been better off financially. However, it all worked out for the best for us." That wasn't just Rosalind's loss. It was Hollywood's, too. With the studios making so little effort to help people parent and work at the same time, how many women must have chosen to limit the choices they made? And once you step off the carousel of work, no matter how briefly, it is incredibly challenging, if not impossible, for most to step back on. With a thriving career in this part of her life, Rosalind has made the leap back. Not everyone does.

A similar problem confronted Keiko. *Star Trek* has never been a show about the characters' domestic lives, and Keiko was there as O'Brien's wife rather than a scientist or a security officer. When Rosalind came on to DS9, she was aware

> Keiko was hardly a passive wife, a common trope for Asian women at the time. She is loyal to her own personal ethics and isn't afraid of confrontation, be it with her husband or the imposing Kai Winn.

that the writers didn't seem to know what to do with that kind of character. As Ira Steven Behr told me, in retrospect he saw Keiko as the biggest fail the writers had in terms of women on the show. They changed her profession to teacher to try to generate stories, but the Miles/Keiko dynamic never really took off. They had affectionate humor between them, but their overriding theme was the tensions that come from being a two-career family.

At the end of the day, Dr. Bashir and Miles O'Brien seemed to have more of an intimate, real friendship. They were genuinely happy to spend time together, and shared activities they both enjoyed. I don't remember seeing the O'Briens do much of that. As Rosalind said, Keiko seemed like a ball and chain. There are those in the audience who saw her that way, too.

As we were shooting the show where O'Brien and Kira get too close while she is carrying the O'Briens' baby, I wondered where the scene between Keiko and Kira was. Wouldn't the two women attempt to figure out the boundaries of this complicated relationship? It never seemed to cross Keiko's mind that Kira could be a threat to her relationship, as she kept pushing Miles and Kira together. But then I read a piece written by Livian Yeh for Startrek.com, and started to see aspects of Keiko through a different lens.

First of all, here was an Asian-American, onscreen, with her story being told in the 1990s. Chao says many Asian-American women have told her that Keiko helped influence their perception of themselves. Yeh said that the character's initial resentment of moving to DS9 and her struggles to adapt represented issues that expats and immigrants often grapple with. Because Starfleet officers know how they fit in by the function they serve on the station, Keiko's struggle to find how she fit was one that television didn't often explore. She also recognized that Keiko was hardly a passive wife, a common trope for Asian women at the time. She is loyal to her own personal ethics and isn't afraid of confrontation, be it with her husband or the imposing Kai Winn. She learned to adapt and change jobs when necessary, and left the station with her children when the threat of war made life there too dangerous. Not the actions of a helpless woman.

With this in mind, I looked at Keiko's reaction to Kira moving into her family home a little differently. Instead of seeing Kira as an interloper and "the other woman," she saw her as a lifesaving and necessary part of the family who made the healthy birth of Kirayoshi possible. She was grateful and empathetic, as Kira was a huge part of saving the baby's life.

I could also argue that her dignified trust gave Miles and Kira the room to come to their own conclusion that their intimacy was only situational, and not something either one of them really wanted to pursue. Even though both writer and actor say Keiko for the most part was a missed opportunity, she was a wife and mother with a career who struggled to get it all right. That's a relatable story and a different flavor of strength: the ability to adapt.

Chase Masterson as

LEETA

If you ask Ira Steven Behr about the women of Deep Space Nine, *he will tell you that his biggest wins were Kassidy Yates and Leeta. I had to take a moment to think about that. Superficially, Leeta was skimpily dressed and performatively female. But that, Ira says, didn't stop her from being a lot of other things, too.*

He told me that at first, the writers were a "little freaked out by the Dabo girls." What, he asks, "was going on in those holosuites?" In order to tell a deeper story of women whose work included wearing the skimpiest of outfits and spinning the Dabo wheel, DS9's head writer wanted to have a Dabo girl with character.

Played by Chase Masterson in a breathy cross between Marilyn Monroe and Mary Tyler Moore, she was sexy, yes, but with a mind of her own. She was empathetic, intelligent, and capable, and had a relationship with Dr. Bashir, but called it over when she fell for the Ferengi Rom. It demonstrated her depth that she chose a partner because of his character instead of how he presented to the world.

UNEXPECTED DEPTHS

This was one of the great relationships, according to Ira. Other characters' judgment of Rom might have been skin-deep, but Leeta saw a little deeper than most. Although she wore the revealing clothes the other Dabo girls did, we saw her resolve in episodes such as "Bar Association," in which she joins the strike at Quark's bar, or "Sacrifice of Angels," when she joins the resistance to the Dominion.

I didn't have the opportunity to talk to Chase, but I read in an article on Trekmovie.com that she saw the value of her character's skimpy costumes. The outfits were created as eye candy during sweeps week, she said. That might have been superficial, but that outfit earned her even more screen time, and the chance to form a relationship with the audience.

Even when she didn't have much dialogue, her close-ups told us we needed to know what this woman thought of whatever was transpiring in the scene. That there was curiosity and intelligence in her face went a long way to the development of her character.

The role is an acknowledgment that women who work under conditions such as Leeta's have an underlying complexity that is sometimes overlooked, and that they are often victims of bias when people think that assumptions can be made from judging their clothes, or lack of them. Ironically, Chase tells a story of another actor during the filming of DS9 being surprised she was fully trained in the arts, with a major Shakespearean role to her credit. Even though Leeta was only a character she was playing, the costume caused other actors to conclude that Masterson wasn't their professional equal.

What makes Leeta one of Ira's triumphs for women characters was the fact he could easily imagine her life outside of the one she had with Rom. In his mind, she continued to live, even offscreen. "I believe Leeta is in the back with the other Dabo girls, telling them how to deal with these asshole men grabbing their ass. How to deal with Quark and how to be a Dabo girl—if that's what you're gonna be—and survive it all."

STAR TREK: VOYAGER

Star Trek: Voyager had something none of the shows that came before it did: a woman co-creator. Jeri Taylor had worked her way up from supervising producer to executive producer and showrunner on Star Trek: The Next Generation *before joining Michael Piller and Rick Berman at* Voyager's *top table. From the beginning, her interest in character development and in advancing the roles of women was baked into* Voyager's *DNA.*

Taylor knew firsthand how strong girls could be. In her own words, her family was "very dysfunctional, extremely so—divorce, alcoholism, mental illness. It just was the whole kit and caboodle." She was self-sufficient and self-reliant because she needed to be as a child; there was no one else looking out for her. At eleven, she watched the Disney film *Dumbo* and was so affected that she decided to be a writer so she could create that same emotional connection for others.

She graduated college in 1959 and was horrified when she was the last of her friends to be married. To be on the single shelf too long meant "you may not get the real prize, which is a man." Three children later, and never expecting to be anything other than a wife and mother, she was divorced and totally unprepared to support herself and her young family. But her chaotic upbringing prepared her for this moment, and she took her shot at being a writer. Once she had put her two-year-old to bed, she would spend the night teaching herself how to write a script. She says her best friends were fear and ignorance: fear she would end up making minimum wage at a job she was unqualified for, and ignorance of what it actually took to make a living as a writer.

Despite the tide against her, she established herself as a freelance writer, working on shows such as *The Incredible Hulk*, *Quincy*, and *Jake and the Fatman*. In TNG's fourth season, she was called in to rewrite a *Star Trek* script. "My heart sank because I literally knew nothing—literally nothing—about *Star Trek*." But it had been a while since she worked,

so she took the job. Her first script was so well received that she was rapidly offered a job on staff and would stay with *Star Trek* for the rest of her career.

I had guested on some of the shows Taylor worked on before TNG, and they were extremely male oriented. I asked her if it had pushed her to double competency, and she said her life had always been a struggle. To survive, she had always felt she had to work harder and be better than anyone else.

Taylor "writes people" and felt that Berman and Piller treated her with respect and "seemed to value what I brought" to TNG. But it was all-consuming work. By the time she was writing and producing, she felt "enormous guilt" at not being a full-time mother for her children. "Television is a nonstop job. It's not five days a week and eight hours a day. I worked every weekend, every holiday. There was no such thing as a holiday where I wasn't writing something."

Taylor more than proved herself. She improved the treatment of the women characters on TNG: It was her idea to give Troi a uniform, and under her influence, the women were included in more adventurous storylines. TNG was going strong, and as the show wrapped up, the ratings were still growing. Most of the production team would transition to *Voyager*, with Taylor in charge of the writing staff.

When Berman and Piller approached her to co-create a new *Star Trek* show with a woman captain, she felt they

didn't need her. They were seasoned at developing storylines and characters: "They certainly knew how to create interesting female characters, but I could see that the perception would be better if a woman was involved."

She says it was "very, very important" to her the new show's female captain was "not a man with boobs, that she would have qualities that I consider essential to women, which consisted of compassion, empathy, understanding, sensitivity, some of those softer things that some women don't want to aspire to because they think it puts them on a different playing field in a man's world."

With her ship being 70,000 light years away from Starfleet (which in the 1990s, still seemed like a patriarchy), the captain would be free to use those female strengths without interference from male superiors. "She had to really

have her fingertips on all the feelings of her crew if they were going to manage to hang together and survive, so I wanted her to have those traditional female qualities."

Taylor herself brought those qualities to the writers' room, where she was a strong leader. To this day, her staff talk about adoring her, and there is little doubt many of them saw her as a mother figure. When I met with her, I saw a warm, self-effacing woman with a sharp intelligence and strong curiosity. Brannon Braga said she was a "nurturing presence in the best of ways, she cultivated talent when she saw it," and ran the writers' room as a safe and inclusive environment. The similarities between Taylor and Janeway are obvious. Braga also saw her in Kes, who he says shared Taylor's compassion and supportive nature.

Even though it was a grind and Taylor always felt

behind, she found the work deeply gratifying; It made her feel productive and valuable. When she stepped away from *Voyager* and retired in the fourth season, she and her husband moved on to the dream they had been planning of living in Northern California. Brannon Braga took the reins, and Taylor remained a consultant until the end of the show's run. Interestingly, she had no input about one of the show's most significant female characters: Seven of Nine, played by Jeri Ryan.

When I asked Taylor for her feelings about how influential the women she helped create were and are, she didn't have a sense of the ripple effect they have had in the culture. "It's wonderful to hear, wonderful to contemplate, and to think this is possibly true is just beyond my wildest imagination."

OPPOSITE LEFT: Janeway was a huge step forward for *Star Trek* and showed that women could be commanding and likable.

OPPOSITE RIGHT: Kes ended up with traditionallly female roles, including nurse and girlfriend.

ABOVE LEFT: B'Elanna is one of *Star Trek*'s great successes: an engineer who isn't afraid to be confrontational.

ABOVE RIGHT: Seven was only introduced later, and was designed to give Janeway "her Spock."

Kate Mulgrew as
CAPTAIN JANEWAY

Captain Janeway is important. The movies and Star Trek: The Next Generation *had established that there were female captains in Starfleet, but they had only made brief appearances, and a woman had never been the series lead. Janeway's fearless style of leadership would act as a model for countless women, and as Kate Mulgrew discovered, would be both influential and inspirational.*

"Mrs. Clinton invited me to the White House to speak to women in science. She'd called a group of eminent, young scientists who obviously lauded Janeway and said she wanted me to come and to speak. And she met me in the China Room, and she said, 'Star Trek: Voyager is the show that Chelsea and I watch together. It's the one thing we really share. It means a lot. So these women are very important women in STEM, and I've gathered them from all over the world.'" The First Lady then asked Kate to make a speech to the impressive assembly of women. "And of course, when I got up there and stood at the podium and looked over the sea of bright, earnest, fabulously intelligent faces, I just took the speech and threw it in the air and said, 'I have nothing to say to you. But you have everything to teach me. So why don't we start at the beginning. And what it is that Janeway has done?' And this young girl—I don't think she could have been twenty-eight, she looked so young—stepped forward. She said, 'If I may say, I was going into research, and then I was introduced to Kathryn Janeway. And I turned to my father, and I said, "I'm not going into the office. I'm going to go up."' And she did. That's huge, Nana."

It is undeniable that Captain Janeway moved the needle for what young girls thought possible for themselves as they watched this latest iteration of *Star Trek* premier. I spoke to scientists working both at NASA and the European Space Agency who were little girls when *Voyager* premiered. The

passionate example of Kate Mulgrew's captain removed glass ceilings from their minds and allowed them to imagine themselves in positions of authority, in science, and in space. In 1966, *Star Trek* put Uhura, a woman of color, on the bridge of a starship. Nearly thirty years later, in 1995, they made a woman the captain. In both cases, the message was that "this is the future and your place in it will be different." And in both cases, little girls grew up and chose paths that seemed possible to them because of the examples of these characters.

It's a sign of how far we've come that today putting a woman in charge of a starship is commonplace, but as recently as 1995, having a woman as Number One on the call sheet and the captain for the entire run of a show was newsworthy. I remember the buzz among women at the time. *Voyager*'s pilot episode even has people discussing what to call her—should she be "ma'am," "sir," or "captain"? (The answer is "captain," although "ma'am" is acceptable "in a pinch.") Just like society at large, *Star Trek* was trying to work out what it meant to put women in positions of power. The example that Janeway—and Kate—gave us would shape the future. "What would Janeway do?" and "Do it for Janeway" were both phrases I was told in various interviews that many women use like a sextant to navigate their day-to-day issues.

Kate was hired to replace Geneviève Bujold, who had relinquished the role of Janeway after two days of filming.

ABOVE: There was enormous concern about Kate's appearance, and several scenes (including this one) were reshot because the studio was worried about her hair.

OPPOSITE: Kate was rushed into play Captain Janeway and had to hit the ground running.

It seems natural that the producers would want the cultural heft of an award-winning actor playing their first female captain, but Bujold had little experience in television and she had a different energetic approach to commanding a spaceship than *Star Trek* had taught us to expect. It wasn't a fit. Bujold recognized it quickly and left. "She knew herself," said Kate. "I admired that."

The production carried on shooting around her, but Janeway was in so many scenes that they soon had to shut

down. A frantic search began, with the producers even considering making their captain a man.

The excitement surrounding a female captain was such that it overcame me as well, and I remember catching Rick Berman on the street in front of Stage 4 and passionately telling him I could do the role. He was kind. He said the obvious: We need you on DS9. I said that I could do both. It shows you what a big deal this character was; for the length of our conversation, I had completely lost my mind. Kate Mulgrew literally came to the rescue, returning from a vacation in Ireland, and giving an audition that left the producers knowing that they had found their captain.

Kate, like Geneviève, didn't know the *Star Trek* world and entered a whirlwind of preparations, with only a week's notice before filming began. "If a week," she told me. "I was absolutely blown out of the cannon."

Brannon Braga said that although the studio didn't really get involved with the writing of the show, they had their fingers firmly planted in the details of casting, hair, and makeup. With such an important role, exhaustive attention was given to every detail of her appearance. One of the ways an actor enters into a character is by believing that the character happens to look, act, and react exactly as they themselves would in certain circumstances—given character traits. With that sense of seamlessness, you are able to stop watching yourself and start simply being. For the entire first year, Kate wasn't given that chance.

Although she understood the issue almost immediately, it took a full season before the production team let her get on with becoming Janeway. Kate met with Rick Berman, who she says she respected and liked very much, and told him to call off the makeup, hair, and wardrobe departments. She recounts that she had ten hairdos in one season. "As if a captain on a starship would have any hairdo. Picard wouldn't have that problem, would he?"

Bald or graying hair on a man would be one thing, but in 1995, the way a woman looked was very important. Bujold had a streak of gray she had refused to cover, and I remember hearing that it was one of the unacceptable parts of her portrayal. Kate was able to explain to Berman that "the more you convince me that my physicality is working against this character, the more we're going to be in deep trouble. You'll be firing me and hiring a man again, and no progress will have been made. Leave me alone." She told me, "We cut the hair...I threw the boobs away...and I said, 'Let's talk now. Let's make her real. I want those twenty-five-year-old guys to look at me as a captain.'" After that, Kate grew to love the role of Janeway. But starring in a groundbreaking role for seven years, memorizing difficult technobabble with two little kids at home, wasn't easy. "It was just the hardest, hardest thing I've ever done."

Taking charge of her appearance was a courageous step that I don't think every woman would have taken. Too often, trying to please the powers that be is the first response if you feel that you aren't, somehow, meeting expectations. Instead, she took control. Talking to Kate, I realize that she understood what it took to get ahead in that world. She made her whole career without using what would be considered stereotypically female strategies, but she is also profoundly practical about the way things were.

Get Kate talking about art, how to deal with growing older, or the women affected by Janeway, and she will get downright poetic. Ask her how to make changes for women that will truly impact their lives, and she is practical and brief. As a political person, she accepts that change is slow and works within the framework that exists. Ultimately, she's very clear about what will make the difference. "Parity. When there's not even the corner of a doubt that I'm going to make what my male counterpart is going to make, then we're going to talk a new day."

I joined a soap opera named *Ryan's Hope* in 1978, a little while after Kate had left it. I remember just about everyone in the cast and crew talking with almost reverence about the young actor they were sure was destined for stardom. They weren't the only ones. She was a fan favorite who had studied acting at the Stella Adler school in New York City. After two years on the soap, where she formed a lifelong and important friendship

with creator Claire Labine, she worked constantly in film and television. Early films include *Lovespell*, *Remo Williams*, and *Throw Momma from the Train*. Television work included TV movies, lots of guest-star parts, playing the title role in the series *Mrs. Columbo*, and *Heartbeat*.

I asked Kate to imagine what could have changed for her in the business if she had been a man. "It was a man's world at that time—1970. The climb was hard, and it would have been a lot easier if I'd been a man. And I watched what my compatriots did: Meryl Streep and Jessica Lange and Sissy Spacek. Hard work. Infinite sacrifice at every turn that the men weren't called upon to make in the same way. It was a constant chess game."

When we spoke about aging in the business, I joked with Kate that women must have died at thirty-five in the 1966

Star Trek universe, seeing that there was so little representation of older women back then. "Are you sure it was 1966?" she laughed. "Some things never change." Looking back on her youth, she said, "I'm not sure what I felt all those years. I've been acting for forty-seven years. I'm not sure I had the time or the depth to look at it squarely until just about now. It's a very interesting choice for a young girl to make, isn't it? I think this business is almost singularly unforgiving and certainly not for the faint of heart."

She saw the sexist behavior in the business, but never fell a victim to it. Her friend Claire Labine cast her at twenty-one to play Richard Burton's wife and threw her a birthday party in Ireland, where they were shooting. Kate remembers being pulled onto Burton's knee, and while he serenaded her with the song "How to Handle a Woman," he draped a mink around her shoulders and gifted her diamond earrings. Her mother whispered to her, "You will return them tomorrow."

I knew Burton around the same age, and I would have had a war of emotions going on if it had been me on his knee: emotions of disgust at the idea of being "handled" with expensive gifts, and elation at the incredibly special moment with such a revered cultural figure.

But Kate was raised with brothers. She loves and appreciates men, and feels that they are often victimized by the patriarchy themselves. "My heart goes out to men, actually. I always sense their tenderness and their inability to expose themselves because society's been very, very harsh in that regard. They think they have to do these things. But I always sense, in nine out of ten good men, that there is a great tenderness, and the female power is to access that. Not only in ourselves, but in them. Don't forget that the most documented word spoken in times of war, since the fifteenth century, is the last words on the lips of a dying man, and that is 'Mama.'"

When I recounted a story about being inappropriately touched by an actor during bed scenes on a soap opera, she asked me how I handled it. I had told him to stop. When I said he didn't, she asked me why I didn't kick him in the balls. Well, I didn't want to be fired. "Bingo!" she replied. "That's why she goes to the door, and he opens the door, and he's in a robe, and he says, 'Come into my hotel room. We're going to talk about the job you want so much.' And then she cries what she cries. But she needs to think a little before that, doesn't she? Don't we all?"

Kate thinks that many women are impatient with the pace of change in the culture. It's taking more time than anyone wants it to, but she thinks it's important to remember that some of the fights for equality we're engaged in now have been moving with glacial timing for centuries. In the meantime, she believes women have to protect themselves from sharks instead of hoping that the sharks can be rendered harmless by cultural shifts. Nor does she see cancel culture or intimacy coaches on sets as an answer. "That's been going on [sexual harassment] since time immemorial."

As far as she's concerned, understanding that there is a slow process for change, and gaining parity with men's paychecks is the way forward. "I think our strength is inherent, and when we own it like men own theirs, it's going to be a new day. Patrick Stewart doesn't question his value, my dear. He simply demands what he demands. And he gets it."

When I brought up the issue of being torn between motherhood and having a career, Mulgrew was again practical. She said it's the same for any woman with a big job, be they politicians, diplomats, scientists, or leading actors in film or TV. If your child is sick, you will not be able to leave a job to care for them. It comes down to getting the work done. She says the answer is, again, parity in pay. If a woman gets a big paycheck, the optics are that she is powerful and therefore has to be kept happy.

Every time an AD or producer adjusts a schedule, they are increasing the chances that things go wrong for the production down the line. Telling a woman that she doesn't

CAPTAIN JANEWAY'S HAIR caused a surprising amount of stress, and as a result, it was constantly changing. In the early seasons, Kate wore an enormous wig that was bundled up on top of her head. It took a long time for her to persuade the producers to let her wear it in a bob. Captain Picard did not have this problem.

OPPOSITE: After a while, Janeway was also allowed to show that she was a warrior who could fight like any other captain.

ABOVE: Janeway's hair continued to be a source of anxiety, and the producers kept changing it, putting Kate in a variety of wigs until they settled on a bob.

have permission to leave set to check on a sick child, even though the schedule might permit it, eliminates risk. "No" is simply safer and easier. If, however, that same AD or producer says no to someone with perceived power, and that person takes their objections up the line of command, the risk becomes personal to the ones denying the request. Production members could even lose their job, which makes considering permission in those instances much more likely.

NATURAL LEADER

In seven years of *Voyager*, you never for a second question why Janeway is in charge. Kate enters any room with a presence of pure authority. She lent that to the captain, who is defined by her self-reliance, her strong opinions, and above all, by her compassion. Watching Kate's performance, I realize why the "A" in STEAM is so important. Inspiration and example from Captain Janeway literally changed the lives of so many of the people I spoke to. Kate has an intensity when she focuses, and Janeway's passion for science, her reveling in the questions it brings and the solutions it makes her reach for, is so instructional. Psychologist Mihaly Csikszentmihalyi wrote a book in which he describes "flow" as the most useful brain state for achieving one's goals. In a flow state, you do something not for gain or because someone

told you to, but because the joy of simply doing it is enough to make you forget to eat lunch. Janeway is an instructional video for what this powerful brain state looks like.

Like Picard, Janeway is so devoted to her job that the rest of her life suffers. Kate sees Janeway as a caring but isolated figure who had to accept that being in charge comes at a price. The question of whether she could have a romance kept coming up. Mulgrew said that her experience of being Number One on the call sheet and having a family made her see how having a committed relationship while being a captain would be impossible.

Most of the women I spoke to for this book had few ideas for how women could work, and have relationships and children, in a way that was successful for all. Having it all without compromise was what we had been told was ours if we worked hard enough, but it seems that even in a sci-fi show in the 1990s, it couldn't even be a projected dream of the future.

The pilot established that she had left a partner, Mark, at home with the dog. In the first two seasons, there are moments when she flirts with aliens, but this was the 1990s. By now, romancing the alien of the week like Captain Kirk seemed a dated concept even for a man, and would be frankly unacceptable for a woman. The writers picked up on the fact that Kate and her co-star Robert Beltran had chemistry in their scenes. As is often the way with *Star Trek*, fans started writing stories about them becoming a couple.

Even though the audience saw romantic tension between them, Kate was firmly of the opinion that Janeway couldn't have a relationship with her first officer and maintain her command. "That pretty much was my call...because I understood to get the men, I had to prove command. To prove command, I had to be alone. It's still true in my life. But I think that's fine. Loneliness is inherent in greatness. It just is." So Kate told the writers in no uncertain terms that they should put a stop to the potential romance.

In "Resolutions," written by Jeri Taylor, an insect bite infects Janeway and Chakotay with a highly contagious virus, and they are left in isolation on a planet until a remedy can be found. The captain works tirelessly to research a way to safely

return to the ship. Chakotay faces the fact that they may be stuck, and starts to make a home for them. There is an interesting moment done with expression alone. Finding Janeway in a bath, Chakotay becomes aware of her as a woman, and promptly leaves. Janeway registers his response to her, but quickly prioritizes her scientific figurings, and finds him to discuss them as if that sexual moment had no importance.

This is one way in which Janeway is so significant, I think. She has the ability to have her own goals and to focus on them with her whole being without being hijacked by a man's desire. The rest of the episode shows its 1990s roots. Sexist stereotypes are flipped instead of blurred, so that Chakotay cooks and acts as homemaker and Janeway struggles with her work of figuring out a way to return to her crew and to get them home.

But the story is about a romance, so a *deus ex machina* in the shape of storms on the planet is used as a device to destroy the equipment. Janeway is left thinking that she may have no choice but to start a relationship with her first officer that is so sweetly romantic that it feels as if we have switched to a Katharine Hepburn movie from the 1930s. When they

are rescued, Janeway moves on, prioritizing her command over her personal life. Beltran says that in his mind it took Chakotay longer to get over his feelings, and that he carried a torch for his captain for another season and a half.

Even though a committed relationship was off the table, Janeway wasn't completely without romance. But having a romance took tricky situations such as being left without technology in an Adam and Eve setting, reprogramming a hologram, having her mind wiped, or playing emotional chess with a dangerous alien.

In "Fair Haven," writer Robin Burger explores Janeway's desire to have a perfect mate. When the ship goes through a powerful storm, Paris keeps a nineteenth-century Irish village holodeck program open day and night to keep the crew's spirits up. When Janeway visits it, she meets a bartender, played by Fintan McKeown, who she spends a game- and booze-filled night with. She decides to reprogram the character to meet her specifications: no wife, with an increase in complexity, curiosity, education, and height. The dilemma for Janeway becomes that what could be a vacation from her day-to-day job is simply the same job in a different setting.

Being in total control of the moment isn't as satisfying as she thought it would be.

Far from home, the doctor points out the positives in the interactions for the captain: She has the choice of a relationship with a subordinate or a passing affair with an alien. Fantasy works to relieve pressure and provides a place where she can "play" with having a life with less authority and responsibility.

It seems very proactive and healthy to me that she finds a way to meet this need. It also seems a bit of 1990s blow-back when some members of the crew get hurt in a bar fight because the bartender is lovesick and doesn't understand where she has gone. A woman just enjoying an affair becomes dangerous for others.

In season seven's "Workforce," we once again see that the fascination for science is in her DNA. Most of the crew is kidnapped and given a mind-altering drug that erases their memories so they can be sent to work in a plant that lacks highly trained workers. She meets a co-worker, Jeff, played by James Read, who expresses interest in her at once. Although you clearly see her priority is her work, she falls into a romantic relationship with him. When he asks her to move in with him, she agrees immediately, saying what is actually true: "I must be out of my mind."

The relationship is close and comfortable, until Chakotay is able to convince her she is the captain of *Voyager*. Her lover helps her escape, and they have a tearful good-bye. When she is back on the bridge, she tells Chakotay that her time on the planet felt like home. When he asks if she is sorry he rescued her, she says, "Not for a minute." Again, my takeaway for the time is: a choice is to be made. You either have a high-powered career, or a romantic life. And if you have a high-powered career, you will choose that over a relationship.

In "Counterpoint," a Devore inspector, Kashyk, played by Mark Harelik, is looking to root out telepaths. They are illegal in Devore space, and he searches *Voyager* for refugees who are, in fact, being hidden there. He is imperious and cruel but follows his orders out of strong ethics. Both he and Janeway play cat and mouse when he reboards the ship pretending to defect and seek asylum on *Voyager*. By the end of the episode, you find out that they had both been using a romantic friction between them as a deception, even though it's clear they developed real feelings.

RIGHT: Janeway acts as mentor to Seven of Nine, forcing her to acknowledge her humanity.

OPPOSITE: The scenes between Seven and Janeway put two women at the center of *Star Trek* for the first time.

They are worthy opponents or lovers because they are a counterpoint. She goes against the Prime Directive to follow her ethics and save the refugee telepaths. He follows the law for the sake of his ethics but perhaps goes against his feelings about it. But in the end, as in every other relationship for Janeway, she cannot choose love or romance.

In the Nineties, there was a lot of media noise about women not being trustworthy in the workplace. Would they steal other women's husbands? Would they get married and pregnant and leave a job after being invested in at work? Could their need for romance and love make them untrustworthy? The climate then, I think, would make Kate and the writers on the show lean in hard to demonstrate the opposite. To prove that people with more feminine characteristics could be trusted to get the job done, the unreliable woman in the workplace had to be refuted.

There may have been romantic frontiers Janeway was forbidden to visit, but when it came to her crew and the aliens they encountered, she had huge capacity and high emotional intelligence. The compassion Jeri Taylor insisted upon is evident in both the scripts and Mulgrew's performance. Very often, there is a trope of a woman in charge being hobbled by a feeling: overwhelming empathy, the ability to feel what others are going through.

I read once that sympathy is felt when you see the object of your sympathy as hierarchically below you and you have no real intention of offering help. Empathy is when you can understand, and even feel, the difficult emotions another is experiencing.

The issue with empathy is that it involves the nervous system, and that can lead to feeling overwhelmed. Once the nervous system is involved, the ancient part of the brain starts "thinking" in terms of a fight, flight, or freeze state, rendering the strategizing part of the brain useless. Empathy is the pathway, however, to compassion. When a firefighter sees someone at the window of a burning building, they go through empathy straight to compassion, which involves specific parts of the brain that supply the body with hormones that help focus them to do what is necessary, and strategize the best way to save the person in need.

Compassion is different to sympathy or empathy because it is activating. This is demonstrated over and over with Janeway. In the pilot, "Caretaker," she puts herself and the crew on a long journey home in order to protect the Ocampa from the Kazon. In "Resistance," Caylem, played by Joel Grey, is determined to break his wife out of a Mokran prison, where, in fact, she died long ago. He sees Janeway as his daughter, who is also dead. Although she tries to disabuse him of his delusion throughout the episode, when he is dying, she shows huge compassion. She hears his confession and forgives him as his daughter, so that he can die in peace. The scene is emotional, but her focus is doing what is compassionate for Caylem in the moment. Whatever thoughts she has for her own experience seem to me to happen once she is back on *Voyager* and in her ready room. Over and over, she puts compassion and accountability for her crew over her own well-being.

These two traits, compassion and accountability, are two qualities that motherhood possesses. It is difficult for me to watch *Voyager* and not see Janeway as a good mother to her lost children. In "Resolutions," Harry Kim seems like an idealized version of a son who will go against authority, do anything, to save his mother figure. The more profound examination of the mother-child relationship, however, is Janeway's mentorship of Seven of Nine.

to media coverage, that sexiness turned out to be incredibly effective. Seven—and Jeri Ryan—got a lot of attention. Although the character was very sophisticated, her complexity wasn't always reflected in the media.

The magazine *SFX* tellingly published an edition at the time that featured a photo of a partially dressed Ryan, on her belly and hair mussed, with a box inserted on the side of the cover promising an interview with Mulgrew. It's easy to figure which is more compelling for the casual male reader: the immediacy of the shot that is a thirst trap, or the promise of an in-depth interview.

In an interview for the Television Academy Foundation, Rick Berman spoke of how active Kate had been during the first three years of the show in championing this new achievement for womanhood: making speeches, going to the White House, and taking on the mantle in the media of first woman captain in *Star Trek* space. A tight catsuit on a very beautiful woman seemed to instantly push all that aside. Looking back, Brannon Braga told me he should have done things differently. He said there wasn't enough communication between him and the cast at the time of Ryan's hiring. Talking to them before filming began could have gone far in helping them understand and accept the decision to add the character and build viewership, which, he told me, increased by 60 percent after the addition of Seven of Nine.

I remember when Michael Dorn was added to DS9 to help up our ratings. We weren't told anything, and I learned of his joining the show at a convention, when I was asked how it made me feel. At the time, I saw it as a threat to my character, especially because I wasn't told anything about his arrival. I thought he would take over from me, as he had from Denise Crosby. I believed, with my understanding of how Hollywood worked back then, that Worf would soon be in the captain's office talking strategy instead of Kira, and I would make appearances as a sort of Bajoran secretary. The communication might have made a difference. But this seemed to be how the world worked at the time.

In reality, as Ira Steven Behr told me quite heatedly, creators are desperately spending their time, which is never enough, trying to come up with interesting plots and to

Much has been said about how difficult Kate found it when Seven joined the show. The powers that be felt that *Voyager* needed some help with the ratings. Their solution was to introduce a new character who, in addition to everything else she brought, filled the "Sexy" box. When it came

OPPOSITE TOP: Kate sees Janeway as a lonely character who could only find love on the holodeck.

OPPOSITE BOTTOM: "The Year of Hell" showed that Janeway could be obsessive and would sacrifice everything for her crew.

LEFT: Janeway is a tactician and a scientist, who was capable of outwitting the Borg.

However tense as it may have been for both actors, the effect of the character is undeniable, and the relationship between Janeway and Seven is one of the strongest and best-written things *Star Trek* has ever done. In "The Gift," Seven wakes to the reality that she has been cut off from the Borg Collective, and is furious and frantic to get back the connection she has lost. Janeway is calm but clear that she knows what is best for her and will execute it whether Seven agrees or not.

I saw this as the true birth experience, the child crying and confused by no longer being in the safe confines of the womb, and the mother giving comfort but knowing there is no going back to how things were. The emotionally difficult job of bringing someone through the stages of human development is demonstrated in all the scenes between them.

THE GOOD MOTHER

Janeway functioned as a good mother to Seven throughout all the stages of Seven's gradual development as she becomes an individualized being. In the early stages of childhood, a mother is a caretaker who makes decisions based on what is best for the child. When Seven's body starts to reject the Borg implants, Janeway is determined to save her and makes the decision to insist on surgery, even though Seven vehemently argues to be allowed to return to the Collective.

The question raised is the ability to choose your own fate, but as a caretaker, Janeway has information and an overview that Seven does not. The Borg had been a little girl named Annika Hansen when she and her parents had been assimilated. Just as a deprogrammer must fight someone deeply embedded in a cult to help them return to who they had been, Janeway stays a steady course to what she believes is best.

Seven's acting out and untrustworthy behavior reminded me of a teenager trying to work their will against rules they don't understand. And just like dealing with a teenager, Janeway limits her new crew member's freedom until she can be trusted.

break stories. The breakneck speed of twenty-six episodes a season in those days didn't leave much time for anything else. And, in those days, there was much less awareness from everybody about how to sensitively think of these things. "You're lucky to have a job" would have been each of our mantras, from the top of management on down.

Brannon told me that Seven was designed to make Janeway a stronger character—to give her a Spock—and that to this day, he regrets not having spent more time discussing this with Kate. Spock, Data, Odo, and Seven of Nine were all characters struggling with their humanity, and they are all characters that activate others in storylines and relationships.

In "The Raven," Janeway continues to cultivate human emotions as well as tools to control them. She exposes Seven to art, with a Leonardo da Vinci sculpting program. Nanoprobes from her assimilation have become active again, and like a sufferer of post-traumatic stress, she starts to have flashbacks of the trauma of the Borg attack on her family. Even though she behaves like an enemy on the ship, destroying and attacking, Janeway continues to look to find the cause of the behavior instead of denouncing it.

By the end of the episode, Seven has come to the other side of the repressed memories, and is able to access the very human ability of imagining. Janeway is supportive and refuses to give up on her throughout.

In "Dark Frontier," Janeway takes the leap all mothers must when she realizes the child has matured enough to make their own decisions and mistakes. When Seven insists on joining an away team that could put her at risk with the Borg, Janeway makes it clear she doesn't agree but allows Seven to make the call.

In "Think Tank," Janeway allows Seven to decide whether or not to join a disparate group of aliens who have superior intelligence. She tells her that Seven has learned enough to make the decision based on what she wants for her life, not based on what the consequences might be for *Voyager*. Like a good leader and mentor, she encourages individual growth outside the group.

The positive example of this relationship was a game changer for many women in the audience. By the end of the 1990s, the Janeway/Seven of Nine relationship showed how women could pull each other up and support each other for mutual benefit. This was the antidote to the catfights between women on so many TV shows and movies at the time.

The Janeway/Seven scenes pass the Bechdel Test with flying colors, and show thoughtful human development taught with patience and compassion.

On board a *Star Trek* cruise, I asked an endless line of people for a total of about eight hours who in *Trek* inspired them. From a widely diverse group, the answer came back again and again: Janeway. She was a leader with ultimate accountability who accepted personal sacrifice in order to do the job. She had the full spectrum of human emotions that allowed people in the audience to witness a woman who could go through a depression and find her way out of it, make tough choices to lead a lost crew/family through uncharted territory to a place of safety, and mentor a fellow woman to embrace her individualism. And as Stacey Abrams said, she did it all by herself, without the oversight of a hierarchy.

In terms of useful storytelling for women during the Nineties and beyond, it's a profound one. For the women of *Star Trek*, it was an essential and unskippable step toward a character who wasn't compelled to make a choice between companionship and her right to authority.

Kate told me of her son's baby daughter, Miro. She hopes that one day, when she is around twenty, Miro searches for her grandmother's name on whatever a computer looks like in the future. "And I hope she'll be dazzled and moved and inspired because I think I've done some work my little granddaughter can be proud of, and that in turn she will do the same for her granddaughter."

ABOVE: *Voyager*'s final episode features a septuagenarian Janeway saving the day. Not something you see often.

OPPOSITE: A hero is measured by their enemies, and Janeway proved herself more than equal to the Borg.

Jeri Ryan as

SEVEN OF NINE

Casting directors Ron Surma and Junie Lowry remember that when the call went out to cast a new character with sex appeal on Star Trek: Voyager, *their assistant fixated on the picture of Jeri Ryan, taping it to the wall behind their desks. Her manager and agents kept refusing to send her in, but the assistant wouldn't give up. After weeks of persistence, Ryan finally agreed to audition.*

She told me the two audition scenes informed her of what she could expect from the role. The "infamous Harry Kim scene: 'You wish to copulate...take off your clothes'" made it clear that her sexuality would definitely be part of the way she was portrayed. But the other scene, which she said was one of the most beautifully written scenes she has ever read, told her this part would also be something special. It was never shot, but in it, Seven recalls her first memory of laughter.

Her son was three at the time and had been diagnosed with autism. Playing someone who was learning how to fit into a neurotypical world made this a very compelling project for the young actor. After a deal was made prior to her final audition, Jeri caught a glimpse of this new show she might join that happened to be airing that night. She hated it and cancelled the final audition. Rick Berman called her (as he did me when I refused the job the first time) and persuaded her to come meet with Brannon, Jeri Taylor, and himself. When she learned not only that they had big plans for the character but also that they had the same opinion of the show that aired (she had no recollection of which episode it was), she believed they would live up to their promise. All these years later, she knows they did.

When I saw the towering Los Angeles billboards of Jeri Ryan's character Seven of Nine sheathed in silver, I wondered where their Number One and captain, Kate Mulgrew, was in the picture. But, as we know, sex sells, and the beautiful blonde in the skintight silver suit that could easily belong to a dominatrix sold *Star Trek*. Brannon Braga said this kind of media attention started the talk of exploitation that only started to fade once people actually watched the episodes and found that Seven of Nine was "a complicated character that served her purpose to reinvigorate the show and the characters."

Brannon, who Jeri said was not only the creator but also the keeper of Seven, had been contemplating adding a Borg as a regular character, but had needed to wait for the film *Star Trek: First Contact* to come out. Stealing the Borg Queen's thunder wouldn't have served the franchise. The success of the movie made the Borg even more compelling, and Brannon called Rick Berman to suggest adding a Borg to the show. Berman, thinking the show needed more sex appeal, added that powerful adjective to the character, and Seven of Nine was born.

As I watch the show now, and interview so many people to whom Seven was important, I see she served as a true Trojan horse. The sexiness brought more people to the show, where they could come for the costume, but stay for a well-acted and developed character. Seven was an avatar many different groups of people could claim as their own in the same way that Spock, Data, and Dax were, but maybe for even a wider group: She was an abused child; she was a survivor of trauma; she was a victim of a cult; she was queer;

165

she was neurodiverse; she was every woman who has been valued for her appearance but is so much more; she was anyone who struggled to find their true self and fit into a world where they felt othered.

Not only did she add dimension to the show, but she also added layers to Captain Janeway. The mentorship of Seven, I believe, helped cultivate one of the most significant and culturally relevant relationships in all of *Star Trek*. The gift to Jeri was every actor's dream: a character with such a

wide arc that she literally started as barely human, and had years to take the journey to becoming her own person. She understood the massive opportunity.

The transformation from evil-looking cyborg to beautiful, mostly human woman is a sci-fi take of the Pygmalion story. When the Doctor presents the alterations he made to Seven of Nine in season four's "The Gift," actor Jeri Ryan's magnetic beauty in a skintight suit is breathtaking.

The outfit comes with a medical justification: It helps regenerate Seven's skin to keep her alive now that she is separated from the Collective. Costume designer Bob Blackman was always challenged to come up with new and provocative designs, and he has spoken about his vision of having the character completely covered while at the same time meeting the demand of appearing extremely sexy.

ABOVE: The idea behind Seven was to put a Borg, and therefore the Borg's point of view, on the ship.

OPPOSITE: Seven may look sexual, but don't be fooled, there is much more to the character.

The effect he wanted was a spray-painted jumpsuit, and the fact that Ryan had the best figure he had ever worked with made it easy. What he said exemplifies how common it was, and still is, to quantify a woman's appearance by using the stereotypical standards of the male gaze: large breasts, small waist, with long legs. It is so ubiquitous that it easily becomes an unconscious bias for so many of us and is accepted as the bar to aspire for.

When I talked to Jeri, she said that these standards have only worsened. Being the mother of a fifteen-year-old girl, she finds the media "scary. Everything is filtered and retouched and photoshopped and tweaked, and it's scary." She feels young women need to know how to stand in their own strength and their own power, and that power comes in infinite sizes and shapes and colors, and not just a single culture's idea of beauty and worth.

But Blackman also stated that as he read the script, the character was more dimensional than the typical 1990s babe, and would require a different kind of sexiness; a low-cut top wouldn't suffice. After several episodes, the costume caused issues with health and practicality. It was so restrictive, it took twenty minutes to get her in and out of it for a bathroom break. The subsequent catsuits were still tight but much more practical. When I learned that Ryan wore a robe over the catsuit, I asked her if she had been uncomfortable in the costume. She answered no, it was simply cold on set. Her only request, which

became a joke during shooting, was that full-body shots be done before lunch, because her lunch would appear in shots done after.

The physical makeover is a man's work, but the emotional work of individuating Seven belongs to a great extent to the captain. In "The Gift," Janeway becomes a caretaker, knowing what's best for Seven. The hybrid-Borg responds with righteous fury and the argumentative reasoning of an enraged child.

When I played the evil intendant, I used the self-awareness of my body and costume to send the message that my character used sex as a tool to get what she wants. With all the attention on the costume and her appearance, Ryan has a wonderful, unselfconscious presence that reflects the character's lost connection to human emotion. If she is sexy, it is the way she is perceived, not who she is. From the moment she appears, she becomes a work-in-progress way more complex than the way she looks.

Seven's traumatic background and disconnection from herself is seen in "The Raven," which tells the audience that this was a little girl with a name, Annika, who lost her autonomy in a violent way. S.E. Fleenor, in an essay for Startrek.com ("Seven of Nine Was Always Queer"), said: "Seven's body is often a site of conflict between her and those that would control, dismantle, or destroy her for her refusal to fit in to a binary." It also makes her a valuable story to people who have been

In season five's "Someone to Watch Over Me," her scientific curiosity about B'Elanna and Tom's relationship leads the captain and the Doctor to think it's time for her to experience a romantic relationship of her own, for her "social development."

It was 1998 by now, and the episode is loaded with moments of the Doctor trying to ready Seven for a date in performative ways. He teaches her to take her date's arm when offered (as if she were in a hoop skirt and unsteady!) and to please him by making small talk. He takes her hair down from its usual updo. All that was missing for me from this ugly-duckling-to-swan trope was a moment in which he would remove a pair of heavy glasses as he breathlessly tells her she is, in fact, quite beautiful. Thankfully, glasses didn't appear.

He then suggests a short, sexy dress for her upcoming date—it is the full prescription of how to attract a man. It turns out, however, that the episode title refers to the Doctor's desires and not Seven's. Although she is game to learn, she decides she isn't interested in anyone aboard ship, breaking the Doctor's heart just a little. Even though she is taught how to be performatively female—and Paris says an issue for men will be her dominant behavior (ironic, given his relationship with B'Elanna)—she decides she is fine how she is. She has agency over how she presents herself and who she chooses. The episode turns out to be more about men's expectations and issues with her, as we discover that she is perfectly comfortable with who she is.

I asked Jeri about the social politics of being a beautiful woman in Hollywood. She said it gave her the power to be more choosy when it came to accepting roles; it allowed her to bypass the typical "mother, girlfriend, victim" roles. In the 1990s, Hollywood was a very male world, and she made friends with people she worked with because there was very little time or opportunity to meet people in any other way. Many were directors and producers; none were women. Her mentors were all older men. Jeri Taylor was one of the first women in a position of power she crossed paths with back then.

Her looks gave her some degree of power when it came to roles, but there was always the belief from many people that because she was beautiful, she must be stupid. She

abused as children, suffered trauma, or felt that they weren't aligned in some way with the culture they find themselves in.

The value, I think, is the example she provides that there can be growth and autonomy after difficulties. Seven continues to grow throughout the series, but wonderfully, the storytelling doesn't require her to conform.

ABOVE: When Seven experiments with normal life, we see someone struggling to understand what it means to be human.

OPPOSITE LEFT: Seven was incredibly intelligent and convinced of her own superiority.

OPPOSITE RIGHT: Seven's costume was designed to show off Jeri's body while revealing the minimum amount of skin.

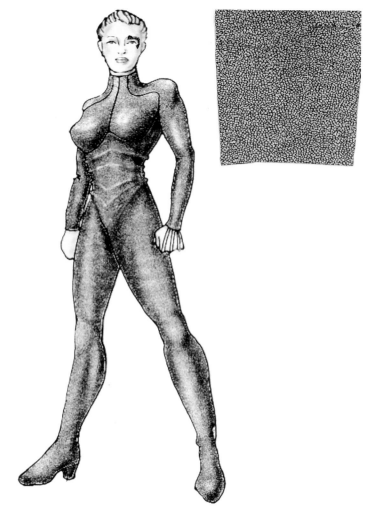

would move quickly to "show them I am not." In fact, she was a National Merit Scholar (something we have in common), and Roxann Dawson told me that more often than not she would have her nose in a complicated-looking book between setups during filming.

The Borg Collective can be seen as a patriarchal society in which you follow the rules to fit in. Seven admits the appeal of being accepted but, before long, resists being re-assimilated. She resists it with her new crew mates, too. In the first scene of season five's "Drone," the Doctor catches her practicing the physical feat of smiling, and later asks her to smile for the camera. She does not. It seems clear in all her scenes that she doesn't see the point in pleasing or meeting others' expectations of her.

Women will recognize the pressure to present as pleasing. The neurodiverse may recognize this as something they deal with, too. A young man with high-functioning autism, Jay, told me he found Seven extremely relatable because she exists in a sea of strangers, with a mentor who takes on the job of teaching her social skills. Like some on the spectrum, she is excellent at her job, highly intelligent, but not familiar with the accepted rules of everyday interactions.

Further in this episode, she explains to the crew that the drone, created from a transporter accident that merges her nanoprobes with the Doctor's mobile emitter, is drawn, like she is, to the Collective. She describes it as a natural desire for perfection. So many people, I believe, can relate to this idea of rigid perfection. Staying an individual entity comes with choices and learning from mistakes, with uncomfortable emotions.

When the drone chooses to die in order to ensure the safety of *Voyager*, Seven feels the emotion of loss. The episode started with her practicing a smile in a mirror. It ends with her looking at herself experiencing a real emotion, one that comes with being alive and hurting. Unlike the smile, it is spontaneous and for her alone. For women, maintaining the fluidity of feeling all emotions without having to be performatively pleasing at all times is real freedom and mental health.

Seven is given the experience of mentoring a child, Naomi Wildman, with whom she experiences a deep relationship. The relationship develops as Seven teaches her geometry and serves as an example to Naomi of how to achieve her goals of someday being the captain of a ship. In season six's episode "Survival Instinct," we see them declare each other family. Even so, Seven doesn't treat her in the stereotypically prescribed way of a compassionate, warm mother figure. Seven is always who she is, regardless of who she is in relation to.

The tone that women were responsible for finding in those days—a tone that would be nonthreatening and obsequious, is totally absent here. Instead of having to shape-shift according to who she is relating to, it is up to others to either accept who Seven is, or move on.

In "Ashes to Ashes," the Borg children under Seven's care let us see a progression in Seven's understanding of their need for play. Too much of a disciplinarian at first, she eventually changes her protocol with them to include unstructured play. The example of being wrong and learning is a big one for everyone, but especially for women, who often have the cultural expectation that they should have been born with an infallible mothering instinct.

It often felt to me that if I didn't meet others' expectations of nurturing, I was simply a bad mother. The fact is, empathetic understanding and compassionate caring can be learned, just as Seven learned them. This kind of three-dimensionality makes for a character who is definitely outside of any kind of cultural box. It also offers an expansion of possibilities for anyone who felt that they weren't able to learn.

In her own life, Jeri found balancing motherhood and working as a successful actress hard. Her son was three when she started the show, and would come to set often early on. Once he started school, it was another story. Their seven-day episodes had brutally long hours, and prosthetic makeup took additional time to take off because it was reused the next day. She felt she missed her son's entire childhood.

When she did a David Kelley show after *Voyager*, he had set up a daycare next to the set. But by then, her son was already in school. When she had her daughter, she was determined not to repeat history and "changed my parameters very, very drastically by what I was willing to do." That, of course, meant limiting her career choices.

During the ancient war between the Greeks and the Trojans, the city of Troy was impenetrable. After ten years, the Greeks built a huge wooden horse and left it in front of the city. The Trojans, thinking it was a gift, pulled it inside their walls, at which point the Greeks hiding inside the hollow horse came streaming out and defeated the unprepared Trojans.

For me, Jeri Ryan's Seven of Nine is a true depiction of what it is to be a complicated, ever-evolving woman wrapped in pretty gift packaging. Her beauty got the show and the character a lot of attention. But I think it's difficult to continue to objectify her as her story unfolds. It would take effort not to see the hurt child, the complexity of spirit, and the progression of someone whose choice was taken completely away and who has to learn, from the bottom up, what it is to be an individual. It's a depth you can't unsee. Looking at a finished painting, you see a picture, and not the first rough brushstrokes the painter made to define the canvas. In this way, the more I watched her episodes, the less I noticed the outfit or the body, but saw a person.

I think Seven was a true gift to women who needed the example of women mentoring women. But her appeal was so broad, including so many groups, not to mention women unfairly objectified for being beautiful, that I consider her a gift to Third Wave Feminism, which strove at the time to include many social issues under one umbrella.

She told me revisiting her character on *Picard* was quite different to working on *Voyager*, which was such a difficult work experience that everything that came after seemed easy in comparison. She noted that what most influences a show to make it feel safe and welcoming is the producer at the top and Number One on the call sheet. Her favorite experience was the medical TV series *Body of Proof*, with Dana Delaney as Number One. But *Picard* offered a chance to revisit a character she had thought she had said goodbye to, and it was a joy. This time, clothes weren't an issue, and Seven was freer and owned her own strength. The relationship with Raffi made sense to her, too. She had heard that Jeri Taylor had pushed for Seven to be nonbinary in some way, but for the sake of the male gaze, that idea wasn't explored. For her character's journey, it made sense to her that Seven would finally explore all aspects of her sexuality.

Today, she is married to an "incredibly modern man" who is a chef and does most of the cooking and cleaning, and who shares equally in caring for their daughter. Instead of having to ask for help, Jeri finds that they fight to be the one to handle the day-to-day responsibilities of having a teenage daughter. They know how quickly that time goes, and neither wants to miss a minute of it.

It's her daughter who inspires her to tell young women, "There is no limit if you don't limit yourself." When I asked her what Seven had left behind in Jeri's personality, she said she hadn't considered that before, but actually playing Seven of Nine had encouraged Jeri to "stand firm in what I want, what I stand for, and what I believe. Thanks, Seven."

OPPOSITE: Jeri's personality is very different from Seven's. They're both very intelligent, but Jeri is much more relaxed and has an obvious sense of humor.

ABOVE: Seven was trying to escape from the Borg but was still drawn to their certainty.

Jennifer Lien as

KES

I had to think long and hard about how to approach writing about Jennifer Lien. One of the main goals of the book was to give insight into the experiences the women of Star Trek *had, to see where they were in their own lives, how they were impacted by the culture of Hollywood and the times, and how different it was (or wasn't) from what they were helping to imagine the future for women might be.*

The other women whom I didn't have the opportunity to talk to personally had given many interviews; talking about *Star Trek* is simply part of being in this community. What they said and thought about their experiences is something they willingly shared. Jennifer rarely gave interviews and has left the business. All I can do is recount what others have said and speculated. It is clear that she had serious personal issues, but women have been denied their voice too often—been told how they feel or what they should be feeling or who they are so many times—that I feel it's better to make a space, an empty space, that she can fill in, if and when she wishes. What I can do, is talk about Kes.

Kes was an Ocampan, which meant she had telekinetic abilities and would only live for eight or nine years. The concept of the character had been to explore how an alien with a short life span would have a different experience and cause the audience to think about their own lives in a new way. The writers thought of her as having "the lifespan of a butterfly," and in the earliest notes, before she gained a name, she was referred to as "the mayfly."

The creators of *Star Trek: Voyager* wanted a beautiful young girl with a delicate, elfin quality that belied the wisdom and calm that usually comes with age. Jennifer Lien was nineteen when she was cast, but her character's short lifetime meant that Kes was already a mature woman, regardless of how young she appeared. She has a fragile beauty, with a voice that sounds like it's out of a 1940s film-noir movie: deep and melodious. Her eyes, for a young person, seem like they've seen a lot of life.

But some ideas work better on paper than onscreen. She is paired with Neelix, played by Ethan Phillips, who was in his forties at the time. On paper, this must have seemed like a relationship that would create many storylines: the wise but young-looking butterfly with the comical, childlike, but kindly alien with lots of prosthetics. Onscreen, however, the age difference is uncomfortable. Even if Kes is mature by Ocampan standards, she just looks like a very young woman. Here is where having more facial prosthetics could have helped as a reminder that this is an alien, which immediately reframes our expectations. The prosthetic ears weren't a prominent enough reminder to me. A twenty-year age difference between men and women was often accepted in the past (just watch Bogart's movies with Bacall), but in today's society, we are acutely aware of the possibilities of imbalances in power. But still, something about this romantic relationship didn't translate well to the screen, even though offscreen, the actors enjoyed a good working friendship.

I asked Brannon why Kes wasn't aged through the years with prosthetics to make the original concept play out in a visible way for the audience. He said it was never even talked about. It's possible the reason was aging makeups, as Braga points out, don't always look convincing—even today. Also,

hiring a beautiful young woman and then covering her up with age makeup seemed counterproductive at the time.

By the middle of the second season, the writers and producers had recognized the relationship between Neelix and Kes didn't work, and purposely avoided showing love scenes between them. A romantic attachment that didn't work, a passive characteristic such as a short life span, and the actor's own personal issues' impact on filming may have contributed to the stalling of the character of Kes.

There was another issue: one that often afflicted women on television. Kes didn't have a very clearly defined role on the ship. In the beginning, she is simply Neelix's girlfriend, who offers an alien perspective, but she doesn't have an actual job of her own. There aren't many storylines that can be generated by growing hydroponic fruits and vegetables. However useful and smart the reality of that is, it's not going to get a writer's juices flowing. They addressed this by putting her in sickbay with the Doctor, effectively making her a nurse.

In some ways, that made sense. Kes had all the very best characteristics of her co-creator, Jeri Taylor. She was nurturing and focused on others, as well as calm and caring. And

Robbie McNeill, who played Tom Paris, said that the character was very influential in developing the Doctor. She argued for the Doctor to have better treatment from the crew, and her caring and instruction to him about humanity went a long way in developing Robert Picardo's character. But it didn't really develop Kes, and it put her in a more traditional role than the other female characters. To be clear, there is no question that the compassionate caretaker is essential to society. Roles such as Kes's allow audience members with similar strengths to experience the story through the character's eyes. But it's a role that too many women have been restricted to, whether they had that attribute or not. Also, in order for a compassionate character to feel three-dimensional, there is a test, I think. When she helps others, what development happens for her? If it's just the other character gaining complexity and depth, she may not be fully realized.

There is a kind of alchemy in the creation of a character. There is a concept, then an actor takes that concept and opens it up by adding elements the writers never thought of, which the writers then spin further. The actor then adds further new aspects. This is the kind of virtual relationship between actor and writer that inspires both sides. Somewhere along the line, that circle was broken, and—for whatever reason—Kes stopped developing as a character.

Although the senior producers tried to help Lien, her problems were clearly serious. Back then, it was unthinkable to publicly share mental health issues without professional and personal repercussions. So much more is understood now, and I hope that things might play out differently today.

Lien left the series at the beginning of the fourth season, but the character returned in the sixth-season episode "Fury." A much older—and more powerful—Kes blames Janeway and the rest of the crew for the terrible things she experienced after leaving the ship. There is time travel involved, leading a younger Kes to convince her older version that she is wrong.

In the last scene, Neelix brings the older Kes snacks to eat for the journey home. He stares into her eyes. She asks what he is doing, and he says, "Just looking." Her face is old, her hair gray. She asks him if he sees anyone he knows. "Only you." His face is filled with love, longing, and loss. I felt that he saw the person he had loved, not the aging body, and the moment was profoundly moving. I thought how bittersweet this storyline could have been, and how capable Ethan was at making it heart-wrenching and beautiful.

In season four's "The Gift," Jennifer Lien's character of Kes is developing her psychokinetic abilities to the point where she is destabilizing the very structure of *Voyager*, and she is destabilizing, too. She comes to the decision that she must leave to safely explore this phenomenon so that she doesn't put the ship in danger of being destroyed. Enter, in the same episode, Jeri Ryan as Seven of Nine. In an interview for the Television Academy Foundation, Rick Berman said his idea was: "What if we bring a babe onto the show?" Jennifer was a beautiful young woman, but the casting of Kes had called for an elfin quality, and Jeri was a bombshell, who, it seemed, the studio valued more. It all looked bad. The truth, however, was much more complicated.

In talking with Brannon Braga, I understood he had been waiting for the right time to bring a Borg character onto *Voyager* for a while. He thought the concept was just what the show needed. Being half-human, she would struggle with identity—making her relatable. Having everyone's worst possible enemy to deal with on a regular basis would create interesting dynamics and storylines, and the recent movie *Star Trek: First Contact* had made the Borgs the hot alien. When he brought the idea to Berman, the idea of adding sex appeal made sense; some male fans weren't buying into this newest *Trek*, and viewership was lagging. There was a plan in place to have Kes leave the show after the end of the fourth season, but suddenly the writers were asked to move it up. I can't think of another *Trek* character who was let go mid-run. Both Denise Crosby and Terry Farrell had a hand in their own exits. Jennifer didn't seem to be asking to leave. Why the rush? What happened?

The showrunners didn't share the real reason for their decision to release Jennifer from her contract. I imagine it was a combination of protecting the actor, the show, and just plain human decency at the time. There was a discretion that is observed even today when I asked creatives and actors about Jennifer. She was having mental health issues, and couldn't be counted on to keep to a shooting schedule. A TV show is hard work that doesn't leave time for much else in your life. Shooting a *Star Trek* show with twenty-six episodes a year was one of the most grueling jobs you could have, and took both endurance and discipline. There were extremely long hours, owing to prosthetics, special effects, and the quality of the work the creatives were trying to achieve. Each episode of *Voyager* cost around $3 million to produce, and every minute a cast and crew is kept waiting costs money and time that will mean a later wrap. Neither crew members who have even earlier calls than most of the actors, nor actors who honored their call times would be happy (to put it mildly) to sit and wait. Being late for your allotted time in the makeup chair is a blood-chilling thought for any actor. Sometimes, young actors have to be taught this basic discipline, and they learn it fast. Jennifer was young, but that wasn't the problem. She had issues and didn't allow anyone close enough to be able to help. Jeri Taylor tried hard to reach her, but couldn't get anywhere. Neither could castmates, who took her leaving their company hard. The character who was most like the beloved Jeri Taylor herself wouldn't make it through the show to the end of her very short life span.

The desire for exploration that caused her to want to leave her home of Ocampa never really played out, until the episode in the sixth season, "Fury," in which her character returns to seek revenge. Three years on, Kes returns and plans to trade passage to Ocampa with the Vidiians in exchange for the lives of the crew of *Voyager*. She is angry

and has obviously been alone too long, and now believes the captain ripped her from her home and then gave her the bad advice of leaving *Voyager* to discover her powers when she wasn't ready. Her method of spreading destruction is a difficult one for any actor. I remember having to get the hang of pointing a phaser and imagining the powerful beam

a message for herself as a reminder that everything that transpired was what she herself had chosen, she remembers the support she got from Janeway and leaves for Ocampa peacefully. The old-age makeup was used in this show, and for most of the episode, I agreed with Braga that it didn't do much other than cover up a beautiful woman.

The importance of how Jennifer Lien and Kes left the world of *Star Trek* lies in the discussion of mental health. To deal with it in any circumstance is difficult, but to deal with it in the public eye, with huge pressure to perform, is brutal. Add the element of shame, which makes it impossible to talk about, and it's disastrous. Back in the 1990s, Jennifer's dismissal wasn't spoken of, and neither was my rape or post-traumatic stress—including how toxic the shame is. A casual Google search showed me how much things have changed. Stars such as Katy Perry and Dwayne "The Rock" Johnson share about dealing with depression. Ryan Reynolds talks about his anxiety, and Selena Gomez continues to work and flourish as she handles her diagnosis of bipolar disorder.

There are many in the public eye who see the importance of opening a channel for this discussion in order to normalize something so many of us deal with. When there is less stigma attached, maybe medications will be taken when they are needed instead of being skipped; maybe people at difficult points of their lives will feel safe enough to reach out for the support they need. It may not have changed anything back then for Jennifer, but maybe it would have. I see Kes, and Jennifer, as an important link in the women of *Star Trek* that needs to be spoken of instead of hidden. What Jennifer struggled with is what many women did and still do. We need to include her story, and them, in the conversation so we can burn the shame off these issues.

OPPOSITE TOP: Jennifer shows her dark side in "Warlord."

OPPOSITE BOTTOM: Kes deals with the issue of what it means to have a child.

ABOVE: A handful of stories touched on Kes's aging, but the series never fully explored what it meant to have such a short life span.

emanating from it that would be added later by special effects. It takes practice to just point and feel like something is happening. Because she is using telekinesis to spread mayhem, she simply looks hard at something. It ends up looking passive yet again, with the actual action done by special effects and not the actor. Once a younger Kes leaves

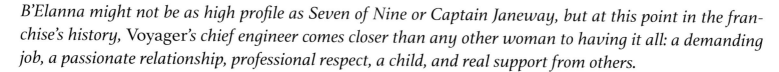

Roxann Dawson as
B'ELANNA TORRES

B'Elanna might not be as high profile as Seven of Nine or Captain Janeway, but at this point in the franchise's history, Voyager's *chief engineer comes closer than any other woman to having it all: a demanding job, a passionate relationship, professional respect, a child, and real support from others.*

She is as far from performatively female as it's possible to be. She doesn't set out to please anyone, and her struggles are normalized by the acceptance of them by those around her. No one questions her competency or suggests that she needs to step back from her job or her life when she seeks help. In fact, the man she falls in love with, Tom Paris, is a study in how men can be a support system for a partner.

B'Elanna Torres was designed to be a classic *Star Trek* character. Like Spock, she is half-human, and like Worf, she has Klingon heritage, which makes her quick temper acceptable in a way that it wouldn't be if she were "just" human. That conflict would generate storylines that dealt with mental health issues throughout the show's run. Just as it did with Kira or with Dax, her alienness freed her from a legacy of assumptions about how women should behave. If B'Elanna snarled, it was because she was Klingon and that made it okay.

Roxann Dawson was instantly attracted to the scope of the character of B'Elanna when she first auditioned. She was told at the time that *Star Trek* could change her life, but she was more interested in the immediate challenge of the role in front of her.

When I asked her if she had ever encountered a "box" that she was put into professionally, she answered with a resounding yes. Because Roxann has Latin heritage, the box Hollywood offered her was smaller than most. Most of the Latina roles back then were drug addicts or maids,

roles that were two-dimensional at the most, but in the 1980s and '90s few people were willing to consider her for anything else. In fact, she once showed up for an audition where the casting director asked her why she was wasting everyone's time coming in for a non-Latina role. It was difficult for Roxann to grasp just how small this Hollywood casting box was. She had worked extensively in theater as an actor and a director, where the strongest performance gets the part, not the person who best matches its physical description.

Star Trek offered her an opportunity to do something radically different. The role of B'Elanna was instantly fascinating to her—not only was the character half-Klingon, but she was also half-Latina as well. This duality was something she had experienced in her own life, so she felt she had something meaningful to contribute to the storylines, which she says explored "the many sides of ourselves, whether it be our heritage, genetics, whether it be an emotional side, a psychological side. We all deal with that."

There were drawbacks, though. In 1990s Hollywood, if you were in your thirties and attractive, you knew it was a now-or-never race, before you turned forty, to prove yourself worthy of the "Beauty" box, which was pretty much the only way you could climb the ladder and become a leading lady. Not being a blonde Caucasian already limited Dawson's chances of landing leading roles. Being made up as a Klingon for seven years must have felt as if she was being asked to give up on the idea completely. Emerging from the makeup and getting cast in those leading roles must have looked almost impossible.

Her makeup tests for B'Elanna had Roxann worried as they seemed to be leaning more toward "horror" than beauty for the character, complete with snaggled Klingon teeth. She purposely didn't make the teeth work when she spoke during the tests, and said she made clear her discomfort with the more extreme makeups. Still, she believed it was the right of the creators to make her look any way they chose. She could have been buried beneath the makeup for seven years, so she was grateful when the look they settled on was a balance between beauty and Klingon. As it was,

with the ridges on her forehead, it was difficult for her to look in the mirror, but it instantly had the effect of informing her of the character's own sense of discomfort with her heritage.

In the *Voyager* pilot, you learn that Torres is combative yet brilliant. It struck me as progressive that her emotions didn't become an issue that got in the way of her work or advancement, and she is given the opportunity to learn. When the Maquis and Starfleet crew members join forces on their quest to get back home, you learn that Chakotay has full confidence in her ability to replace *Voyager*'s dead chief engineer. But convincing the Starfleet crew would take some doing.

TAKING COMMAND

After fighting with Lt. Carey, who hopes to take over engineering, she comes up with the correct solutions and earns Janeway's trust. As she deals with the engineering team that is now under her command, you see her start the shift into the role of leader, realizing she needs everyone's support and knowledge to make a collaborative workspace. This instantly gets her support from her former rival for the job. From then on, every episode seems to only further prove her competency at a job that was at the time considered primarily for men. B'Elanna is not only an engineer; she's also a leader and, like Janeway, a scientist. Early episodes often show the two women working side by side to solve scientific problems. In episodes such as "Eye of the Needle," "Emanations," and "Prototype," Torres describes the awe she feels for science and creation. Her determination, curiosity, and tirelessness provide a primer on how to succeed with any personal or professional goal, inspiring more than one woman to pursue engineering.

Andrea Boyd, professional engineer, mining control system specialist, and *International Space Station* flight controller, was a young woman when *Voyager* first aired. She told me how much she appreciated seeing a woman as chief engineer, which normalized it for so many. Torres's duality also helped normalize Boyd's life. "Having two different races [was meaningful] as I have two different citizenships and very different family backgrounds, and being able to see that on the screen was very refreshing...to be able to see that in pop culture."

B'Elanna's temper could have sunk her into the trope of what writer Allison Yarrow called a "Nineties Bitch." It was yet another box that society designed for women who dared to step over the line of acceptable behavior by being confrontational or unlikable in any way. But Torres had what Brannon Braga calls the secret ingredient to make a character instantly relatable: She struggled with her identity as a half-human. B'Elanna is a twenty-fourth century character, and according to Gene Roddenberry's rules, humans had resolved any behavioral issues by this time. B'Elanna could still explore them through her struggles with her Klingon heritage.

EMOTIONAL STRUGGLE

Her mental health is a recurring theme throughout the series. In season one's "Faces," she is abducted by a Vidiian scientist trying to discover a cure for his people, who are suffering with a deadly disease called the Phage. Because Klingons are resistant to it, he separates her into two distinct beings in order to be able to conduct experiments on a pure Klingon. In order for B'Elanna to escape, her two distinct selves have to work through their differences. Meek and scared, her human side wants to think her way out of the situation. Her Klingon entity sees force as the answer. The two halves learn to compromise, with the human seeing the benefits of bravery and the Klingon starting to utilize reason. Through the process, Torres comes to understand herself better, and in the end, she feels more peaceful as a human. But because she won't survive without Klingon DNA, the Doctor reintroduces the Klingon genes to her body. She understands that although there will be a lifelong struggle between her two selves, she will be incomplete if she denies the way she was born. Many people in the audience could identify with this. Accepting multiple parts of ourselves is challenging to anyone, but for a

woman of mixed heritage to see their different characteristics as a toolbox instead of a roadblock is perhaps an empowering concept that can prove useful within the narrow strictures of whatever dominant culture they find themselves in.

In season six's "Barge of the Dead," she fights the boxes she is put in, asking what particular version of B'Elanna is called for—daughter, Maquis, Starfleet officer, lover? The story is about her resistance to her Klingon heritage, but also brings in her spiritual beliefs, making her character even more dimensional.

"Extreme Risk" from season five deals with depression head-on. One response to trauma is a disconnection between body and mind as negative emotions are shut down. When B'Elanna learns that her Maquis compatriots have been killed, she starts putting herself in perilous positions in order to feel something. She orbital skydives and

OPPOSITE: B'Elanna had to deal with an aggressive Klingon side that gave her a real temper.

ABOVE: B'Elanna starts to take on a leadership role when she is made chief engineer.

fights Cardassians in the holosuite with safety protocols off, but says, "I'm not trying to kill myself; I'm trying to see if I'm still alive." She isn't able to comfort herself—an ability that is essential for emotional health. There is a scene in which she tries to eat banana pancakes—something from her childhood that traditionally made her feel safe, but it doesn't work. After she is counseled by her friends, the last scene proves their support is what she needs in order to restore her ability to self soothe: She eats banana pancakes again, and this time they provide the feeling she has been looking for.

B'Elanna's emotional problems aren't just tolerated by her colleagues; over and over again, they offer her a support system. She gets nurturing from Neelix in "Prototype." He is a supportive, compassionate friend again in "Day of Honor" when everything goes wrong for the engineer. In "Juggernaut," her "emotional volatility" causes Chakotay to order her to meditate. The Vulcan Tuvok is in full "therapist" mode as he attempts to teach her how to control her thoughts. Chakotay is again a friend when she learns of the massacre of their fellow Maquis, and Janeway talks to her about mental health in the same episode. But the biggest and most evolved support comes from her relationship with Tom Paris.

Watching the Torres/Paris scenes, my present-day lens sometimes picked up a lot of Nineties tropes that surrounded relationships at the time. But, for the most part, their relationship works in an extremely modern way.

In "Blood Fever," a Vulcan crew mate, Vorik, enters *pon farr* and chooses Torres as his mate. Because she refuses, in a violent and succinct manner, he has to get through this sexually charged chemical imbalance either by meditating or physically fighting to win over B'Elanna. Adding to the complications, he initiated a telepathic mating bond, which now puts Torres into a highly sexualized, almost crazed state herself.

She desperately tries to have sex with Paris, who we know already has feelings for her. He refuses, telling her he wants her, but not when she isn't in control. It's a scene that could be used in schools to show how to honor the full woman by wanting both her body and her mind, and that someone out of control isn't in a position to give consent.

When meditation doesn't work for Vorik, he attacks, interrupting B'Elanna and Paris, whose resolve is starting to weaken. But wait—it isn't Paris who fights him, but B'Elanna, who deals the knockout blow that frees them both from their hormonal haze. So, she is allowed to be sexually voracious (okay, it's a Vulcan mind thing, but still), fights her own battle to choose who she is with, and has an evolved man wanting the entirety of her, rather than a quick encounter. Pretty solid stuff for the 1990s.

In season seven's "Drive," Tom has a chance to enter the *Delta Flyer* into an alien rally. He learns about the event when a Terrellian named Irina challenges him to race her. He is excited by the idea and forgets a romantic holodeck getaway Torres has painstakingly arranged for them. She is

hurt, and reverts to her tendency to run before Paris does.

She states that they are "machte," a bad match. When Seven says she actually supports Paris, Torres rethinks her position and decides to join the race. If she can't have the romantic getaway, she will join the activities that are meaningful to him as a form of support. She thoughtlessly inserts herself as co-pilot and gets rid of Kim without thinking about how Paris and Kim wanted to experience the race, but even this is kind of refreshing. A lead woman not taking care of everyone else's feelings first? Interesting.

I also liked that the jealous woman trope was avoided. Irina is alluring and a racer like Tom, but he isn't interested in her in the least. A catfight is not on the menu here. The woman's perspective is clear in moments such as B'Elanna thinking about marriage and liking the ring of "Tom Torres,"

and Paris stopping mid-race to talk her through their feelings for each other. Both are a Nineties flip of expectations, but we had to start somewhere. And stopping to talk it out had an important side benefit: If he hadn't stopped the flyer, a terrorist explosion would have killed them and others.

One of the things Roxann is proudest of is that B'Elanna was used to explore meaningful issues, a fact that was brought home to her when she got a call from her daughter saying,

OPPOSITE TOP: Tom and B'Elanna have one of the most realistic relationships we've ever seen on *Star Trek*.

OPPOSITE BOTTOM: As an engineer and a scientist, B'Elanna inspired a generation of women.

ABOVE: Roxann started her directing career on *Voyager*, proving that she had what it took to lead the company.

"You aren't going to believe this, Mom; they're talking about you in science class." Dawson's daughter, a scientist at MIT, was at UCLA when her teacher used the episode "Lineage" to open a discussion about the ethical pros and cons of making genetic changes in the womb. In the episode, Torres struggles with having a child who will go through the same painful experiences she did growing up multicultural in a biased world. She considers removing the Klingon genes from her unborn child to save her from the internal conflict. In the end, we learn that her biggest fear is that Paris will be unable to handle having a Klingon wife and daughter and will ultimately leave, as her human father did. Roxann has said that B'Elanna's relationship with Paris forced her character to evolve. Having a father who left his family caused her to not only struggle with identity but also to mistrust a man's commitment to her. Her temper and her tendency to want to end the relationship before he could were protection against future abandonment.

In the final episode, when B'Elanna is heavily pregnant, she calls Paris "Flyboy" more than once, which struck me as a way to stereotypically box him as the sexy, breezy pilot who isn't to be counted on to put her above his love of speed.

But when she gives birth, it's clear it's a device to keep herself safe. He tells her he isn't going anywhere, and when she says that he will "leave her alone to change diapers," he tells her, "Not a chance." Paris's steady reassurance and patience slowly allow her to build trust and heal some childhood wounds. This is a couple who fight fairly, and where the woman is allowed not only her emotions but also room to heal her wounds. She isn't forced to be a Nineties sexy babe, yet has so much enthusiastic sex with her partner that Seven comments on overhearing it regularly. It's a truly healthy, intimate relationship. She has a husband who supports her as a partner, mother, and professional, and friends who recognize her worth and help her through her personal struggles. This was definitely a character that was a hopeful example for women back then, and still is today.

TOP: B'Elanna always struggled with her Klingon heritage.

ABOVE: The series ends with B'Elanna giving birth, and you believe that she and Tom will have a happy family.

B'ELANNA WASN'T THE ONLY ONE WITH AGENCY. Dawson has it, too. Her goals of directing weren't handed to her: She worked incredibly hard at becoming an in-demand television director. Before *Star Trek*, she had experience directing theater, but knew TV had very different demands. Within the first year, she approached Jeri Taylor about learning the craft. Taylor and Berman had opened the Director in Training program, and she spent her nights and days off observing other shows filming at Paramount, spending all-nighters on downtown shoots with *Buffy the Vampire Slayer*, only to go to her trailer at 4:30 a.m. to get a quick nap before the shooting day began on *Voyager*. I wonder if all the male actors who had directed the shows to this date had put in this extreme effort. The end result was that she learned the craft and became respected and trusted as a director. She put in the time to learn what she could from all the different departments, although interacting with the writers was something she had always done.

I had almost no interaction with the writers and producers once I got a new script, but Roxann actually kept her phone nearby when the script arrived so that she could call with her notes and suggestions. Torres's struggle with her duality, and the episode "Extreme Risk," were a direct result of her input.

By the time she was ready to take on directing an episode, she was pregnant with her first child with husband and casting director Eric Dawson. She chose to wait until season six and debuted as a director with "Riddles." She was terrified throughout the experience, as one is when attempting something new that involves a lot of people and a lot of money. At the wrap party that year, Rick Berman told her he had liked the job she did, "so I'm going to give you another chance to fail." Roxann didn't take it as a sign of support, but she took that chance and went on to direct episodes in well over fifty series, including *Star Trek: Enterprise*. It sounds to me as if Berman recognized the grit and talent she had.

When I asked her what young women needed to know today, she cautioned them to be prepared. In her experience, women in our business are being given more opportunities to work in different career paths, such as producing and content creating, that they had previously been locked out of. Awareness of gender bias is causing more doors to open. Some jobs, such as directing, can be prepared for up to a point, but the rest is learned from experience. Women have been denied this experience for years, so the learning curve is steep and can be brutal. Education and preparation, as much as possible, is key. When they haven't armed themselves with enough knowledge to do those jobs, it's too easy to dismiss them when they don't succeed and make it a reason to not give more women chances. Strategize what you need to know before you put yourself out there, so that you are ready to succeed when given the chance. It's certainly what worked for B'Elanna, and what worked, and continues to work, for Roxann Dawson.

ROXANN DAWSON AS B'ELANNA TORRES

185

STAR TREK: ENTERPRISE

I had never seen Enterprise *prior to preparing for this book, and I skipped around episodes to get a feel of how it portrayed its female leads. The show struck me as stylistically similar to a submarine movie from the 1950s: The ship is tight and militaristic looking, with lots of weapons, tense situations, and testosterone. It is set before Kirk's time and takes place in the twenty-second century, one hundred years before Kirk commanded his* Enterprise, *and it's clearly meant to echo the original show.*

What I initially saw led me to believe the women's issues may have warped back to the 1960s, too, but keeping some of the trappings of the decade that show was created in. I had just finished watching *Voyager* and had expectations of women such as B'Elanna, Janeway, and Seven. I was surprised to find it quite different.

In season one, I saw a decontamination scene between T'Pol, played by Jolene Blalock, and Trip Tucker, played by Connor Trinneer, that struck me as extremely objectifying to both of them. She is dressed in a T-shirt, with no bra; he is in underwear. While Trip makes his feelings known about his discomfort with her presence on the ship, they massage what seems to be oil all over their bodies, helping each other with the tough spots.

Their minds are not on their bodies, but ours are, thanks to the camera that catches a hip there (with the speed slowed slightly) and a pec there. This struck me as a sexy gift to the audience, but one that seemed to leave the characters out of the moment.

I would see T'Pol again take off her clothes, dropping her robe in front of Trip later on in the series. By now, they are in a relationship, but the camera doesn't give us Trip's perspective, which would include us in an emotional connection between the characters. The camera is behind her to direct us to see what the camera finds interesting: T'Pol as naked as was allowed at the time. Not her pleasure and emotion, and not even his.

Skipping around, I watched "Shockwave, Part II." The Suliban have taken over the ship, and the fight is on to regain control. Ensign Hoshi Sato, the communications officer played by Linda Park, acts heroically to save the captain and the ship. She must travel through air vents to deliver a hypospray, especially impressive because she does so in spite of her claustrophobia. But to end the scene, she falls through the ceiling and lands in front of Malcolm Reed, the chief security officer played by Dominic Keating. She loses her shirt, but wait—there is a camera shot explaining how it snagged before she fell! This isn't pandering by giving a view of the youngest member of the cast. This could happen!

She stands before him, covering her breasts, and tells the shaken Reed that she doesn't want to hear whatever he had to say, and tells him to retrieve her shirt. It seems like a moment engineered to both titillate and excuse the titillation by Hoshi's take-control reaction. What was a powerful and intense scene that showed Hoshi's dedication to her ship and crew ends with a little sexy joke.

To be fair, the first officer being naked and the communications expert losing her shirt was balanced with plenty of shots of half-naked men. Trip was in his underwear, and the captain seemed constantly shirtless, but there's a lot of history of women being objectified, and in the early 2000s it still had a very different context.

Both of those scenes happened in season one and season two, so I went to season four to see how a show would approach Orion slave girls, the green beauties first featured in the original *Trek*. This show deeply disturbed me. You see, all along, this episode explains, the men have been slaves of the women: not the other way around. They emit pheromones that make men helpless and without a will of their own against the women's agenda. Their mere presence on the ship causes all the men, including Captain Archer, to turn violent. There was even a gym scene: Beset by the Orion sisters' pheromones, Reed and Travis are forced to lift heavy weights while trying to maintain their control over their impulses. Only T'Pol (being Vulcan) and Trip (being in a relationship with her) are immune to the pheromones. The other women aboard react by getting headaches as a natural way to eliminate competition for these Orions. Chaos takes over, with fistfights and disobeyed orders abounding.

The captain almost destroys the ship, stopped only by T'Pol. It's a strong moment for the Vulcan, but from the first scene of the Orion sisters dancing seductively to the last, when they simply leave because their sexual power is the only power they have, the messaging seemed black and white: Men are helpless and can be dangerous but not held accountable if women use their sexual power.

Harrad-Sar, the Orion male who appears to have more agency than the slave he turns out to be, brings it home when he says, "Women are the same throughout the Galaxy, aren't they?" They use sexuality to make men delusional and highly aggressive? They make men forget rules and regulations and missions? This truly does seem less advanced than even the least enlightened episode of the original series. But I was looking at the show with a *Star Trek*–trained eye. This show, and the decade it was created in, was something different.

By the time Brannon Braga came to co-create *Enterprise*, he felt every bit of the decade he had spent writing for *Star Trek*. He was exhausted and wanted a moment to allow ideas to germinate before he jumped into space again. But, with DS9 ending and *Voyager* wrapping up, Paramount asked for one more *Star Trek* show to keep the franchise on the air.

Rick Berman wanted to partner with Braga this time around, and came to him with an idea that felt fresh. The show would take place one hundred years before Captain Kirk's voyages. Prequels may feel ubiquitous these days, but back then, it was a relatively new idea for TV. They liked the idea of using modern vernacular and backstories that would be familiar to audiences. They would even be able to address a complaint some had of the modern iterations: Other than the fabulously successful addition of Jeri Ryan as Seven of Nine, the newer *Star Treks* just weren't that sexy.

What Berman and Braga wanted was to get back to the

feeling of Kirk's original adventures. They wanted a show that was both rougher and tougher, and also more light-hearted. The 1983 movie *The Right Stuff* served as inspiration. The movie detailed the Apollo program and followed Chuck Yeager, a World War II veteran and test pilot who broke the speed of sound. It's definitely testosterone-driven, and the women represented are the wives of the seven military pilots who started space exploration. It has the flavor of a Western, and Berman and Braga wanted that. Brave men took huge chances with their safety to conquer unknown territory, and needed courage, an adventurer's spirit, and a camaraderie with their crew mates that felt deep but very hetero. There would be mutual trust, rough talk, and throwing off any kind of earnestness with a laugh. These would be men who craved adventure, and knew the potential price they might pay to have it: space cowboys.

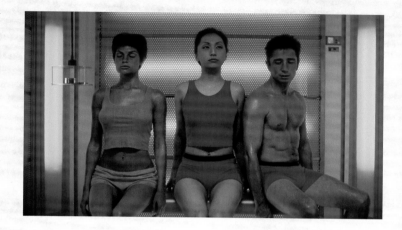

The restrictions Gene Roddenberry had introduced in TNG would be gone. This story would be told without the Prime Directive and before humans reached a stage of perfection that eliminated friction between crew mates or rash acts based on uncontrolled emotions. The show didn't even include the words *Star Trek* in the title until Paramount insisted on it being added in the third year, to see if it would rally the audiences again.

I saw the difference in the opening credits: The theme song has male vocals and is very contemporary for the early 2000s. The first few episodes hit the cowboy feel hard. Captain Archer is quick to smile and eager to get on with the adventure. He indulges Reed by allowing him to practice blowing things up. Trip Tucker is the chief engineer and cannot wait for the away missions, pushing the captain to allow him to go. Archer is understanding of his men's eagerness. This was inspired by a movie that was inspired by Westerns.

Adventure! Danger! Unknown!

The unfortunate thing is that by looking back to an earlier era, they unconsciously (I *think* it was unconscious) picked up some old-fashioned ideas and forgot that the battle for women's liberation was far from won. Only two of the series regulars were women, and one of those, Hoshi, is afraid of going into space.

When I spoke to Brannon, he pointed out that they had spent seven years on the social issues of women on *Voyager*, and thought that they had built a solid structure. They believed the audience would keep in mind the advancements that all the previous *Star Trek* women had made as they watched this new show. And strong women characters that had been such a part of *Star Trek* during those years were now popping up all over the TV landscape. Shows popular by this time included *24*, *Alias*, *Law and Order*, *Crossing Jordan*, and *Six Feet Under*, all starring interesting, layered female characters. Not to mention *Buffy the Vampire Slayer* and Dana Scully in *The X-Files*. A lot of work had been accomplished in featuring complex women in stories. Where the earlier shows had felt the need to show women living in a more enlightened future, *Enterprise* took it for granted. That T'Pol and Hoshi are simply individuals on the crew is maybe progress in itself. Yet in all the interviews I conducted, the only names I cannot recall being brought up as inspirational were the two from *Enterprise*. Why?

Jolene Blalock as

T'POL

The role of the Vulcan T'Pol was destined to be in the "Sexy" box from the start. When I spoke with Junie Lowry and Ron Surma, casting directors for all but the original show up to this point, they told me that casting Star Trek *was fun, because they were "just casting characters," not meeting a laundry list of physical requirements.*

For Lowry, casting is "a very personal, interesting snapshot of an emotion, of a situation, of life, of characters. And it's kind of like being in these little, mini therapy sessions that you get to witness" without having to be a participant. The variety of interpretations that different actors bring to a part, sparking the creativity of others, is one of the things that keeps her engaged after all these years.

Seven of Nine marked the first time ever they were told to cast a "sexy" *Star Trek* character. Jeri Ryan had increased viewership dramatically when she arrived on *Voyager*. It must have felt like a good bet that the part of T'Pol could do the same for *Enterprise*. Rick Berman mentions in an interview he gave to the Television Academy Foundation that Blalock's first audition wasn't a good one because she wasn't wearing makeup. He asked supervising producer Merri Howard to tell Jolene to come in full makeup for the next audition. She did, and she got the role.

But T'Pol wasn't a carbon copy of Seven by any means. When I asked Brannon Braga what archetype he used to create T'Pol, he said he believed that "Vulcan" was in the zeitgeist enough to be considered its own archetype. He has a point. This was the first female Vulcan who would be a lead character. Berman and Braga made the decision that, at this point in time, Vulcans are still mistrustful and contemptuous of humans. They have forbidden the mind meld, and have treated a disease caused by participating in it the way many people treated the AIDS epidemic, with prejudice, fear, and no compassion. To add to the drama, they are governed by a High Command that we learn in the fourth season is secretly controlled by the Romulans.

From the start, T'Pol would have a conflictual relationship with the captain. T'Pol's function is to keep a reasoning watch over the humans, who the Vulcans judge to be reactive and more than a bit untrustworthy.

The Vulcans of this century are so logical that they border on frozen, without the deep spirituality of the Vulcans who come later. T'Pol meditates, but uses it to control her emotions, not allow for them. Brannon reflected on the fact that Spock being half-human opened the character to stories that T'Pol was locked out of.

Her alienness also made her harder to relate to. Spock, Data, Seven of Nine, and B'Elanna are all shown dealing with the complexities of the human part of their makeup. One human strength is curiosity, and Spock was constantly "fascinated" as he observed human behavior. It allowed us, too, to see what he saw with some degree of objectivity. The fact that he rarely passed judgment made it sting less if the human behavior he was observing revealed our own folly.

In the early shows, T'Pol is like a judgmental school monitor trying to keep the boys under control on the playground. What makes it difficult is that she is with all these men eager to get to their outer-space adventures, and we are told Vulcans don't like exploring.

The cowboy response? Very often it's a condescending smirk and a look away for the captain, who seems determined to make her start thinking more like him. He tells her to "smile" when they take a commemorative picture together, seeming to ignore what he knows about the Vulcan culture.

She tells the captain and Trip about a matriarchal society they are about to explore, and the two men bond with smiles over what that could be like. If a Vulcan could roll her eyes, this would be the moment. In the episode "Strange New Worlds," she takes a science team to an Earth-like planet. The guys want to come and stay in a tent for the night, too. T'Pol says, "It's not shore leave, it's a research mission," to which the captain immediately says with a smile that it can be both and grants Trip and Ensign Mayweather permission to camp for the night. When she spends time with visiting Vulcans who are exploring emotions strictly not encouraged in their society, the captain wonders where she is. There is a feeling their tension might turn romantic, but instead she eventually becomes his trusted first officer.

OPEN A CHANNEL: THE WOMEN OF *STAR TREK*

The writers may have thought T'Pol's killjoy attitudes were simply to do with her being a Vulcan. The problem is that society has a stereotype about women stopping men from having fun. That kind of disapproving attitude makes it hard for an audience that came for action, adventure, and exploration to empathize with her.

T'Pol did deal with social issues of the time: Metaphors for AIDS and drug abuse were both looked at through her lens. In "Fusion," she is forced into a mind meld with a visiting Vulcan who defies the Vulcan authorities. This will start an arc for the character that shows her ethical resolve. We learn that she has contracted the supposedly fatal disease Pa'nar Syndrome. In "Stigma," she refuses to reveal that she contracted the illness from what was basically a rape, because it would earn her sympathy and not align her with others suffering with the disease. Through several episodes, ending with "Kir'Shara" in season four, we learn that it is curable, and is caused only by improper melding. The fact that the Vulcan High Command insisted on shunning the ill means that T'Pol's solidarity with them shows us her strong moral compass, even though it didn't quite deal with the question of her mind rape.

In "Impulse," the *Enterprise* makes contact with a ship of what turns out to be Vulcan zombies. They have lined their ship with a neurotoxin called trellium-D, deadly to Vulcans, and it has made them violent. When our heroes board the Vulcan ship (where T'Pol once served), it's a shooting gallery filled with Vulcan zombies that just won't stop coming. It looks exactly like a video game, where the only point is killing as many as you can.

In "Damage," we find out that her exposure to the neurotoxin has made her an addict, but when you are at war, it seems, there isn't much time to contemplate ethics such as stepping down from your post. You have to get on with serving the captain and crew who need you, as best you can. The idea that the doctor keeps the secret, when she could very well take down the ship, seems questionable. But what T'Pol found addicting—and I have read that Jolene didn't like—was that as the drug wore off and she became less aggressive, it helped her feel emotions, especially with Trip.

OPPOSITE: As a full Vulcan, T'Pol often came across as a disapproving character who wanted to stop the male characters from having fun.

ABOVE: Jolene on set re-creating the original series look.

PAGE 191: Despite her Vulcan nature, T'Pol is still presented in a sexual way, and Reed, in particular, fantasizes about her.

With T'Pol's natural Vulcan controls turned off, the romance between them could become a continuing storyline. Feelings of jealousy and strong desire become a part of T'Pol's emotional lexicon. She has a nightmare where she is in the shower with Trip, and her passions get too strong and literally turn her into a monster. It made me think of Jess Zimmerman's book *Women and Other Monsters: Building a New Mythology*, in which she examines the trope of how, when women's emotions are "too much," stories turn them into monsters like Medusas and sirens that are feared and need to be controlled.

Being a feeling Vulcan must have felt like a watering down of the character she had agreed to play. And finding a romantic partner that you are attracted to because "he's

a gentleman, he's great to be around, and he has very nice arms" doesn't set up a relationship that will go terribly deep beyond some sexy scenes.

During her time on the show, Jolene met and married Live Nation CEO Michael Rapino, and after many movie and television appearances, gave up acting to raise their three children. The work she has done since then is impressive. In 2010, they created the Rapino Foundation, whose mission statement is to "protect and uplift underserved people worldwide." She supports other humanitarian causes as well, and the foundation has evolved into R3volve Haiti, which she has said she helps by amplifying the voices of the people there and supporting their creativity.

T'Pol may not have felt like an obvious step forward for womanhood, but she was a senior crew member without explanation or excuse. She forged relationships and worked toward common goals within her community. To say that Jolene Blalock has done that and more in her life after *Trek* is no exaggeration.

ABOVE: T'Pol's relationship with Trip explored the differences between Vulcans and humans.

OPPOSITE: Jolene was cast because of her beauty and her unusual looks as well as her talent as an actor.

Linda Park as

HOSHI SATO

Hoshi was conceived of as the kind of person most of us would actually be if we were asked to serve on a starship. Enterprise *was an origin story for many of the things we were starting to take for granted. Transporters were reliable machinery in the* Trek *we had seen so far, but what about agreeing to have your molecules rearranged in its experimental stages? What about first contact with aliens before any kind of rules were in place, without the guardrails of the United Federation of Planets?*

According to Brannon Braga, the writers gave Hoshi anxiety and claustrophobia to make the character relatable. Allowing a young person to have vulnerabilities at the start of their story and not have it all figured out not only allowed the actor room to bring who they were, but also inspired an arc of growth. In addition, working on internal issues—such as overcoming fears—is as heroic as you can get. Where the men couldn't wait to mix it up with aliens, Hoshi was frightened, which made it all the more courageous when she did. Sounds like the setup for a complex character.

But here's the thing: By making Hoshi nervous, the writers played into outdated ideas about women. After all of *Voyager*'s achievements, they might have thought that wasn't an issue anymore, but you don't have to dig into today's politics too deeply to realize it's still way too soon to think that having a young woman scream with fear will be a bit of fun. Examining these issues with an anxious male character on the bridge of their starship, on the other hand, would have been an interesting choice in this male-driven show.

Once again, I will say that doctors only stopped treating women for hysteria in the 1980s. Those stereotypes weren't—and aren't—a thing of the distant past.

That's not to say that issues such as claustrophobia and anxiety aren't important to examine. But, for Hoshi, I can't help feeling that we need to be given entrance into what it costs her and how she experiences it, not just what it makes her do. In *Enterprise*, the boys embrace the adventure, while Hoshi worries and T'Pol disapproves.

That said, there is a lot to admire about Hoshi Sato. She is, without a doubt, written as a brilliant human. She was involved in the development of the Universal Translator and was an expert in extraterrestrial languages. She is teaching in Brazil when Archer asks her to join him on the *Enterprise*, and although she feels she is not cut out for the uncertainty and danger, she agrees and becomes the communications officer and linguist.

In "Fight or Flight," Archer commands a nervous Hoshi to join him on an away mission to an Axanar ship, in case her skills are needed. When they discover that the inhabitants are all dead and are being harvested for their fluids, we are shown how humans who aren't used to space exploration might react. Hoshi screams, and feels shame and doubt about her ability to continue with the *Enterprise*'s mission. In a scene during which she has lost her nerve to translate, Archer yells (he yells at her a lot, actually, also using the occasional shoulder shake to get Hoshi to pull herself together) that this is a dire situation. She overcomes her fears to speak to the Axanar, who is under the impression that the *Enterprise* and her crew are enemies. Hoshi is successful, and Archer tells her she has saved the day. It's a beautifully done scene, as are all the scenes in which Hoshi is given a chance to take some airtime.

As the show progresses, you see a quiet assurance replace her initial uncertainty. Even in episodes where she is not the focus, she is a professional presence on the bridge. Over and over again, her knowledge of language shifts the outcome of the story, proving her importance to the crew. In "Broken Bow," her knowledge of the Klingon language stops a war with the Suliban. In "Sleeping Dogs," she is able to get a ship running under its own power enough to be able to be rescued by the *Enterprise*.

Every time, she overcomes her anxieties to prove her dedication to the captain, crew, and ship.

Duty is important to Hoshi. In "Exile," when the alien—who has talked the captain into leaving Hoshi with him on his isolated planet—tries to convince her to stay with him for the rest of her life, her first answer is, "I just can't abandon my duties." This is even before she considers what she would choose for her own life. In "Countdown," when the Xindi-Reptilians drug her in an attempt to get her to give the codes for the weapon that will destroy Earth, Hoshi attempts to kill herself rather than help them. At one point, tied to a chair, frightened of the torture that is sure to come, she spits in the face of the alien menacing her. She is tough, in spite of her fear.

In the next episode, she is horrified to have helped them, even though the drug they administered took away her ability to refuse. This is another opportunity to see a human

overwhelmed by dire circumstances and unable to think themselves past their nervous system and do what's necessary. Too many times, though, what it takes is Captain Archer shaking her and yelling, as he does in this scene, "Pull yourself together!" Unfortunately, this scene harkens back to a time when there was a trope in storytelling of overly emotional women needing a strong man to get them back into control.

There were other things I saw in episodes that made me want more for Hoshi. Her backstory included the fact that she was something of a loner, with few close relationships. I watched an early interview in which Linda hopes for scenes with the other woman on board, T'Pol. They eventually do have scenes together, but it was perhaps difficult to write relationship-developing material for a Vulcan and a loner.

At issue, too, was that the focus of the show was often on action, and this is something Hoshi is initially excluded from, like plenty of girls who grew up in the 1980s and '90s. Even when Hoshi is central to the story, the episodes are rarely about her and what she experiences. By the third season, the show is all about the Xindi war, and a military group, the Military Assault Command Operations, boards the ship to fortify its ability to defend itself. In "Countdown," even though the story is centered on Hoshi and her capture by the Xindi-Reptilians, the emotional heart of it is Malcolm and Hayes, the MACO commander. They have a contentious relationship that grows into a respectful one. There is one episode in which they endlessly beat each other up to prove physical superiority. When Hayes dies rescuing Hoshi, there is an emotionally charged scene between the two men, followed by a scene in which Malcolm informs his men that Hayes is gone, and that he needs four volunteers for a dangerous mission. All the men step forward for the mission as one.

ABOVE: Hoshi is shown to be a reluctant explorer who is unnerved by aliens. The problem with this is that there is a stereotype that women are less adventurous than men.

OPPOSITE: Hoshi is tough and resists the Xindis' attempts to torture her, but we didn't see this side of her character until the third season.

In "Zero Hour," although Hoshi is again at the center of the action, and needed for her linguistic abilities, the real story is the captain's sacrifice. When he is believed dead, the crew members gather to comfort each other. It was telling to me that Hoshi hugs Trip and turns her back to the camera. We see his devastated reaction, but not hers. The camera guides us to what the real emotion is that we are meant to be empathizing with, and most of the time it seems to be between the men.

Also, there seemed to be many times when people tell Hoshi what she is really feeling, even when she has just told them. The alien in "Exile" is extremely reminiscent of the Beast in Disney's *Beauty and the Beast*. He insists she stay with him in his lonely lair, is handsome when he comes to her, and hideous in his natural state and desperate for a relationship. Even he tells her what's best for her, regardless of what she has expressed. In "Duty," Hoshi is told that her vision of an intruder is simply her anxiety over the war. Because the

other characters think her anxiety is controlling her, her voice is quieted and her feelings are ignored. Not being heard is a result of bias that affects women in all aspects of their lives, including those concerning medical issues.

I tried multiple times in different ways to get in touch with Linda Park but without success. During my research, I found a podcast she recorded during the pandemic called *Imagine Talks*. In it, she spoke of being an Asian-American, the child of immigrants, with the clarity that can only come from lived experience. Because I didn't manage to talk to her, I've used her interview to grasp what her intersectional experience was.

Hoshi Sato's most significant attribute was that she was an Asian character on TV. There just aren't very many of these. There is an episode in season two called 'Vanishing Point' that reminded me of how Park described her experience growing up as a child of immigrants. Hoshi is anxious about using the transporter, a new and not always reliable device, to return to the ship. It turns out that almost the entire episode is comprised of the eight seconds she spends stuck in a kind of dream state while her molecules are unable to reassemble due to a malfunction.

QUIET PRESENCE

In her mind, she rejoins the crew for normal life aboard *Enterprise*, but she knows something isn't right. She feels uneasy, and when she tries to share this with the others, she is ignored or told she is wrong. She seems to only be able to watch, as opposed to being part of the action throughout the episode. She sits unnoticed and ignored, as her crew mates joke, eat dinner, and make plans without her. She feels unseen as she walks down the ship's corridors, until she eventually starts to see herself becoming literally invisible, with no solidity and no agency in even the smallest everyday events of life. She stops taking up space.

When aliens, during her dream, plant a bomb, she manages to defuse it and she even dares to follow them in their mobile transporter they have brought with them to escape. Scared to the point of refusal the first time she was asked to use a transporter, on this occasion she acts without thinking twice. At this point in her dream state, the *Enterprise* crew is finally able to fix the transporter bug, she is finally reassembled completely in the transporter, and her ordeal is over. That marginalization is something many minority groups have experienced. Too often they are told this isn't their story, and they are ignored.

The sense that Hoshi is there to support the other characters is there throughout all four seasons of the show. Her strength seems to come when she acts for her crew mates or the captain. Even in the story that is in Hoshi's head, she is on the outside looking in at her shipmates' lives, and doesn't become activated until they, and the ship, need her expertise.

As Linda described it in a podcast, she didn't see herself in popular culture as a child. She loved old movies, but always felt left out of the story. Leading ladies, secondary characters, even tertiary characters never looked like her.

She was taught by her parents to be grateful for what America gave them, and to show it by not taking up too much space or questioning her experience. "Don't ask for more," was her parents' refrain. She didn't have a place in a system that "squashed the fullness of her being," and she saw herself—not the system—as the problem. To her, as a child and as a young person, she simply had the wrong features, the wrong color skin. It seemed her parents didn't want the young girl to question why Asian-Americans were left out of storytelling and the country's history: America was making a new and better life possible for the family.

Linda came to the USA as a child of two from Seoul, Korea. Her parents struggled at first to make a new life for their family in Northern California, and the first school she went to was rough. She describes it as being ruled by gang members, and if you didn't choose sides, life was dangerous. She learned to survive by being willing to fight and having a large chip on her shoulder.

As the series progressed, the writers tried to give some of Linda's toughness to Hoshi. In "Observer Effect," Trip and Hoshi catch a highly contagious virus and are in isolation

for days together. She tells him, as the illness takes them down, that she got kicked out of Starfleet for running a floating poker game and breaking the company commander's arm when he tried to stop it. It was a toughness that seemed at odds with what I knew about the character to this point, but it made sense to me when I realized I had forgotten the complexities of being human.

I met Linda once at a convention, and would never have guessed she'd had a rough childhood and an ability to fight. When you see her fend off two aliens who attack the doctor in season four's "Affliction," there is no doubt that Hoshi has a steeliness that belies her anxiousness.

Not fitting in at school, not even having the same cultural experience as her parents, left Linda feeling anger and loneliness. By the age of eight, she found community theater as a place where she could take up space—"more than you were allowed in real life." In a childhood where her nervous system was constantly in fight or flight, she could give herself permission to relax and just be. The theater became an outlet through which she could feel the full scope of her emotions in a safe environment.

Her father was entrepreneurial, and when he hit upon LED lights as a business, the family moved quickly to an upper-middle-class life, and Linda was sent to Notre Dame, a Catholic girls' school. She took every opportunity to make this new environment include more theater—the only place where she felt she belonged. She somehow got the school to hire an acting teacher and convinced them to turn an unused space into a black box theater, where Linda acted and directed.

All the more impressive is that she did all this while she struggled to understand the health issues that were afflicting her. It was discovered she had the autoimmune disease lupus, and spent a full year as a young woman in the hospital.

When she came to Los Angeles, the audition for *Enterprise* happened very fast. She had already filmed a day on *Jurassic Park*, and had recently learned that she had gotten the leading role of Roxanne in San Jose Rep's version of *Cyrano de Bergerac*. She was favoring going back to do the stage role. Theaters were beginning to offer more and more

nontraditional casting, and pieces that may have been cast as all Caucasian were now open to all ethnicities. The young woman who had felt locked out of some of the greatest theater pieces could now get her teeth into important roles. She wanted this opportunity.

Those around her convinced her that *Star Trek* was a "once in a lifetime experience," and she listened. She was thrown quickly into signing contracts, and even getting sized for her own doll. She considers her time with *Star Trek* her grad school. She watched and learned film technique in her scenes with Bakula, and he and John Billingsley were important mentors to the twenty-one-year-old.

The fact that *Enterprise* made the comm officer an Asian woman was an important step for the women of *Trek*. The representation of Asians in a story about the future is hugely important to Linda. Significant, too, is her brilliance and her arc from anxious young woman to able professional.

Looking back, Brannon told me that the concept of Hoshi being "how some of us would be on a fancy warp starship" was all about making her relatable, but most of the time the focus was elsewhere, and without deep emotional connections with the other characters, Hoshi—and Linda—were underserved. "Linda did great work with what little she was given," said Braga.

OPPOSITE: Hoshi is always a professional presence on the bridge, but rarely shows the joy of exploration.

ABOVE: The Mirror Hoshi gave Linda Park the opportunity to show some range and that she could be badass.

STAR TREK: DISCOVERY

A lot had changed in the twelve-year gap between the end of Star Trek: Enterprise *and the debut of* Star Trek: Discovery *in 2017. The Me Too movement opened a channel of dialogue for women and raised awareness. Other franchises had a much more female focus: Scarlett Johansson's Black Widow had kicked ass in Marvel movies, and when* Star Wars *returned in 2015, the new lead character, Rey, was a woman. Having the lead of* Discovery *be a young Black woman made sense for a show that takes us into an equitable future.*

There were economic changes, too. In 2017, *Forbes* stated that women controlled or influenced 70 to 80 percent of all the purchase decisions in the USA. The worldwide "value of the female economy" was $18 trillion. That's a lot of power. When CBS All Access was joining the streaming business, these numbers must have played into their decision to launch their platform with two women-centric shows, *The Good Fight* and *Star Trek: Discovery*.

Because streaming was able to operate so differently from networks, where getting as many viewers as possible is still key, a different kind of show was given a chance. Niche audiences could find shows that appealed directly to them, and diverse audiences suddenly found representation. Freed from the pressure to appeal to everyone and offend no one, *Star Trek* was ready to double down on ideals of diversity and inclusion.

Most people agree that the latest version of feminism is an umbrella for all kinds of social issues, and the show demonstrates this. *Discovery*'s showrunner at the time of my interview, Michelle Paradise, told me "*Star Trek* has always made a mission of giving visibility to underrepresented communities," but *Discovery* has gone further than any of

> They filled [*Discovery*] with diverse, unique people, some of whom would have historically been outsiders, and put them at the center of the adventure.

Trek's previous iterations. There is a loving gay couple: Paul Stamets (played by Anthony Rapp) and Dr. Hugh Culber (played by Wilson Cruz). In the third season, Ian Alexander was added as a transgender character, and Blu del Barrio became *Star Trek*'s first nonbinary character. This was a leap from the metaphor of Dax that many LGBTQIA+ had used as proof that they were included in a positive future. They also went as far as featuring older women in powerful roles—including Michelle Yeoh, as Captain Giorgiou, who can teach the world a thing or two about the capabilities and appeal of a woman over fifty. Oh, if only I had been able to interview her.

It's not just that there are many more women in this show. The fact is, *Discovery* could have been filled with women characters who still played by the rules of stories created for the male gaze. Instead, they filled it with diverse, unique people, some of whom would have historically been outsiders, and put them at the center of the adventure.

Importantly, that seems to be true behind the cameras, too. I read a quote from the Geena Davis Institute's website (Melissa Navia guided me to it) from Meryl Streep: "Progress will happen when men take a stand." It seems to me

that Alex Kurtzman did just that. For the first time, women were working at every level in production. The show has women directors and technicians, Michelle Paradise was elevated to executive producer in season three, and Sonequa Martin-Green was made an actual producer. From what I've been told, the men in elevated positions have been diligent in doing their part to shift what Mike McMahan called the "broken system" they inherited.

There is something happening between the content creators and the studios that is new to me. I remember grumbling and tension from production when studio executives came on set when I was working even ten years ago. They were often thought of as "The Suits" (pretty dehumanizing, actually), who would have notes that were restrictive and basically just thought of as an ego flex on their part. The impression was that they always wanted to play it safe, to do what had been proved to work already, and to please as many people as possible. But Michelle Paradise has had a completely different experience. She tells me there is true collaboration between the network, the studio, and the production team. Instead of the relationship being adversarial and a power struggle, she sees their notes as being useful and an opportunity to see the work with "fresh eyes."

This bouquet of social causes in one show would have been unthinkable sixty years ago. But even when *Discovery* premiered, in 2017, Sonequa Martin-Green told me that she had the strange experience of seeing the show being greeted with both joyous celebration and nasty vitriol. Some viewers were overjoyed to see more diverse representation, but there were also people who are uncomfortable with change and who yearned for a more patriarchal show with a captain like Kirk or Picard.

Discovery is filled with science, beautiful visuals, great character development, plots that temporarily tied up my brain with twists and turns, and beautifully unique people.

There is something Michelle and I shared that made us both laugh. Every new iteration of *Trek* has had to hear the dire news flash that this is the show that is ruining *Star Trek*. From *The Next Generation* on, we have all heard it. Maybe the universe can use a little expanding, and with time, we will all find our corner of it.

OPPOSITE: Women are everywhere on *Discovery*. In fact, there are barely any men on the bridge crew.

ABOVE: Michelle Yeoh is a huge presence who shows that a captain can be both female and over forty.

Sonequa Martin-Green as

MICHAEL BURNHAM

Michael Burnham is something different for Star Trek. *By the time we get to the end of* Discovery's *second episode, she is a complete outsider. She is not only the first mutineer in Starfleet's history, who has been stripped of her rank, she is also a human raised by Vulcans, Black, and a woman. In the future portrayed by* Star Trek, *none of those things will be a problem (apart from the mutineering), but watching TV in the early years of the twenty-first century, they are a big deal.*

Before *Discovery*, *Star Trek* was overwhelmingly told from the point of view of the establishment, which was often White and often male. The establishment had expanded to include Black captains such as Sisko and women such as Janeway or Seven of Nine, but it was still there, and they became part of it rather than radically reinventing it. What *Discovery* does is shift your perspective—the hero isn't the captain, it's the disgraced officer, who stands for all the outsiders. The story literally has a different point of view. When we meet *Discovery*'s male captain, he isn't the Starfleet leader we have come to expect. We cannot expect the same hierarchical rules to apply here; things are more complicated than that. The court-martialed Burnham will become a great leader, and Captain Lorca will be revealed to be an evil interloper from the Mirror Universe.

When *Discovery*'s co-creator Bryan Fuller started to think about what he wanted in a new version of *Star Trek*, he was determined that the series' lead character would be very different from Captain Kirk. It wasn't important, said Fuller, that she was a Black woman, "she just needed not to be White." *Voyager* had achieved getting a White female as captain; this project had to go a step further. The experience of women of color was a story that comes with trials and difficulties unique to them alone, and he wanted to explore that.

When Bryan started to develop Michael in more detail, he says he had "three DNA icons for who she was: Mae Jemison, the first Black woman in space; Ruby Bridges, the young girl who crossed segregation lines to go to school; and Holly Hunter in *Broadcast News*." From Hunter's character, he would give Burnham the quality of always being the smartest person in the room, which would lay on her shoulders the heavy burden of always coming up with the answers.

During the many conversations he had with Mae Jemison, he came away with the understanding that the curiosity in the search for knowledge and the thirst for science were

her driving factors. Because he is a White male, he spent many interviews with Jemison in order to authentically understand who Michael might be.

Ruby Bridges would find her way into the character via Burnham's irrepressible desire to go to the Vulcan Academy, even with her parents telling her only Vulcans may attend. It was her strong internal compass that allowed her to go against what most would tell her was prudent.

That same code of personal ethics allowed her to think for herself and not always follow the rule book. When she believes the Klingons will attack and kill Captain Georgiou and the rest of the crew, she decides saving them is more important than listening to her commanding officer. Burnham "colors outside the lines," and pays the price with being court-martialed, stripped of position and connection in her society.

It's important that Burnham is an outsider. As she says in "Magic to Make the Sanest Man Go Mad," "I am among others, yet apart." The loneliest feeling in the world. *Discovery*'s creators wanted a series that focused on the characters who had historically been marginalized, so the series is told from the point of view not of the captain, but of a woman who has lost her rank and is trying to find her way.

To Bryan's eyes, women often represent all the people who have been excluded from power. Iconic women in sci-fi such as Carrie Fisher and Sigourney Weaver are the characters that touched him as a boy. He used them as examples of how a human behaves, and they were the characters he wanted to support and live through. "They were women who had ethics and morality that were outside any sort of gender role. It was just a human role." He grew up wanting to be R2-D2, Princess Leia's most valuable asset. He felt that the biggest movie released in the 1970s told us that the most important person in the story was the princess, because she was the most humane and altruistic.

In lots of ways, *Discovery*'s first season is the story of how Michael Burnham learns that her humanity and compassion are more important than the cold logic that led her to suggest firing on the Klingons before they can start a war. Streaming meant that *Discovery* wouldn't have to be anxious about serialized storytelling, and that opened up the chance to explore real character growth and demonstrate how much it takes for personal change to take place. In that sense, it's the spiritual heir to *Deep Space Nine*, which it combines with *Voyager*'s emphasis on female characters.

That emphasis on kindness, compassion, and understanding is resolutely at the heart of the show and has led to it being the most inclusive of all *Star Treks*, certainly when it comes to gender. Those values aren't exclusively female, but watching the show, I no longer felt we were living in a man's world, and—despite *Voyager*'s incredibly strong female cast—that felt like progress.

A NEW KIND OF HERO

Discovery is a woman's show, with a young Black woman finding her personal truth and her place in Starfleet and coming to a hard-won understanding of the Federation's values. Michael Burnham failed and found her way to stand back up, applied critical thinking to her problems, and struggled to understand when being the smartest person in the room wasn't enough. She had deep friendships, sensual relationships, complicated family dynamics, and became a leader with a man in her life who supported her. The idea that anyone would even think of objectifying this character seems impossible. That tells me how far women in this franchise have come. I can't imagine that *Discovery*'s creators could have found any other actor to equal what Sonequa Martin-Green does with such an iconic role.

Sometimes, the actor who is Number One on the call sheet can project a depth of character and authority on screen that you hope is true off camera as well. Very often it isn't. I had spent some time at a convention in Germany interviewing some of Sonequa's castmates. When I asked

about Sonequa, the response was almost exactly the same, to the point where I wondered how she cast her spell. Could she really be that, well, wonderful? Was it a choice they had made to rally hard around their star because, although the show was met with joy, it was also met with hostility from some? When I finally got to sit down and talk to her, I very quickly realized it wasn't a spell; it was her. I met a woman who was grounded, giving, had humility, was a superb critical thinker, had been through a lot, and took *Star Trek* and being Number One on the call sheet very, very seriously.

Sonequa grew up in the South, and her experience of being a Black woman in the world was deeply affected by that fact. She is quick to say that the South has love and richness of every kind. "Hospitality is real," she says, but she experienced many things that were "just so soul-crushingly sad about systemic racism." She explained that you start to take it on—the attitude that "if you're not White, you're not right"—as a trauma response. You start to believe it.

OPPOSITE: From the beginning, *Discovery* is told from Michael Burnham's point of view and is about her journey.

ABOVE: In this world, the captain turns out to be unreliable and the disgraced officer is the hero.

PAGE 207: As soon as Burnham arrives on the *Shenzhou*, Georgiou becomes her mentor. That kind of relationship between women isn't shown enough on television.

It wasn't until she graduated from college and was traveling on a New York City subway that she started to become aware of the limitations caused by that trauma response. Whereas in the South, in every kind of circumstance, "you will be met with some kind of resistance," she realized that everyone on the train was a different color, and no one was paying any attention to her. It started a healing that she said was sped up by taking her role in *Star Trek*. As I well know, playing a woman with agency helps you trust that you indeed have it yourself.

New York opened up the young actor to the possibilities of life and culture, and she took every opportunity to learn the lessons of not only acting, but also what it takes to lead a set. In 2008, she was in a film called *Toe to Toe*, where she learned the power of a film family. It's not a blood family or even a friend family, but it's powerful nonetheless. She saw what could be accomplished when "you are all in this together." In her role in *The Walking Dead*, she watched Andrew Lincoln lead the cast with care, and it caused a further paradigm shift for her. She felt it was an "honor, privilege, and a blessing" to be able to establish that kind of culture with her *Discovery* family from the very start. She said, "You don't get that [feeling of a film family] without everybody agreeing," and praised Alex Kurtzman, Michelle Paradise, Olatunde Osunsamni, Jonathan Frakes, the cast, and the Canadian crew with agreeing to the idea, and saying yes to this radical support system that they became to each

other. My thought was if she could have named everyone involved at that moment, she would have.

When she talked to me about the politics of Black hair, it reminded me of the painful situation in the first season of *Deep Space Nine*. Avery Brooks asked for his own hairdresser, one who understood the care of Black hair. Production didn't accommodate him. It was an all-White group of people, and I'm imagining that they couldn't understand what the big deal could be with giving a short buzz to hair, whether it was for a Black or a White man. But this was ignorance, and worse, because they refused to listen. When the hairstylist cut his hair the first time, Brooks was left with shaved holes on the back of his head, and had to report to set like that. I can't remember if they colored them in, but I imagine they did. After a lengthy struggle with the subject, Avery was given his own hairdresser: a man of color.

When I see the long braids Sonequa eventually wore on the show, it feels like a victory, but it was a long personal road for her as well. In the industry, "Black hair is a sociopolitical statement." It was pounded into her at a young age that you could not consider yourself beautiful if you didn't have straight hair; having natural hair for a Black woman wasn't just accepting that beauty has many different forms, it was also actively rejecting the European standard of beauty. Being a Black woman with braids in a *Star Trek* show helps dispel that thought for anyone who watches.

This remarkable woman spoke to me about becoming a producer on the show in season four. That's a first for any female member of the cast and shows just how inclusive today's producers are. Like Burnham, she is thoughtful about it and shared that it wasn't a linear road she traveled on to

ABOVE: Burnham has complicated relationships, but they are always shown from her point of view.

OPPOSITE: As Spock's adopted sister, Burnham explores what it means to be human.

get there. George Floyd's murder and the Black Lives Matter movement was at the forefront of this time, and she lost her way trying to be the producer who would "do it for women, do it for Black women, do it for my people, do it for my ancestors, do it for Nichelle, do it for Whoopi, do it for Avery." Instead of trying to be in all places and do it for all things, she started to recognize her strengths as a facilitator between people—what she calls "nurture culture."

It seemed to be effective. Her emotionally intelligent efforts to build trust and support were repaid when her second pregnancy turned difficult and required her to be less active. The cast, crew, production, and CBS supported her, sometimes, it sounds, in ways that would cost them. They never made her feel that it was a burden to them, and she welcomed a healthy baby girl. While she was filming the

seventh episode of season four, she lost both her father and her mother, who died one day apart. She was immediately told, "Go right now. We'll be okay," even though she was in almost every scene. As she herself said, it doesn't happen like this without an agreement from the top: in this case, Michelle Paradise and Alex Kurtzman.

How far it has progressed from the time when I asked to go to my sick infant when there was a huge gap of hours before I worked, and I was told, "You should have thought about things like this before you took this job." The fact that it was a woman AD who told me this proves the point: It starts from the top.

That attitude to the cast is a sign of progress, and it's no surprise that the writers have extended it to their characters. Connection is baked into the story of *Discovery* and how it can lead someone to act with more nobility than they ever expected. When the choice is theirs, the entire crew decides to go with Burnham into the future. Importantly, that willingness to make a sacrifice comes out of genuine friendship and an emphasis on relationships. When the crew was there to join her in the ultimate unknown, I felt a cavalcade of emotions, and not just for the star of the show. It made for a special moment that the show had earned by taking the time to fully develop all these highly individual characters. As Michael tells her brother Spock as she says goodbye, "There is a whole Galaxy of people out there who will reach for you. Let them."

ABOVE: Burnham's relationship with Book is one of equals, showing just how far gender roles have come.

OPPOSITE: It's still rare for women to take the lead in an action-adventure show.

Her friendship with Tilly, played by Mary Wiseman, is deep and not without bumps. But you never doubt their love and utter support for each other. Mary told me it was true offstage as well. Sonequa was someone she could come to, over and over again, for ballast or advice. I can't help feeling that what was true on set made what was onscreen all that richer.

But being responsible for the Klingon War and the martyrdom of the Klingon T'Kuvma is just our entry point to the arc this character would take. She is our point of view, and we take the journey with her. It would be the first time we meet a captain who isn't already on the bridge in a *Star Trek* series, and it shows what it took for her to get there. As Sonequa put it, "You have to see the fight before you get to utopia."

CAPTAIN OF THE SHIP

When she steps into the captain's role, we see, in Bryan Fuller's words, "a complicated leader, because she has her own barometer for right and wrong and it's not always accurate. She gets herself into situations and then she has to learn and grow." Learning from mistakes is a gift many women are still denied. Roxann Dawson still warns women to know everything they can before attempting directing, because once a woman fails, it can be used as a reason to not give other women a chance, as if we exist in a monolith.

We see the struggle it takes to come back from personal devastation. In "Battle at the Binary Stars," Sarek, the Vulcan who raised her, tells her, "No matter your shame, gather your strength," and she does.

In season three, Michelle Paradise joined Alex Kurtzman as showrunner and we are now in a scary future. It's the year 3188, and the Burn, caused by the explosion of most of the dilithium in existence, has wiped out everyone's ability to travel around the Galaxy and led to the partial collapse of Starfleet. The United Federation of Planets is no longer in charge. After a year of being without *Discovery*, but with a new relationship with a courier named Book, Burnham finds her ship in a glacier. In "Far from Home," she is able to free it from the parasitic ice it was trapped in. She is, once again, the answer to the problem.

I went into the dreaded chat rooms and found that some audience members had issues with this. Their criticism is that Burnham is always the answer, and as with Kirk or Picard, the most character development belongs to the absolute star of the show. The difference to me, however, is that, firstly, it's a Black woman in that position this time. If the hero being very different to them makes some uncomfortable, think how women have felt all these years watching these stories. Equal time for viscerally experiencing imbalance in a story may be uncomfortable, but it may not be a bad thing. It may lead to more understanding of how storytelling without diversity feels to others. As Sonequa told me, *Discovery* is just "one example of what it takes to build a world like this." Just one example.

Secondly, I see so much more detail in the nuance of the struggle it takes to be a leader without having the absolutely taken-for-granted support from Starfleet. Answers don't just appear for her; being the smartest person in the room seems to come with knowing the time and effort it takes to arrive at solutions.

When she tries to get information from Vulcan, which has left the Federation, Michael calls for a *T'Kal-in-ket*, a trial based in unearthing deep truths. The president cannot refuse this, and her hand is forced. She is assigned an advocate. Guess who? Her mother, who has also traveled to the future.

Her mother tells her she is lost—a fact that Burnham is aware of. Here is yet another interesting examination of what humans may experience. She is in a liminal space of not being who she was before the time jump, and not knowing who she wants to be in the present. Or what her relationship to Starfleet should be.

Burnham is forced to do some deep critical thinking, and stops trying to achieve her objective without thinking of the cost to others. She withdraws her request when she realizes it will tear apart the tenuous peace the Romulans and Vulcans have so far achieved. Of course, this gains the president's trust. This moment of growth is truly a step for women, who are too often fearful that there won't be a

network, as there has been for men, that will catch them if they fail. To avoid failing, many women never dare.

In this same episode, there is a beautiful bed scene between Burnham and Book, exactly the kind Penny Johnson Jerald wanted on *Deep Space Nine*. Their lovemaking is filled with tender, deep, and vulnerable beauty, and it's more than clear that this is love and not just sex—the quality Penny wished she saw more of on TV between Black people. At the end of the episode, her win at work doesn't mean trouble in her relationship, and with his arms around her, they each say that they are home. A woman is allowed a deep, vulnerable relationship, and by the end of the season, the captain's chair.

The outsider has been accepted. Yes, she has learned and grown, but it's not without struggle, and she hasn't compromised her values. To me, that's *Discovery*'s real achievement: Starfleet had always had ideals about inclusion, but in the past it felt—at least to me—that the inclusion was about allowing everyone to join the club rather than allowing them to take it as their own and to remake it. Over half a century ago, Nichelle Nichols made a dignified and important decision to remain on the show so that people of color saw themselves in the future. That social consciousness continues in Sonequa Martin-Green. She told me, "There is no 'I' in 'legacy.' You are on the path somebody else paved for you, that you, in turn, pave for someone else." To me, *Discovery* has benefited from two thoughtful leaders: Micheal Burnham and Sonequa Martin-Green.

Mary Wiseman as
SYLVIA TILLY

At some point, how a Starfleet woman should behave and look became its own kind of box. In Roddenberry's future, it seems as if all women are sensible, emotionally controlled, and incredibly athletic and thin. That was meant to be aspirational, but it's also limiting. So many women would look at that future and not recognize themselves in it. Mary Wiseman's character, Sylvia Tilly, breaks that box into pieces.

In Mary's words, "I can't be Patrick Stewart—dignified, cool, slick, impressive. My seams show and I've learned to love that about myself, and I think it's what I have to offer as an actor. I know I can't do that version of the captain, of the hero. All I have is this messier thing, which is trying to be really honest and really transparent."

Watching *Discovery* and talking to Mary, I realized how important an achievement Sylvia Tilly is for all of us. As played by Wiseman, Tilly doesn't play it safe by trying to fit a standard: one of the biggest traps that women can fall into. She has full access to her emotions, and her humor proves that she's a critical thinker. She is also able to

turn her gaze inward for a self-assessing look. With self-determination and agency, she is a great example of a full-spectrum human. Assessing the actor herself, I think Mary is our best example of why A.I. will never be able to perform to the levels a human can. Her humanity is too complex, and it's beautiful to see. Her face changes like a kaleidoscope with what she is feeling, but it isn't an emotional loop just for her.

When I spent time with her, she connected to me in a way that made me feel more human, too.

Tilly loves "feeling feelings," but make no mistake, like Wiseman, Tilly's emotions and unique personality don't get in the way of the job at hand. They are a secret weapon. For all her "messiness," we know that Tilly is exceptional at her job. She simply hasn't crammed herself into some "acceptable" version of a Starfleet officer. She is uniquely herself, and brings the gifts of that to the storytelling. Seeing self-acceptance modeled by someone who doesn't fit a mold gives countless people in the audience the idea that they may be enough, too. Ability comes in all different sizes.

When we meet Cadet Tilly, she is introducing herself to her new roommate, Michael Burnham. She doesn't seem to have any filters when she speaks, and nervousness just makes her talk more. She babbles the worst thing she can say: "The only other Michael I ever heard of was Michael Burnham, the mutineer. You aren't her, are you?" Although it's obvious it's more energy than Michael wants to deal with, Tilly doesn't give up on a friendship, getting Burnham to speak about her feelings by normalizing actually having them.

Tilly is kind and trustworthy: virtues that help the crew in more than one situation. In "An Obol for Charon," an alien species is in danger of extinction. As Tilly is encased by fungal growth, the alien speaks to and through her, desperate for help. The ensign is brave throughout the ordeal, which includes having her head drilled into so that a communicator can be inserted to allow the alien to speak. A quick word here about the men in *Discovery*, who have developed a much larger emotional range as well. In *Enterprise*, the captain had a one-note approach to leadership, which entailed a kind of bullying physicality. As he prepares to open Tilly's skull, Stamets never once tells her to "pull herself together," or shakes her in order to proceed with the business at hand. He asks her to sing her favorite song with him to engage her mind away from the terrible events happening to her. That's refreshing and emotionally intelligent progress.

Tilly's personality may be bubbly, but you never forget that she is "the best theoretical engineer on the ship"—and, like so many engineers I met through working on this book, absolutely fascinated by her job and excited by math and science. Working with Burnham and Stamets on understanding the spores, she bursts out, "You guys, this is so fucking cool!" Instead of disapproving, Stamets says with a little smile that "yes, it is." Instead of what could have been a dead-eyed look from the two other characters that would convey to us a negative comment on her ebullience, there is acceptance and affection for her. Tilly could be the most lovable character ever created, but if the other people in the story don't accept her, we won't either.

In every life-threatening situation, she comports herself like someone who knows the risks of the life she signed up for. She seems to me to know what the desired outcome should be, and what she needs to do to help get there.

Even when she could get blown up at any second, she is naturally funny without ever letting go of the acknowledgement of the threat the moment holds. In "An Obol for Charon," the alien May leads her through what appears to be the abandoned *Discovery*. May darkly tells Tilly, "Maybe they died trying to save you," to which she replies, "Hey, thanks for that." Later, she tells May to take cover behind her. "Fall in. That's soldier for get behind me." It's a testament to Wiseman that those lines don't really read as funny as they are onscreen. She is a natural comedian who can infuse a line like "I am very high. But you need to listen to me" with both humor and dread, even as she sits atop a volcano that Captain Philippa Georgiou is getting ready to bomb. She makes you smile even as you register the danger everyone is in.

CHANGE IS HARD

Tilly is one of the most vibrantly human characters to ever appear in *Star Trek*, so it was difficult to hear Mary talk about her experience with a certain faction of the audience, but it is essential to share. There were some who felt the show was "shoving diversity down their throat," and that diversity included a Starfleet cadet with more curves and bigger hair than they were used to expecting from the franchise. In her extremely gentle way, she apologized for naming her tormentors. "Sorry, they tend to be men that think I'm too fat to be in Starfleet. Somebody said I should be ashamed of myself, that I had such a good opportunity on *Star Trek* and I wasted it. And that really hurt."

She apologized for being emotional, too. But it made me think of what incredible courage it takes to simply say yes to a job offer, do an outstanding job, get bullied for your appearance, and continue to show up—not just for yourself but for so many in the audience.

According to a recent study, the average dress size in America is 16, not anywhere near the size of most women we see modeling them in magazines and social media. That's a lot of women who need more realistic representation. Being conscious of our weight was for sure something the women in *Star Trek* had to deal with in the 1990s. Terry Farrell recounts a time of being called to the offices and told to drop ten pounds. I remember being at the craft service table and picking up a cookie after lunch. An older crew member

came up behind me and warned me to "lay off the cookies." I didn't "want to gain weight," did I? He was well-meaning, I know, but the fact that he felt the freedom and responsibility to check me, a grown woman, for what I ate with my coffee made me feel owned and shamed.

I can't imagine that happening today. Audience members brought up with a specific aesthetic (which older iterations of *Trek*, caught in their own time's cultural bubble, contributed to) have a sense of entitlement, perhaps, to judge how a woman in space should look. The viciousness with which they communicate it is devastating—not only to the actor, but also to the women who watch and finally see themselves represented as deserving of storylines and romances. These vestiges of the narrow lane women have been allowed in the past are broken open by people such as Mary, who somehow finds a way to not run from internet bullying, but find purpose in staying put and remaining who she is.

I understand. Not everyone who watches *Trek* is on board with this expansion of how *Star Trek* portrays people.

In Jessica Nordell's book, *The End of Bias*, she points out that the human brain is constantly making predictions. When the predictions match fact, we feel in control and get a little hit of feel-good chemicals in our bodies. "Holding and confirming stereotypes make people feel good, it provides them with certainty in uncertain situations." Some people who have watched *Star Trek* most of their lives, multiple times, may feel that Tilly takes them out of their comfort zone. At my age, I have learned that growth only happens when we are out of that trancelike zone.

Playing Tilly has had a reverse-engineering effect on Mary's view of herself as a woman. By looking at Tilly's strengths, she has reached a greater understanding of her own. Self-acceptance has eluded her most of her life; she

PAGE 215: Tilly is an expansive character with a love for science.

ABOVE: Tilly is shown to be a genius who can keep up with Stamets.

felt her body, her personality, and even her hair have always been wrong in one way or another. But being who and how she is on the show has offered hope to people who felt as though imagining themselves in Starfleet, even in fantasy, was somehow wrong.

Being young was tough for Mary. With three older brothers and a mother who had a tenuous relationship to her own body because of her interpretation of their religion, she had no one to guide her as she navigated the passage between child and young woman. She became curvy almost overnight, and the changes caused her confusion and a new stressful vigilance when she was around boys. She was on her own to figure out a way of being in the world, and says, "That put me in difficult situations." The culture of her environment was male dominated and required a girl to be delicate, subtle, and small. Mary had big energy with a sense of humor, and that wasn't appreciated, leading her to feel wrong-sized and lonely.

That description struck me as the kind of woman author Jess Zimmerman refers to in her book *Women and Other Monsters*: women who take up space, energetically or otherwise, and are made to feel as if there is something wrong with them. Like so many others I spoke with, Mary found the stage a safe place to be her authentic self.

"It felt like the only place I could go that could hold me, where it was a good thing for me to be who I was." To finally be seen without having to make herself smaller gave her a moment to start building the self-confidence that she feels led to where she is today. Her unique qualities were suddenly a good thing, and there wasn't a need to try to conform in order to be palatable. But unless she is on a stage, Mary still struggles somewhat. When I asked her what advice she would give her eighteen-year-old self, she spoke of compassion and trusting kindness in another person. When asked what her eighty-year-old self would tell her now, she said, "I would tell her that the cruelest thing a person can say is not the truest thing they can say, which I think is a mistake (believing cruelty is truth-telling) I made for a really long time."

Being a *Star Trek* actor comes with responsibility, and Mary has taken it on. She knows firsthand the positive effect the portrayal of women can have on young minds. Mary watched TNG when she was growing up and found Marina Sirtis's character empowering. Young Mary had her emotions readily available, and there was Troi earning a place on the bridge because of her skill in intuiting emotions. The curly hair she wished she didn't have was a sign of beauty on Troi, and helped Mary see herself in a different light. When she married her husband, Noah Averbach-Katz, she inherited a Trekkie as a mother-in-law and clinical proof of the influence storytelling can have. An article in *Forbes* describes Rachelle Averbach as someone whose holidays included *Trek*-themed decor and who taught her son life lessons based on the show. As a therapist—"somebody who has seen the breadth of human experience"—she uses the example of *Trek* with her patients, and was able to communicate to Mary the importance the show has in the lives of people from the whole spectrum of humanity.

Because empathy for others is easier for her than empathy for herself, Mary found a way to "rise to the occasion and not just fake it" for the people who find representation in Tilly. On set, she will find the courage to be an advocate for Tilly by thinking about a woman she met at a convention: "I'm not going to do her like that, by not showing up for Tilly and not showing up for her."

Like so many other *Star Trek* characters, groups that have been marginalized in the past find an avatar in Tilly. I asked her about the fact that neurodivergent people feel seen with her depiction of her character. She answered that because she is herself a nonlinear thinker who has issues with hyperfocus, and her character has the tendency to use a lot of words, people tend to project themselves onto Tilly as a representative for people with a range of cognitive abilities.

She is aware that in the 2020s, however, there is good reason—ethically and otherwise—to have, say, an autistic character played by an autistic actor. She trusts that if the intention had been to make the character autistic, production would have cast the part accordingly. She has never intentionally played Tilly as on the spectrum, but she adds, "I know I project myself onto plenty of people [while] watching television…[and] I don't want to take it away from anyone." By allowing the audience to take what they need from her character, while not presenting herself as the expert, Mary demonstrates her respect and understanding of the platform she has been given.

It's important that although Tilly may not look or behave the way some people expect Starfleet officers to, she is admirable and her actions are Starfleet through and through. This character has great agency. She starts as a cadet, is moved to ensign, and is first officer after Burnham is removed from that duty by Captain Saru. Even though Burnham is her friend, Tilly stalwartly advises the captain to report her to the admiral after she behaves insubordinately, proving that her emotions don't cloud a decision that needs to be made objectively. After helping Stamets with the spores, she asks if Saru would recommend her to the Command Training Program, as she has always dreamed of captaining her own ship. But when she examines herself with the help of Dr. Culber, she realizes her path may be elsewhere.

She changes course to teaching at Starfleet Academy, which takes her out of the main action for the rest of *Discovery*'s fourth season. The Great Resignation during the pandemic that was raging as the show was filming may have influenced this storyline. Many took the time to think through what they wanted the rest of their lives to look like,

and quit jobs they had thought they should want for new paths more aligned to their personal values. Tilly's self-determination is a bold step, and I can't think of anyone better to inspire a new generation of Starfleet officers. As Saru says in "Far from Home," when he chooses her to go on an away mission in search of new life, "We are introducing ourselves to the future. You, Ensign Tilly, are a wonderful first impression."

ABOVE: The Mirror Universe version of Tilly shows that she is capable of efficient brutality.

OPPOSITE: Tilly might not be a traditional hero, but she saves the Earth and her cadets.

Mary Chieffo as
L'RELL

Watching the rise of Klingon Chancellor L'Rell, I found myself thinking about the Star Trek *canon. Even though her reign takes place before Captain Kirk begins his adventures, there is never any mention of the powerful chancellor—or Mother, as she preferred to be addressed. After her reign, it seems Klingons become a very patriarchal society. The Klingon women we'd seen in the TNG era were fierce and have agency, but they weren't running their world.*

Of course, I know the reason we hadn't heard of L'Rell before is that *Discovery* is a prequel, and no one had thought of her. But the way she seems to have been erased from Klingon history reflects something that happens in our own world. In the history written by men, powerful women have been erased from history again and again. In science, erasure of women is called the Matilda Effect. Women philosophers such as Christine de Pizan and Émilie du Châtelet are relatively unknown. People who watch old movies know the name Hedy Lamarr as a glamorous actor of the 1940s, but did you know she was also an important inventor? She developed a system to prevent the enemy from decoding messages during World War II. It's the basis of the system the Navy still utilizes.

One early example of a woman ruler being erased from history is given by UCLA Egyptologist Kara Cooney. Pharaoh Hatshepsut has a lot in common with L'Rell. She was an incredibly successful leader who called herself king because, in Egypt, the word for queen meant "king's woman." After her reign, all monuments belonging to her were destroyed, effectively wiping her out of easily accessed history. When asked why this would be, Cooney said that her successful reign caused a cognitive dissonance. "An ambitious woman leader is usually maligned in history as a conniving, scheming seductress who foolishly brings down the men around

her." King Hatshepsut, the Pharaoh of Egypt, was not that. But admitting that women are capable of leadership could create competition, so many men thought it was in their interest to keep them down. As historian Amanda Foreman noted, one of the first laws in history, from circa 2400 to 2300 BC, stated that "when a woman speaks out of turn, she will be smacked by a brick."

I can see how Mother L'Rell would be erased. I looked up the place of women in Klingon society and found this at Memory Alpha: "Klingon women were treated as equals, except in politics and matters of inheritance." So, not equal, at all. They were powerful in the home, where they educated their children in the way of the warrior. They had influence, as Lursa and B'Etor would later prove, but going down a rabbit hole of Klingon history, I found that after L'Rell, the Klingons once again were a patriarchal society. In terms of law and leadership, the women were powerless. Equal to the men in terms of ferocity, and in the bedroom, maybe, but not in society.

Discovery set about correcting that, even if it meant that L'Rell was an anomaly in Klingon lore. She is one of T'Kuvma's commanders and an ardent supporter of his plan to unite the Klingon Houses. Her costumes denote her positions. There isn't the emphasis on breasts we have seen with other female Klingon outfits. She is dressed for war, and then as a leader; her clothes emphasize her face and power, not her body. She rejects Kol's power grab, and ends up escaping to prison on *Discovery*, which she knows will ensure her survival, because there is no death penalty in Starfleet. This will to live, rather than die with honor, isn't what we expect from Klingons, but it turns out to be what saves her homeworld. When Emperor Georgiou plants a bomb that could destroy Qo'noS, Burnham gives the detonator to L'Rell, handing her the power to take control of the Klingon Empire.

However, she responds to this by replying that she is no one. Her time imprisoned seems to have broken her spirit. It takes a man to change her mind. But men who encourage a leg up to women have always been essential allies. This man is the Klingon Voq, who has been transformed into Ash Tyler via a torturous surgery that we are treated to in flashes. His Klingon side reminds her that although she was happy to have Voq take on the mantle of power when T'Kuvma died, "it's time for you to leave the shadows" and rule.

POWER COSTS

When L'Rell becomes the leader of the Empire, she demands what she deems a more significant title than chancellor and chooses Mother, but in the end she is denied real motherhood. To save the son she had with Voq, she hides him in a monastery on the planet Boreth. She cannot have a relationship with

the man who has been by her side, and their child. She has to choose: leadership or family, and she chooses leadership. But she is an effective leader, uniting the Klingon Houses and even introducing a new class of starship, the D7.

Mary sees her role as L'Rell to be the Mother Archetype, but in a Divine Feminine way, not as someone who is in service to the child. This means she offers a different kind of leadership, which as L'Rell points out, is no less fierce. She lives outside her society's norms, but ultimately, she can only redefine them so much, and the price she has to pay is the loss of her family.

Throughout the episodes featuring her, Mary Chieffo does a remarkable job of giving a nuanced, powerful, and believable performance. Her scenes with Admiral Cornwell are thrilling. I sensed that they were complete intellectual equals who show courage and commitment to their own goals. When I fought an alien woman in DS9, we weren't given the airtime for an extended fight, nor the complexity of a scene that makes you wonder which way it will turn out. The will to survive, and the ability to stay the path, even when it looks hopeless, is a hero's response, and both these women do it justice. That Mary accomplishes this behind a complete mask of makeup and prosthetics makes her performance all the more remarkable.

One of the first impressions I had when I met her was that she likes and supports other women. She made a point to come up to me, heart wide open, and say what my character had meant to her. At six feet tall with strong features, she has a powerful presence that seems to push out the walls of any room she's in. She is enormously attractive and compelling but, like L'Rell, she challenges Hollywood's ideas of femininity. So, I wondered how she would fit into the boxes that have been made for actors.

The child of character actors, she watched her mother deal with the limitations of what it meant to not be an ingenue in the 1970s. Her mother warned her, "Okay, here's the thing: With your features, with your voice, you're probably going to be put into these very dynamic, very fun roles, but not necessarily leads." In typical media, the character actress is the woman lead's girlfriend, mother, crazy aunt,

coffee shop owner. Those roles usually have the most memorable lines and defined characters, but what Mary feels she has the chops for is the chance to propel a storyline forward.

Mary was often cast in male roles at school. Playing Macbeth, Iago, and Othello gave her a taste of the hero's journey, and she wanted to find roles that allowed her to be a protagonist and be in the center of the storytelling, not on the periphery. She watched her mother work within the boundaries set for her and become very successful. But, Mary, who graduated from Juilliard, wants something else. She is very firm that she doesn't want to be a leading lady by forcing herself into the impossible position of being a delicate beauty who looks like she needs saving by the lead. Frankly, Mary doesn't give the impression that she needs saving by anyone. What she wants is those character parts to be brought to the forefront in movies and TV, so that they can be explored and have their own hero's journey.

When I mentioned Jess Zimmerman's quote that "women are often on a diet of the body but always on a diet of the heart," Mary responded: "I feel morally, artistically, that's where I live. I think my frustrations with the industry now are 'I'm ready, y'all.' There are people, I've found, who do get my voice, but for the most part it's frustrating to be up against the industry that is slowly but surely changing."

Being passionate and having a big energy hasn't been an asset in the business for Mary. She says she has felt the need to make herself smaller, more acceptable. One habit that formed for her is apologizing. Laugh too loud, apologize; say something intelligent, but follow up with, "But what do I know?" Being socially acceptable as a woman isn't just about being able to fit into your community, but also about being able to pursue your goals as an actor and support yourself.

In this interim period of time, people in the industry now know enough to not tell someone "we aren't hiring you because of your weight," but not enough to actually hire the same person. Mary isn't sure this is better, but maybe it's part of the journey of change. The hope for her is that all the people ascending to new, powerful positions in the business who aren't attached to the old ways of thinking "don't succumb to the norms of before."

I studied the game when I was Mary's age and would transform myself with platinum hair, makeup, and an accent

that made me seem more naive to get jobs where looking like I needed saving by a man was key. Then after a while, I would change to dark hair and something a little closer to the truth of me, and get cast as the bad girl or killer. It was so predictable, it was almost funny. I felt I was getting what I could, being outside the leading-lady ideal, but I never thought of the consequence of this, as Mary has.

Not only is she learning not to apologize for who she is, but she also realizes that the stereotypical ideal is a long way from reality anyway. She makes the point that media is a powerful way to influence lives. If someone doesn't have the experience of knowing others in their immediate community who are like them, whether that is based on "ethnicity, sexual orientation, or gender identity, then the only exposure you have is what you're seeing on TV."

If TV standardizes people by giving them token characters who represent a community, then the viewer is being told that this narrowly defined character is the way they are supposed to be. "Oh, am I in that box? Is that the only way I'm allowed to exist?" The cyclical effect is people narrowing themselves to fit into the box created by the media. This is also true for the representation of women. If we have many different versions of strong women characters in the arts, my idea of what a strong woman is and yours may be different, but we can both find versions to be our avatars in stories.

There is a leap I see in how the present-day women of *Star Trek* operate. Mary is grateful for more people being their authentic selves and bringing it to their work, and the women she worked with on *Discovery* have acted as mentors, friends, and a social network. She talks at length about the compassion, inclusion, and community built by the women creators on *Discovery* and especially by Sonequa Martin-Green.

The real test to Mary of how women fit into leadership roles is whether they are given the room to make the occasional inevitable mistake, to recognize it, and to grow from it. Michael Burnham epitomizes this. When women, such as L'Rell and Cornwell, are allowed to show mutual respect, despite the fact that they "screamed in each other's faces," it goes way beyond the Bechdel Test of having two women in conversation not talking about a man.

Mary says that having women in production, on the writing staff, on the crew, and leading the show as actors creates an environment that feels safe and inclusive. Creativity flourishes when there isn't the constant energy drain that happens when you are vigilantly protecting yourself from threats. A nonsupportive fellow actor, a subtly sexual comment from a crew member, or being put in your hierarchical place by a producer can all make people defensive in a space in which actors need to be wide open. There are many ways one loses energy by trying to control a nervous system that mistakes social aggression for real physical threat.

Mary is always confused when people approach her at conventions and say: "But you're so beautiful. Why did they put that stuff on you?" "I really found L'Rell to be very beautiful and Klingon. Not in typical societal norms, but she's a gorgeous Klingon." When questioned about what beauty meant to her, she said it wasn't what culture seemed to think it was, which to her seems "neutral...Often it's the safe choice. It's the thing that won't offend anyone as opposed to challenge in an exciting way. I mean, I find beautiful is exciting and challenging and unique." Just like Mary.

STAR TREK: LOWER DECKS

How did a self-proclaimed "Mr. Silly Guy" get to tell a Star Trek *story? Well, he got to because the smart creator of the animated series* Star Trek: Lower Decks *successfully puts a humorous filter over what* Star Trek *does best: pose questions that are worth asking ourselves. Mike McMahan had been working on a show with two White male leads when he decided to change his focus and take his shot. He grew up with the show, and sees it as a feminine entity. It could be because he always watched it with his mom, or because Dr. Crusher made a big impression: a woman with a career, a kid, and no husband! Troi's seat on the bridge next to the captain impacted the young boy, too. He got the message: Women were intrinsic to the crew.*

When he wrote a parody version of what an eighth season of TNG would look like for Twitter, he found he ran into the same problems other writers had with the character of Troi. He saw that she wasn't as fully developed as the others and saw it as a missed opportunity. This lesson would heavily influence what he did next. His animated show would fit into the current understanding of parity and focus on a female ensign with a lot of growing up to do.

But being able to tell a *Trek* story felt like an impossible dream. So impossible, he didn't think he had a real chance of succeeding and did what the lawyers always warn against: named some of his characters after real people. When he made his pitch, his lead character, Beckett Mariner, was named after his beloved sister. He wanted to tell the story of the people in the background during the first five minutes of a TNG episode, before the important action took place and our stars took over.

Lower Decks would be different because the focus would be on people at least a decade younger than the officers who were usually up front and center in the stories. Anyone who is in Starfleet is the best of the best, but being an ensign means there's a road to finding your place in it. Beckett Mariner is sometimes her own worst enemy in this process. A woman with flaws being given the opportunity to self-examine is a huge win for female representation on TV. The show being animated may go some way toward what alien makeup did for women back in the 1990s. It's less threatening to see a woman who doesn't fit the status quo if she's drawn.

Mike doesn't see his show as a patriarchy or a matriarchy, but an experiment: a found family. The main characters support, accept, and challenge each other as they try to find their way in the world.

Besides the space travel, cultural, and scientific aspects, Mike says a part of *Star Trek* has always been the question: What are you discovering? There is personal challenge in finding out that the things you thought were true may not be after all. Questioning yourself and the culture around you are integral to the storytelling on the show.

Mariner has seen a lot of different sides to Starfleet, as she keeps managing to get herself knocked back down to the same job placement while others get promoted upward away from it. This puts her in the unique position of being able to judge the institution, and she doesn't always like what she sees. What she continually has to grapple with is whether what she is seeing is a flaw in Starfleet, or herself. The show, with gentle affection, suggests that to respect a system you are a part of may require questioning it at times. It may even require updating the system or maybe your own

understanding of it. At all times, if you are sentient, you need to be questioning yourself.

When the characters look deep into themselves and find a flaw, it usually turns out to be some form of dishonesty. The only solution is usually, in the end, being honest with themselves and others. Because the lead character is a woman, this examination will help us understand her in a granular way. It's proven that girls need to see examples of themselves to cultivate ideas of who they wish to be. Mariner's self-examination allows girls to anticipate the struggles that sometimes come with the work of building self-respect.

Mike sees being human, in all its infinite variations, as our true power. This ethos is not just about what you see on screen, but also in the work culture he created. When I worked on *Star Trek*, the show's production offices were dominated by men. I am delighted to see how much that has changed, but as Mike told me, making that change takes effort. When he entered the business, he could see "the remnants of a system that wasn't always inclusive." Most experienced upper-level writers were not women and certainly not women of color.

By 2012, he was insisting on parity for women in his writing rooms. When he would ask agents to submit writers, they would inevitably send him a list of exclusively male names. He would then have to specifically request a list of woman writers in order to receive one. But the fact is, he says, there have always been more women in animation. It's "the weird kid's table, so the men's table fell apart pretty quickly." He has worked with a lot of women in executive positions, and noted he was mentored by Jennifer Howell, who was at the time head of animation at Fox. She "taught him everything."

McMahan says young people need to question everything in their world, including themselves. *Lower Decks* gives us a lead character who is a woman of color, and we can witness all her mistakes, all her victories, all her growth, all her human aspects, and all of her complexity. Sometimes, as Mike told me, shining a light on yourself is harder than finding a new planet. Outer space has tools that are ready-made to aid in discovery, but venturing into inner space has fewer tools and, at some point, is something you do alone.

ABOVE: *Lower Decks* features the kind of women *Star Trek* has never shown before.

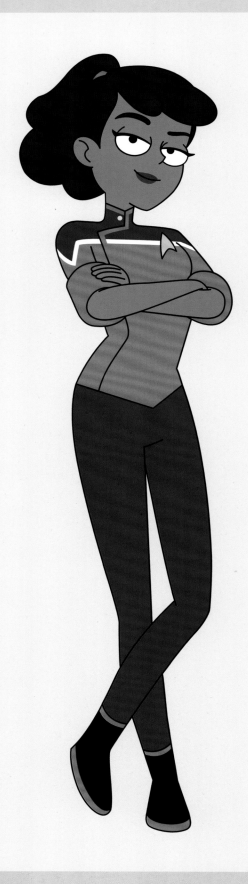

Tawny Newsome as
BECKETT MARINER

When I guest-starred on the sitcom Night Court, *Marsha Warfield kept me in stitches on the set. She had a running joke: If she saw someone do something truly astounding or physically difficult, she would deadpan, "I could do that. I just don't feel like it right now." Over and over again, Beckett Mariner seems capable of doing everything any* Star Trek *captain can accomplish. But, for some reason, she finds a way to be sent back to square one and the title of ensign. Maybe she just doesn't feel like it right now.*

Played with fast-paced flair by Tawny Newsome, Beckett Mariner gets to do everything that used to be reserved for male characters. This is truly a woman character unleashed. She has a rich, almost unbelievable past; she is smart, funny, and irreverent; and she thumbs her nose at authority. She has been on five different ships, mostly because of her rebellious belief that she is right and the system is wrong, which gets her sent to the brig more often than not. The daughter of Captain Carol Freeman and Admiral Alonzo Freeman, she ends up on her mother's ship, the *U.S.S. Cerritos*, as she tries to figure out life and her relationship to Starfleet.

That's important in all sorts of ways. At the most basic level, Mariner gets to do and be all the things that little girls used to be told weren't for them: She is energetic, adventurous, and insubordinate. We might sometimes think she is unwise, but in the world of *Lower Decks*, everybody can make mistakes, and there's no question that Mariner is the show's hero.

All too often, women have been told that they have to be perfect, but Mariner has more flaws than we are used to seeing in women characters who are leads. Actually, she has more flaws than most characters of either sex. She is insubordinate to her mother, the captain, and goes against the Prime Directive. For example, she decides to stop rat aliens from eating lizard aliens. She strikes a heroic stance as the rat monument is pulled down. That is, until her mother shows up. She has it wrong: the lizards are raised for food, plus, you know, the Prime Directive. She is enraged to hear she is being sent to therapy instead of the brig.

Mariner gets to make mistakes. She is impulsive, and clearly knows so many of the things she does are wrong in hindsight. Even if they come from a good original thought, they can have disastrous outcomes. When she has the idea to power-wash buildings on the planet Apergos, it activates an energy source that transfers monstrous, deity-like powers to the first officer, who begins attacking the *Cerritos*. Although the captain realizes his attack is being fueled by his feelings of insecurity, because she has been favoring her daughter, what really stops him isn't the captain building his ego back up, but Mariner simply kicking him.

Most of the time, even when it seems like a foolish idea, Mariner is right—maybe not in theory, but in getting a result. Once the crisis is over, she tells her mother that although it's best that they don't work so closely together anymore, she loves her. Then Mariner sets off to the place she knows her behavior deserves: the brig.

That's just not something women have gotten to do on TV. Mariner is impish and irrepressible. Her constant rule-breaking is the kind of behavior that has been seen as admirable in men, who are described as roguish, but

RIGHT: Mariner is disobedient and disrespectful, but she is still the hero.

OPPOSITE: Mariner is allowed to indulge in the kind of wild, anarchic behavior normally reserved for male heroes.

normally rejected in women, who are more likely to be regarded as dangerous and unhinged.

Mariner is also free of the kind of ambition that defines most *Star Trek* characters. *Discovery* details the long and difficult making of a captain. Here, we see a woman who doesn't seem to care about the status of leadership as much as she cares about having an interesting life. It answers the question of what life is like for all the people brilliant enough to get into Starfleet but whose stories never get told because they aren't officers.

Even the ship isn't an important one. They are more of a "land on a planet to take care of an animal control issue" kind of ship. What this means for Mariner is a lot of room to make mistakes, make friends, grow up, and figure out if the Starfleet life her parents chose is the right one for her. She doesn't just fall in line; she also makes her own way.

She has a complex relationship with her mother, and isn't above calling her a bitch when she is sent to therapy. She sets up an elaborate hologram featuring an alternative-universe

> Here, we see a woman who doesn't seem to care about the status of leadership as much as she cares about having an interesting life.

Mariner, called Vindicta, and lives out taking the ultimate revenge on her mother. But at the moment Vindicta is about to kill the captain, Beckett appears to fight the evil side of herself. In the fight, she realizes that if she was as badass as she thought she was, she would "do the hard thing and be a good officer." She comes to the conclusion that she doesn't hate her mother or the *Cerritos*. "I may hate protocol, but I would do anything for the captain." The idea that her motivation to break rules may come from others' expectations is a big realization for the ensign, who decides excitedly that "therapy works!"

Most of the characters in *Lower Decks* could be played by either gender. They are individualized by life experience, special interests, and alien identity. But even then, stereotypes are challenged. Mariner thoughtlessly insults her Orion friend Tendi by calling her a pirate and thief, but mostly because it serves her purpose for both of them to appear badass. When Tendi confronts her and says some Orions are like that but not her, our hero apologizes sincerely.

While Mariner is more likely to take physical risks to get out of a situation, her friends Boimler and Rutherford find the thrill in compromise. Confronted with dangerous rogue Ferengi, they develop a power point to show them how much more latinum they would make by building a sanctuary for mugatos rather than poaching them. The male characters are allowed to step away from stereotypical aggressive behavior and make intellect look cool. Mariner supports this in her friends and tells them to kick ass in their own way, not hers.

The Bechdel Test of looking for scenes between two women where they don't talk about men is too low a bar for this show. Beckett and her friend Tendi go on an away mission with the shout "Girl's trip!" It seems less and less fun as Mariner, by following the beat of her own drum, messes up the mission, which keeps getting more and more dangerous as a result. The two are friends, but find out on this trip that they don't know that much about each other. Tendi is surprised to find that Mariner has many types of people she is attracted to. "Sexy bad boys, bad girls, bad gender-nonbinary types, ruthless alien masterminds, bad Bynars" As they get to know each other through the adventure— "People who work together soon will be people who get their ass kicked together"—there is a shift. Instead of just worrying about themselves, they start caring about the outcome for each other. To keep Tendi from getting in trouble for breaking an heirloom, Mariner decides to ram the shuttlecraft into the *Cerritos* as an excuse for the damage. She practically takes herself to the brig. It's a good example of women supporting women, and taking responsibility for their actions, although it's obvious that her method of crashing is less than ideal. But...funny.

Her sexuality is less about who she is in a relationship with, and more about what happens in every relationship, regardless of who is involved. Her girlfriend is Jennifer Sh'reyan, an Andorian who used to have a contentious

the actor who plays her, says, which gives her someplace to grow to and made her the perfect *Star Trek* character for Newsome to inhabit.

"I tend to have more fun when the character can be a little on her back foot, when she can be, like, trying to catch up. That's one of the things I love about Mariner. She's both very high status and very in charge, but also a kind of fuckup and kind of chaotic and sporadic, and I think that's true to me and true to life." These kinds of multidimensional, funny roles weren't available to women of color when Newsome first started out in theater. "You could do *The Color Purple*, you could do *Ragtime*, you could do *Lion King*." Theater hadn't yet evolved into the habit of nontraditional casting. Today, the quirky roles now being written for women that she would love to play go to people in their thirties. In her fourth decade, she gets offers for snooty society women, stern judges, and frustrated moms of teenagers. Her roles in filmed comedy were as the grounding woman to the male leads, who "were big, dynamic people who would make mistakes but you love them anyway. I'm

relationship with Mariner. The stories look at things such as fear of intimacy, or meeting your lover's friends for the first time—things that are universal to everyone.

From the beginning of the show, we are shown a "badass" who slowly reveals the reasons why she is the way she is. She keeps her past vague on purpose. To make close friends and truly reveal herself would only make it more painful when they are separated, either by the person being promoted or by Mariner herself being sent to yet another ship. She fights her mother, but loves her deeply. She struggles with the rules of Starfleet. But, in the end, she wants her life's work to have a greater purpose. To stand for a greater good.

When, at the end of season three, her mother mistakenly thinks Mariner spoke badly of the captain to a reporter, she sends her daughter to the dreaded Starbase 80. Mariner quits Starfleet and travels the planets with archeologist Petra Aberdeen. Once she learns that the *Cerritos* is under attack, Mariner commandeers Petra's ship and brings every *California*-class ship with her to defeat the enemy. When faced with her mother, she takes responsibility for not being trustworthy for so many years, which had led her mother to mistakenly believe the worst of her. She recommits to Starfleet, and asks for the first officer to be her mentor as a true indication of her concession that she may not know everything.

This is a character who is supremely human: flawed, self-righteous, prickly, but able to admit mistakes, have true agency in her life, see herself clearly, and choose to evolve. She is "wrong-footed" much of the time, as Tawny Newsome,

OPPOSITE: Tawny Newsome got to play a real-life version of Mariner when she made a guest appearance on *Star Trek: Strange New Worlds* in the fan-favorite episode "Those Old Scientists."

TOP: Mariner has a tendency to act before the thinks.

ABOVE: Mariner has frustrations, though, which she acts out on the holodeck.

just, like—write me like one of those men!" Because she realizes that once you inhabit a box, you may be relegated to it by the industry, she will turn down parts in order to wait for opportunities like those roles. Beckett Mariner was exactly the kind of opportunity she waited for.

When I asked her about the freedom of playing a character who is sexually fluid, she is quick to say that she doesn't identify as queer, and always wants those roles to go to the many excellent queer actors out there. But "Mariner was created without a ton of defining characteristics," and her sexual fluidity was added after Tawny was cast and the show was underway. So she is happy with the representation she helps bring to life, but says her ideal would be a decision like that being made prior to casting.

Mariner is funny and quick, and Newsome's years in Chicago at the famed improv theater Second City honed her comedic talent. But there was a culture to the improv group that would unconsciously lock the women out of some of the work. She was involved from 2012 to 2015, and the men she worked alongside were "all lovely people." They seemed to understand that women now needed to be given their comedy shot, but there wasn't a thought about how to integrate them. "They would kind of step aside—okay, now here's the girls' song." While the women got to do a song about dating, the men would do a scene about life.

When I met Tawny at a convention, I quickly learned the new star of *Lower Decks* absolutely was a fan of *Deep Space Nine*, and more specifically of Major Kira and Lt. Dax. Her mother is "an extremely tough person" and has spent her life in law enforcement, and she saw the two characters as extensions of who her mother was and what she taught the young girl at home. With a charismatic Black father who reminded her of Avery, watching the show "just felt like my house. But in space." She would have liked to have seen more representation for women of color in lead roles, but was grateful for the recurring characters of Keiko and Kassidy. She loved that women in DS9 were sexual beings without that fact driving the story. "Relationships were just a bonus, and I was like, 'God, that's how life should be, right?'"

There is nothing like personally understanding the importance of finding representation in characters to make you understand the responsibility of being in a *Star Trek* show. At one convention, she met two members of the SyFy Sistas, Yvette and Tamia, who created their podcast as a place for "nerdy Black girls" to share their love of sci-fi. It wasn't only the representation of Mariner onscreen that made them grateful to Tawny, but also her outspoken presence as a longtime fan of *Star Trek*. Every time Tawny posts about being part of a fandom on social media, the idea of Black women who love science and science fiction becomes a little more normalized, and the conversational circle they helped create grows.

I asked her about the power of being a nerdy Black girl, and she told me, "We have a secret lens into the world." Being Black and being women means they are often overlooked, "but what that allows you to do is see without being seen," and it gives them a uniquely layered world perspective and an interest in what *Star Trek* so often examines. They are like "humanity scientists."

Like many women of color, Tawny saw it as her responsibility to also be a "crusader" in the business, and it was only

after the fact, each time, that she would realize how much precious time and energy it cost her. And often, it was effort done with no payoff. She remembers working very hard to get a producer, who she had a good relationship with, to understand the Bechdel Test, and the fact that their show was failing it. She sent him articles and emails—he was grateful and thanked her—but she waited for a scene with another woman, which didn't come until the last day of shooting. "Per your note," he said, and had her stand next to a background woman with no character name, for them to be seen talking in the shot, with no written dialogue.

Lower Decks has women writers and women animators. There are even a few who have been Trekkies all their life and now get to work on a *Star Trek* show. The lines blur between fandom and the creative team, and that's only a great thing for a show that is so devoted and gets to be wonderfully irreverent to the franchise. Watching Boimler try to get his commemorative Tom Paris plate autographed when

the pilot visits the ship is an example of how it couldn't get any funnier to anyone intimate with the culture.

All the new iterations of *Trek* give good representation to women of color, but Tawny has a soft spot for Mariner and *Lower Decks*. "All Starfleet is competency porn, and I think we can always use more humor. I think that especially for Black women, the ability to be competent and in control and all those good things, but we can also be, like, deeply, innately very, very funny. I think culturally, Black people are just some of the funniest people on the planet because we have no choice sometimes, and so you see us, like, strong and stoic and cool and collected. I'm like, yeah, but we're also hysterical." Yes, Tawny, you are.

OPPOSITE: More than anything, Mariner is about her friends.

ABOVE: Mariner's relationship with her mother is at the heart of the show as they seek to find a balance.

STAR TREK: STRANGE NEW WORLDS

When Alex Kurtzman signed a deal with CBS to expand the number of Star Trek *shows, he imbued each one with the same DNA, even though the stories and styles are all quite different. There is diversity and inclusion, not only in the scripts but also on the stages, in the production offices, and in the writing rooms. Is it perfect? I doubt it; but from everything I have been told, every effort is made to hear everyone's point of view and to make diverse hires throughout the company. There are women executive producers, like Michelle Paradise and Jenny Lumet, and women directors and creatives on every level.*

Actors are told what their arcs will be, and are encouraged to give their ideas to the creative team, even in decisions about makeup and hair. That was almost unheard of in my day. The sexualized costumes are gone, with everyone dressed in space outfits and shoes that look ready for adventure. Women come in all shapes and sizes, not one ideal, and that is absolutely represented here.

There seems to be a respect for an actor's personal life as well. I read that Anson Mount was often absent from filming the second season of *Star Trek: Strange New Worlds* because he had just had a baby. When Alexander Siddig and I had our son, the baby arrived in the middle of the night. Siddig stayed throughout that long night with me but then was told his early morning call was still in place, and he had no choice but to leave his hours-old son and go to work—not one change to the schedule. I have never seen him more upset, before or since. It makes me want to weep with relief that people aren't treated with so little humanity anymore.

Along with this humanizing of the conditions comes another thread of DNA I see in all the new shows: gentle, affectionate humor. It was telling, to me, that Captain Pike is not only allowed to be silly but can even get close to getting on his crew's nerves. After they defeat pirates who take over the ship, he does a corny pirate imitation that his crew needs him to stop doing immediately. What was interesting to me is that this moment didn't undercut his authority at all.

Pike doesn't lead through intimidation or patriarchal rules. There is no authoritarianism. He listens to his crew, getting their feedback before he makes a decision. He is aware when one of them may be in emotional trouble, giving them a chance to talk it through without trying to "fix" it. He understands what makes them tick, and motivates them accordingly. When he makes a joke, the vulnerability he shows to his crew by doing so demonstrates the intimacy and trust between them.

Unless you are a professional comedian or don't care about other people's feelings, you don't joke if you aren't sure it will land on friendly ears. Even when his pirate joke doesn't land, you can see how safe and unbothered he is by it. These vulnerable moments help us understand these people at a deeper level. The captain is allowed to be a full-spectrum human, and he is a great leader of a mostly female crew.

The humor extends to the franchise itself. As Jess Bush told me, there are so many people working here that grew up on *Star Trek*, its lore is like a second language to them. This familiarity allows them to affectionately tease out the humor in some of its tropes without ever crossing a line that might be disrespectful to the show or its audience.

I noticed something in the first season of the show that I hadn't seen before on TV. There have always been women hired or fired to accentuate the storyline and character of a man. I have read that Nurse Chapel was created to accentuate Spock's alien ability to control his emotions. But in this show, Chief Engineer Lt. Hemmer, played by Bruce Horak, was created to be a mentor (!) to Uhura. She is a new cadet who isn't sure Starfleet is her life's path, and Celia Rose Gooding's performance makes seeing Uhura enter the bridge for the first time in uniform a powerful moment. This Uhura has many facets to her personality, and they are given plenty of screen time to develop. Uhura is finally getting the attention and care she always deserved, and Gooding plays her with a sweet, open manner; a sharp intellect; and, like Nichelle, a beautiful singing voice.

It's interesting to watch Uhura in the original series with this in mind. That a male Aenar was, as Horak himself put it, a kind of Obi-Wan Kenobi to Uhura adds dimension and a

bittersweet history when you see Nichelle on the bridge. It's also a lovely nod to the fact that the Reverend Martin Luther King Jr. was himself a mentor to Nichelle Nichols when she wanted to leave the show, giving her the broader perspective of her importance in the community so that she didn't quit. Hemmer encourages the young Uhura to go on in Starfleet, too. He shows her the importance of keeping her heart open, even when there is inevitable pain when you do so.

Now, the original series' Uhura seems like a human who did the hard work of evolving when she faces down the perils of a life in space, not simply someone who had the correct emotional makeup for the job. This is such an important lesson: There isn't always a clear and easy path to commitment, and there is always a steep learning curve at the beginning of every career. Evolution is a personal process as well as a societal one, and it isn't always a breeze.

I didn't have the opportunity to speak to Celia Rose Gooding or Rebecca Romijn, who plays Number One Una

Chin-Riley. This is another woman who has been given a history and storylines that enhance the original character she was created from. She is trusted by the captain, and she is an essential and respected member of the crew.

CHARACTER REBORN

Number One can speak to so many who join an institution with an idealized belief that there are no cracks in its foundation that may need repair. Una wanted to be in Starfleet since her childhood. She saw the beauty of all the different species from all the different planets working together as a crew. The problem lies in the ban Starfleet imposed on genetic enhancements because of the Eugenics Wars. As an Illyrian, she herself was genetically enhanced for strength and immunity to disease. She has to lie about her heritage in order to be in Starfleet, which, of course, made me

think, "Why would they deny someone good at their job and devoted to the institution because their body is a certain way?" And that's the beauty of this character, who fights for the right to serve, avoids court-martial, and makes Starfleet history as the first person to serve as an acknowledged Illyrian on the bridge.

The DNA of the original *Star Trek* also runs deep in this show. The promise of Roddenberry's bold ideas is brought into our present understanding of what the future should look like, without missing a beat of the fun.

OPPOSITE: *Strange New Worlds* is set before the original series but shows a much more gender-balanced world.

ABOVE: The crew of *Strange New Worlds* seem to appreciate what they've got and to enjoy the inclusive nature of the show.

Christina Chong as

LA'AN NOONIEN-SINGH

La'An Noonien-Singh is the kind of role most actors would kill for, and Christina Chong knows it. She combines vulnerability and toughness in a way that makes a character incredibly compelling and a joy to play. It's a characteristic she shares with Seven of Nine. In lots of ways, she also shares DNA with Tasha Yar—another character who suffered terribly during her childhood and is passionately devoted to the Federation's ideals. A lot has changed since 1988, though. Back then, Denise Crosby left the series because she wasn't being given enough to do. Christina admits that she worried that might have happened to her, too, but the reality has been very different.

When Christina got the role of La'An, she grudgingly prepared herself to play a role she had played a hundred times before. Christina grew up in England, and early in her career played token Asian roles, or as she puts it, "the first character to be killed off."

Because she is biracial, with a Chinese father and a Caucasian mother, she says she wasn't seen as fitting into either the Caucasian casting box or the Chinese one. It took an agent with an imagination to start pushing casting directors to see her for roles with more meat to them. After reading three scenes and getting the role on *Star Trek: Strange New Worlds*, she thought the part would be the typical straight, reserved sci-fi woman that would serve to round out the rest of the cast. But she took the job anyway because "it was Covid, the goalposts in the business had changed, and, after all, it was *Star Trek*."

When she met with executive producers Henry Alonso Myers and Akiva Goldsman, she was blown away with what they had planned. She now sees La'An as a huge gift. Even though most shows have caught up to *Star Trek*'s diversity and inclusion, you simply don't find roles filled with endless possibilities and complexity for women like you do on *Strange New Worlds*.

One of the proven ways to give a character richness, agency, a way to grow, and issues to deal with is to give them a history. If writers can look at a character and see an immediate list of possible stories, they will write them. The audience can spend time getting to know and love them, or hate them, because there will simply be more of them in the story. I benefited from that as Major Kira, and that was one of the things that excited me about the role. Predominantly, it was the male actors who were given the more thoughtfully constructed character backgrounds to bring to life. Things have definitely changed.

La'An is chief of security, with a tough exterior and a depth in her eyes that tells you she has seen too much trauma. She endures pain, refusing painkillers from Nurse Chapel while undergoing genetic modification. It's almost as if she inoculates herself to physical pain by bearing it, or maybe it's the punishment for the survivor's guilt she feels? The ensigns don't like training with her because she is an unforgiving and strict teacher. Lesson number two for them is "there are no breaks in security because threats never take a break." But even though her friends admit they see her as "where fun goes to die," she doesn't shut down. Instead, she

OPEN A CHANNEL: THE WOMEN OF *STAR TREK*

makes it a mission, with the help of her friend Number One, to try to see what others see in this thing "fun." Because of her horrific childhood, she never learned how to play.

The themes of La'An's life are love, loss, and shame, with the redemption of eventual acceptance of self and the opening of one's heart. There are parallels to these in Christina's life as well. We learn that La'An is a survivor with severe post-traumatic stress. As a child, she saw her entire community on the *U.S.S. Puget Sound* be captured by the Gorn and either killed or slit open and used as breeding sacs for the Gorn young. Her young brother Manu died making sure she survived, and she was rescued by a Federation ship, the *U.S.S. Martin Luther King*. On board was Ensign Una Chin-Riley, who took the child under her wing, becoming an important mentor and friend. It was because of Una, who we come to know is First Officer Number One, that La'An joined Starfleet. That's important because, unlike Tasha Yar, La'An isn't just a woman who is prospering in a man's world. She is also part of a community of women. Mentors are very important to Chong, too, and she has three at the moment: her mother, her life coach, and her acting teacher.

For Christina, *Star Trek* has the added benefit of a grounding in philosophical questions and social issues, dealing with stories that aren't gendered so much as human. In fact, the character she plays is fully human. In the 1990s, La'An would have had prosthetics on her face to allow her to step out of performatively female expectations. She wears, in fact, little makeup at all, other than to enhance her eyes, which she feels heightens La'An's intensity.

Although she isn't a legacy character like Number One, she is connected to two heavyweights. She is the descendant of Khan, one of the tyrants who ruled Earth during the Eugenics Wars. Being connected to Khan is a source of great shame for Noonien-Singh during the first season. When people hear her name, there is an immediate association with evil, and she protects herself by adopting a closed-off attitude. In fact, she says she "finds people challenging," but so do most people who have been bullied and ostracized when they are young.

Here again, Chong is able to connect to the shame felt by her character because of racism she herself experienced when she was little. She told me of being six years old, onstage at school, displaying her artwork in her hands. In the front rows sat some boys, who pulled the edges of their eyes and sang "Ching Chong Chinaman" to her. I asked her how her mother helped her deal with things like this, which were a daily occurrence during her childhood. She said she felt too much shame to tell her mother, but simply took it on in silence, until it was just a part of her. Through listening to her interviews for *Trek*, her parents have been shocked to learn of this aspect of her life, and it has been a starting point for conversations with her father, who experienced racism in England during the Vietnam War.

In the second season, in the wonderful episode "Tomorrow and Tomorrow and Tomorrow," La'An falls in love with James T. Kirk and finds self-acceptance by stopping a time-traveling Romulan from killing her ancestor Khan as a boy. She is thrown into an alternative timeline in which Kirk

OPPOSITE: Christina was amazed to discover just how much the show let's her do and was surprised to find La'An transformed into a fairy-tale princess.

ABOVE: As the *Enterprise*'s security officer, La'An has echoes of Tasha Yar, but Christina has no concerns about not being given enough to do.

is captain of the ship she suddenly finds herself aboard, and together they are shot back to present-day Toronto. They are forced to find a way to blend in as they figure out what exactly their mission is.

There's something very important about the romance with Kirk. For almost all of *Star Trek*'s history, we've seen romance through a man's eyes. This time, we are given the story through the lens of the woman's eyes. A half-open drape in a clothing store's changing room allows La'An to glance at Kirk's torso. She quickly turns away with an intake of breath, letting us know it has affected her in a visceral way. But it's not lascivious, because we see the questions she is asking herself reflected on her face. It let me know there is full emotional engagement; this moment means something to this woman who has a hard time letting people get close. The idea of healthy female desire is not something you saw on TV until recently.

In another scene that gives us La'An's point of view, she cannot sleep in the room next to Kirk, and gets up to quietly watch him as he sleeps, then turns and walks away. The energetic pull from her gaze causes him to wake and look at where she had just been. The indefinable, palpable air that exists between people who are falling in love is caught onscreen, and there is no objectification in either direction.

REAL CONSEQUENCES

This seems so appropriate for *Star Trek* the franchise because it's in step with all its other humanistic themes. Things have moved on since the 1960s. Then, in most—but not all—cases, Kirk's romances wouldn't have much lasting impact, and we certainly wouldn't think about the effect they had on his lovers. He would romance a scantily dressed woman and then move on. Now, the character's feelings are first and foremost examined; it's not a sexy performance to catch an audience's attention. Because we can recognize the humanity in the love story, it's not only respectful to the characters but also to us as well. It works to connect us to the two of them, and then to feel the loss, as La'An does, when he sacrifices himself to achieve the objectives of their mission.

The story is ultimately about La'An learning to accept herself. She kills the Romulan who would destroy the terrible history of Khan by assassinating him as a child. At this point, she knows that Khan could still be killed, but she would survive it because of the time-traveling device she holds.

Yet, when she opens the door and finds a small boy, with artwork and schoolwork surrounding him, she comes to terms with the fact that his part in history should not be changed. He is "exactly where he needs to be" in order for all the stages of growth and peace to take place that occur after the destruction he causes. As lawyer Neera Ketoul points out in the previous episode, she is merely "born with the capacity for actions, good or ill." She decides to lay her fears to rest that her genes will win over her personal choices in her life from here on out.

When she is back in her own timeline, she is told by a temporal agent that she must tell no one what has happened. That she gets in touch with this timeline's Kirk, just to see his face again, tells us that this storyline is a thread that will be picked up again. Her flood of tears at the loss at the end of the show gives us insight into a complex character in the painful beginning stages of opening her heart. This is the first time ever we have experienced a love story with Kirk through the woman's eyes. I have to say, he comes out of it, for me, so much more likable, complex, and human than he ever has before. No sexiness is lost in the translation.

That I am not the only one to feel this way is evident in the outpouring of responses Christina got from both men and women who felt this episode spoke to them personally.

That kind of storytelling shows how *Star Trek* is evolving. *Strange New Worlds* often tells the kind of stories you'd have seen on the original series, but it brings far more focus on the characters' inner lives, and unlike in the 1960s, the female characters are absolutely central to the story. That offers the actors opportunities they'd be unlikely to get in other shows. As La'An, Chrissy Chong gets to use her background in dance in fights and sparring matches with the doctor; her difficult childhood helps inform her complex character; and she gets to tell stories of love and to wear princess dresses in episodes that let her flip her character on its head. She also examines heavy ethical questions we may want to ask ourselves. I can't think of many other shows that offer an actor all those things. Chong is a singer and songwriter, and recently wrote these lyrics:

> **"I get to choose 'I'**
> **This is *my* life."**

For a woman who rarely saw herself in the storytelling and is now the one given the close-ups, the screen time, and the storylines, the perspective she offers to the rest of us isn't gendered really at all. It's human.

OPPOSITE: La'An's romance with a young Kirk is shown from her point of view rather than his.

ABOVE: La'An is constantly struggling with her past and sets out to find the family of a girl who survived a Gorn attack.

Melissa Navia as
ERICA ORTEGAS

Star Trek has been waiting since the '60s for Erica Ortegas. José Ortega never made it out of Gene Rodden-berry's notes. By the time Trek's first pilot, "The Cage," was filmed, he had morphed into José Tyler, who was very blond and blue eyed. In fact, the entire cast was scrapped save Leonard Nimoy for the next—ulti-mately successful—pilot, leaving it for the best part of sixty years and the casting of Melissa Navia to give the character new life. Strange New Worlds's Erica Ortegas (yes, there's an s on the end, and yes, plenty of Latinos spell their name that way, says Melissa) has links to the past but drives us straight into the future.

Sixty years ago, it seemed inevitable that the *Enterprise's* pilot would be a man. In those days, the characteristics of a hotshot pilot seemed fundamentally male, and the person flying the ship was bound to be inspired by John Glenn or Neil Armstrong. *Discovery* had already put Emily Coutts's Detmer at the helm. *Strange New Worlds* would double down on that.

The breakdown for her character described a Latinx pilot, a soldier who could handle a gun and crack a joke, was capable and confident. Her exuberant "abso-frickin-lutely" while flying the ship demonstrates that she isn't caught up in her head like José, worrying about instruments and cal-culations, but piloting from passion. The character is free from any kind of stereotypes about performative femininity or limiting ideas about what it means to be a woman, and that's something that Melissa seems to share.

She grew up wanting to be just like her philosopher/writer father, even wearing jackets and ties when she was young. Rather than wonder at this, her father taught her how to tie her ties. In fact, Melissa told me that her entire family gave her the belief that there wasn't anything she couldn't accomplish in life, and that whoever she chose to be was who they would back. They may have been the only ones in her life not to put limitations on her dreams, but

their influence was so great, she was effectively inoculated against being placed in any kind of cultural box.

As a tomboy Colombian-American with short hair, Melissa never saw anyone like her onscreen, but that didn't stop her from dreaming. The roles she saw that made her want to act were "the male roles. Those," she says, "were the ones who were cool; those were the ones with the most lines, the most adventures. They didn't have to be perfect. They could be a number of things, like we are in real life." So she simply co-opted the roles that appealed to her, like the Ninja Turtles and Indiana Jones, and decided that these were the kinds of characters she would play.

When I asked her about the Hollywood box, I learned she had absolutely refused to get in one. She was always told she wasn't enough: not feminine enough, not butch enough, not Latina enough; but instead of being performative to fit expectations, she refused to compromise who she was. It made it difficult to get auditions, but the roles she got were consistently intelligent, nuanced, and interesting. She nar-rowed her options, ironically, by insisting on holding on to the different facets of her character.

When one man told her, "Fifty years ago you wouldn't have made it in this business because you aren't a blonde bombshell," she answered, "I would have made it fifty years

ago because I am me!" "And you know what he did?" she asked me in that intense but unbelieving tone I have seen in Ortegas when she's facing down the captain. "He laughed." He has since been removed from her life.

Ortegas offers Melissa the chance to bring a more evolved idea of what women can be to the screen. She loves that she was seen by the producers as who she was and that it was reflected in how they wrote for her. In terms of representation for women, this is a very different prism we are getting for a main character on *Star Trek*. She has hair that is short, shaved on the sides like we rarely see for women on screen, and like every other crew member, she is blessedly in a uniform with sensible boots. When the crew find themselves living out a fairy tale, she wears the stereotypically male-gendered clothes of a knight, Sir Adya.

She told me that the way she presents physically brought all kinds of assumptions with it from people in the business, and the audience as well. That's fine with her, as long as the person defining her or her character isn't doing it with judgment attached.

She told me that she gets overwhelming love from the audience, but a small percentage "assume certain things. If you use the assumption to attack women that don't fit a standard of femininity that works for you." Some of the comments are from people who assume that Ortegas must be gay. They are "so homophobic, so bigoted, so bizarre," she has to address it. She does it to support the little girls who may be outside the gender standard, as she was, but may not be as supported as she has been. Not everyone gets inoculated.

When I asked her if she had ever been told by anyone in the business that she had to be "fuckable" to get a job, her answer made me happy. She had been in a series called *Dietland*, playing a revolutionary who went after abusive men. She was watching it with her mother, and there was a scene where actresses are talking about having to be "F-able." Her mother turned to her, asking, "What's wrong with being affable?" It was the first time that she too had ever heard the phrase. Hopefully, it's a piece of excrement left in the social amber of the '90s.

Melissa has played soldiers and pilots more than once in her career, and even played an astronaut on the series *Billions*. At conventions, people in military service tell her that Ortegas is spot on, and those who have seen combat say, "I have fought alongside someone like her." The tiny percentage of trolls she has encountered included those who left comments on the internet before the show aired. After the promo of *Strange New Worlds* was released, people said, "That character looks like they checked off a box," "she has the acting ability of a piece of wood," and "Pike needs to put her in her place." This last was from a woman, who I insist on believing must have changed her viewpoint once she saw the show.

SHE FLIES THE SHIP

When I went over the first season to remind myself of her scenes, I was shocked that there really weren't that many. She is such a strong presence, I think I kept her in mind as living on the bridge even when the action didn't take place there. In many ways, she seems made for the part. There's no question that Ortegas has resonated with the audience in a way that few characters do.

In "Among the Lotus Eaters" in season two, the crew is hit with memory loss so severe, they forget who they are. At the top of the episode, Ortegas is excited about being a part of the landing party. She is feeling a little stuck just flying the ship, and wants more. She doesn't get to go, because of course, no one can fly the ship like she does. Later on, she is affected by the memory loss, and barely makes it to her quarters, forgetting her name, and even why she is on a starship in the first place. All she has is the computer's voice, who finally tells her who she is and what she does. "I am Erica Ortegas and I fly the ship!" She repeats it over and over, as she allows her instincts to take her to the station and do what she does best. We have been told that the loss wipes out everything in your brain, but cannot erase what you love, which will act like a beacon to guide you back to who you are. She finds that even when everything is taken from her, the thing she was finding tiresome was something she deeply loved, and allowed her to save not only herself but everyone else. A little Indiana Jones-ish, if you ask me.

The relationship between Pike and Ortegas is one of the most satisfying and truthful of the series. It is full of humor, as relationships are that are built on mutual admiration and trust. Their lives, and the lives of the rest of the crew, depend on the shorthand intimacy of two people with immense training and focus. The humor between them speaks to the lack of ego the captain has, and the joyful self-confidence Ortegas needs to do the impossible again and again. We understand the stakes by what she says, and understand that he uses challenge to motivate her. In "Memento Mori," he asks her to fly into a brown dwarf, to which she says, "Didn't our Science Officer just say that would crush our ship? Just asking, sir." When he tells her if anyone can do it, she can, that's exactly what she needs to take up the challenge. "Now you make it almost sound fun." In "The Serene Squall," Pike tells her to fire gently at the *Enterprise*, which has been taken over by pirates. She fires. He reminds her he said gently. "What does firing gently even mean?" Her humor happens in staff meetings, too. "No shields. No weapons. What are we supposed to do, throw luggage at them?"

Her humor never takes away from the drama of the moment, but heightens it. For someone to trust their actions and abilities under high stress, they need to stay out of their nervous system. The best way to do that is to stay in the part of your brain that strategizes, plays chess, and yes, makes jokes. Her focus is always on the job at hand, and the challenge in front of her is always made real by the look of resolve in her eyes. She adds that she understands why gender parity in representation is important, and that not everybody has the mindset "I can do whatever I want." She knows that "if I can see it, I can be it" is an important way for storytelling to widen the worlds of people in general.

It is interesting that I feel the need to break down the fact that she is a hotshot, wisecracking pilot. We have seen plenty of these in countless TV shows and movies. We just aren't used to a woman in the role. It's a good thing it's Melissa Navia playing her; I believe she will cut a wide swathe for other women to follow her, and fill these challenging, exciting roles with unique, unbridled humanity.

OPPOSITE: Ortegas and La'An are both soldiers who perform duties that were traditionally male, without anyone commenting.

Jess Bush as

NURSE CHAPEL

We've come a long way since 1966. Back then, Majel Barrett had to settle for the role of Nurse Chapel. Her part as the ship's first officer was axed, so she worked with her future husband, Gene Roddenberry, to craft a new character. Even though she was involved in creating the part, she was famously unhappy with its two-dimensionality and with Christine's "soppiness." The original Nurse Chapel spent a lot of time thinking about men: the fiancé who transfers his mind into a robot and creates a bombshell robot companion, and Spock, whose Vulcan characteristics are destined to make romance impossible. She was, mostly, on the receiving end of things, rarely took charge, and had virtually no agency. From what I saw, this was nothing like Majel, but it did play into all sorts of ideas people had about women.

Fast-forward to 2022, when *Star Trek: Strange New Worlds* introduced us to a new version of Christine Chapel, who is now played by Jess Bush. When I asked Jess if she could imagine playing a character like the original Christine, she said: "No, it wouldn't fly, thank God. The audience would reject it. I think we've evolved past that. It doesn't reflect people's experiences or desires."

Jess's Nurse Chapel has a mad sparkle in her eye. There's a rogue joy she seems to get from doing her job. She exclaims, "I'm gonna mess with your genomes!" when La'An, Captain Pike, and Spock need to have genetic enhancements that will allow them to go undercover on an alien planet. When La'An reduces the procedure to a hat trick by saying Chapel "makes disguises," Chapel pushes back and demands respect. Without any nastiness, Chapel lets her know that's a simplistic explanation of her work, and right away we know that this woman has healthy boundaries. She's brilliant and can take care of herself. That's a massive improvement. This Christine has an extra dash of passion for her job that offers a reminder that this is Starfleet at its finest.

Whereas the original version of Chapel often seemed worried and distressed, this new version has a sense of fun. When one of the aliens in their care suddenly makes a run for it out of panic, the doctor tells her, "You catch the rabbit." Thrilled for the hunt, she answers, "You always give me the fun job," and off she goes in a chase that seems to be an exciting challenge for her. When she corners the alien, she assures him, "It's not what you think!" But with a nanosecond's reflection, adds, "Well, maybe a little bit," before hypospraying him.

With her platinum hair and white jumpsuit, she seems like a futuristic mad scientist who loves her work, is compassionate, thinks science is the coolest, and loves her part in it. She can fight with the best of them. Like Dr. M'Benga, she resorts to injecting herself with a cocktail of drugs that turn her into a super soldier who is more than capable of taking out a group of Klingon warriors. Not something I can imagine the original Chapel doing.

When it comes to men, the new Chapel has taken a massive leap forward. The original Christine had taken a demotion to search for her fiancé and pined after Spock, who never

seemed to give her the time of day. Men aren't everything for this new version of the character. Away on leave, Ortegas wonders if she is going to have to play her usual part in freeing Chapel from another romantic entanglement. This time, Chapel disentangles herself from Lt. Dever, because, well, he's boring. She has agency and is the one who wants to avoid anything too serious or being tied down.

A woman on TV taking control of her sensual life and not treating everything as a matter of life or death is still

ABOVE: The modern version of Nurse Chapel is a supremely competent medic who is in the thick of the action.

OPPOSITE: Chapel and M'Benga are shown to be equals even though he is the senior officer.

unexpected. According to Jess, this is an area where there is still progress to be made. For most of human history, she says, female sensuality has been defined by men. One of the things she was taught as a young girl that she found limiting was that it wasn't safe to be sensual because it could only be part of some kind of power game with the opposite sex. Her understanding of her power got warped in the process. It was okay to commodify it, so that it could serve others, but it wasn't something for Jess herself to own. "Patriarchy's mission," she says, "is to separate women from their power by making them afraid of it."

In *Strange New Worlds*, her relationship with Spock is far more complicated and definitely not one-sided. When Spock has to convince Captain Angel that there is no tie between him and his fiancée T'Pring anymore, he passionately kisses

Nurse Chapel. It is one of those kisses that you experience in a visceral way; both seem to be aware of nothing and no one else. Even though it's done as a ploy, they are lost in the moment. And though they must deal with the realities of their lives after that kiss once they are out of danger, Chapel feels what she feels.

I went back to "Plato's Stepchildren" to see the only kiss between the original characters. In that episode, the aliens are controlling their bodies and forcing intimacy for their own pleasure. Chapel says, "I am so ashamed. Please make them stop," telling me that she knows she has no power here, but hopes the man does. Spock answers, as if he was failing her, "I haven't the power." He kisses her as if he is having a fit, to show how hard he is fighting what is happening. She tells him, "I wanted to get close to you; now all I want is to crawl away." Even with feelings for him, she must be ashamed in the moment. How different.

After the kiss, in SNW, Nurse Chapel respects Spock and his choices, even when they don't align with her feelings. She may be falling in love, but there is no pining. Her world doesn't begin or end with this man.

In "Charades," she shows she is an advocate for herself by applying to a fellowship for archeological medicine, which would involve her relocating to Vulcan and away from Spock. By now, we know she has strong feelings for him, but her response is to get on with her life.

In the episode, Chapel and Spock are in a shuttle accident that Spock only survives because some inter-dimensional beings "repair" him. The problem is that the aliens don't have the instructions and make him completely human. Chapel works tirelessly to find a way to bring the Vulcan side of him back. She is so focused on her work for

Spock that she is even late for her interview with a snippy Vulcan for the proposed new job. When she comes to the conclusion that they don't have the technology to return Spock to his natural form, she goes back to the anomaly to ask the inter-dimensional being to "fix" him as he was.

It's a wonderful moment for women in *Star Trek*. Chapel convinces her friends Ortegas and Uhura to help, and the three women go off on a dangerous mission together. Flying so close that they end up in inter-dimensional space themselves, Christine argues her case with the alien, an experience that turns out to be hilariously similar to getting caught on a call to your pharmacy, trying to talk to a human. In order to convince "Yellow" to help, she has to reveal that her feelings are more than friendship, something both her friends convince her is necessary. She says she misses him as he was, even though communicating with him as a human would connect them so much more. It's clear she is working hard because she can't imagine not putting this wrong to right. As the doctor says, "when Christine sets her mind to something, she is hard to stop."

This is a big step away from the messaging women have been given. In 1962, there was a song from the movie *Bye Bye Birdie* sung by the young ingenue:

> *"How lovely to be a woman*
> *And have a job to do*
> *To pick out a boy and change him*
> *And then when you are through*
> *You've made him the boy you want him to be*
> *Life's lovely when you're a woman—like me."*

The false idea given to women is that you can bend some-one to your will, without respecting their wants and needs at all. Scary for absolutely everyone. Was the song written by a man for a young woman purposely tongue in cheek? Probably. Did young women get that irony? I doubt it. I see this messaging being passed down, even now, in our culture. Go, Nurse Chapel, go.

Unlike the 1960s Christine, this one ends up kissing Spock for real. When they kiss this time, it's sexy as hell. Sexy, I think, because the kiss isn't for us, it's for the char-acters and they own the moment. It's true to the characters. As they break for a moment, Spock says, "What does this mean?" Nurse Chapel, owning her moment and her feel-ings, answers, "I don't know. Shut up," and they kiss again, falling out of frame.

NEW STORY

For the rest of the season, they are involved with one another. Chapel is no longer pining for Spock. If anything, she is the one who makes decisions about the course of their relationship. After Boimler visits from the future and tells her how important an emotionless Spock will be to history, she clearly develops doubts. She applies for another fellowship—this time with Roger Korby—and in the musical episode that follows, we learn that she is more than ready to take up the post she has worked so hard for, and that if that means leaving Spock, she won't fight it. This time it's Spock rather than Chapel who looks heart-broken and leaves the room. The story has been rewritten, and this time the woman has a much better role and a lot more control.

There's more to the story, too. It's clear to see the shifts that have happened not just *for* women, but also within them. Jess's experiences as an actress are a world away from the 1960s or even the '90s. She has had nothing but a positive experi-ence with every part of *Trek*. Talking to her, it sounds as if the production has really caught up with the values of inclusion and diversity for women that it preached for so long.

There is a preponderance of women throughout the cast, crew, and production team and writers, and they enthu-siastically support her dream to direct the show eventually. "The ethos of *Trek* is palpable on set," she says. "It permeates the crew. I also think that to work on *Trek* is a dream held by a lot of people in all avenues of the industry, and a cer-tain type of person, who holds the worldview and hopes of a Trekkie, is drawn to the job."

I asked her about "The Box," and if she had been given similarly constrained roles in her past because of it. She talked about an interesting phenomenon of productions trying to have a more politically correct approach to cast-ing, but it ends up being "pretty transparent and tokenistic." Descriptions of characters would be: "She's pretty, but she's smart too." Ah, that "but" does give it away.

She had a box when she was in her twenties, because she wore her hair short. "I inevitably got typecast as either gay or troubled." However, things are getting better now, according to Jess, with the parts she goes up for being more realistic and nuanced than they used to be.

I asked her if she had had the "you need to be fuckable" talk from anyone in the business. She looked genuinely shocked and said, "Absolutely not. It would cause a building fire. It's sickening. It's unheard of." Her response is healthy and comes from awareness of women speaking up and to each other.

Jess hopes Nurse Chapel is an opportunity for "young folks to embrace all complex aspects of their womanhood, and not feel they have to compromise, bend, or abandon their femininity, their womanhood, however it manifests, to obtain power and safety.". She, and *Strange New Worlds*'s Nurse Chapel, is a powerful example for all of us.

OPPOSITE TOP: Chapel now has a much more involved backstory, where she and M'Benga fought together in the Klingon War.

OPPOSITE BOTTOM: Chapel's relationship with Spock has been turned on its head. She is no longer simply pining after him and takes the lead.

JESS BUSH AS NURSE CHAPEL

CONCLUSION

Writing this book caused an earthquake in my life. Most of the interviews were filmed. I asked questions that I thought would help the women reveal how it had been for them. Rewatching them, many times I felt that the questions I chose and the words I used revealed me, too, in ways that weren't always consistent with who I thought I was. Doing this project forced me to take a hard look at myself.

When I started defrosting how the 1980s and '90s had formed me, I realized for the first time the degree to which I had been groomed and educated to shape-shift into someone the culture could be okay with. I saw how that took energy from my goals and dreams.

Instead, I focused on pleasing others, becoming one of the boys to laugh off a sexist joke, accepting that men had priority, and taking personal responsibility for, well, for just about everything. Once unfrozen, I couldn't unsee how much I had accepted that phrase "That's just the way it was/is."

As I started to loosen the cultural amber I was stuck in, the effort caused a large quake in my personal life that took some months to recover from. Newly vigilant and unwilling to compromise another minute, I became impossible to be around. Two male friends goading each other to be brave and not act like "pussies" caused me to immediately throw down the gauntlet. In the past, it would make me uncomfortable to hear a woman's body part being associated with weakness, but I wouldn't have thought my discomfort mattered as much as making sure the men weren't offended by my laying down a boundary.

My newfound zeal caused me to be relentless. At one point, no one in my personal circle was talking to me. Eventually, I learned how to take up space in my new world without pushing everyone out of it. But I am unquestionably different now.

I am starting to recognize biased language and behavior, and that understanding informs how I choose to respond to it. I have given myself license to emanate from the inside out, instead of the other way around. I realize where in my body a stray sexist comment lands, and I no longer accommodate it. I paid attention to old, deep thoughts of other women being threats, and burned them out. In their place, I see potential connection, collaboration, and support for every woman in my life. And that is the most satisfying joy.

The women I talked to for the book turned various lights on in different parts of my consciousness, and it has stuck with me. When I asked Jess Bush if anyone in the business told her she needed to be "fuckable" to get a job, she told me that if they had, there would have been buildings burned. Back in the 1960s, Grace Lee Whitney felt she had ruined her career because she refused to sleep with "the Executive." Her fault, her poor choice, her responsibility—in her mind.

Today's leading ladies of *Star Trek* have a different perspective on what they are required to be silent about, and their voices are part of what is responsible for a huge improvement for both the female characters of *Trek* and a steady improvement of the treatment for the women who played them.

What if Whitney could have understood that it was not a weakness to want the ability to say no? I imagine her approaching this new way of thinking with intellectual curiosity. "That's just the way it was" isn't a lazy choice; it's having no other options you can fathom.

This is all very serious talk for a book about *Star Trek*. But after hearing from a multitude of audience members of how it shifted and guided their lives, it's hard for me not to be serious. There will be those who argue it's just a TV show. Does all media and art have to be instructional? Can't it just entertain? As Gene Roddenberry proved, it can do both.

And, it turns out, being asked to think about issues while we are being entertained is very engaging. There are too few things in our lives that ask us to just reflect. Not shoot out a bullet of opinion, but just think about something.

Star Trek has spanned decades and shows a significant change for how women interact with the world. But it's important to remember that what has been achieved can very quickly be taken away, and that all the accomplishments can be buried. Thoughtful television can go a long way to building a community that won't allow history to repeat itself.

I wasn't aware that women had been huge players in the early days of Hollywood. In the era of silent films, the industry was a wilder medium and mostly written and produced by women. The men were away fighting World War I, and women wrote stories that centered on women's lives and concerns. As soon as the technology for sound was developed (by a woman, by the way), banks started investing, and prioritized the men. There were fewer women creators and fewer women telling women's stories onscreen.

The Women Film Pioneers Project by Jane Gaines and Radha Vatsal list the jobs women filled in Hollywood in 1923: They did everything you can think of, from plastering to editing, writing, and distributing. But as Hollywood was organized into a hierarchical corporate system, women started to be shut out. Quoting a *Photoplay* article from the time: "Women were not team players and not organized to maximize profit." Some women directors and writers managed to continue to work, but the free-range ability to create and produce was taken away.

Some people fear change. We have become so used to stories being told from the male perspective that a more balanced representation can feel disorienting. The way I see it, we are all actors who were given scripts by a culture that herded us into stereotypical silos. As women start to be able to play to their strengths in the community, so will men. Using everyone's talents and points of view will lead to stories that are more truthful to our world and our interests. We all suffer with the stamp of stereotypes.

The systems that aren't accountable for the human lives within it are remnants of the patriarchy, no matter what gender is in charge. You can run away from a system, fight it, or work within it. How, I had to ask myself, do you work within it and still maintain your own integrity? I think of all the words I heard used and argued about during the making of this book; the most useful one is Mike McMahan's: "Question." If we question ourselves—if we can honor the systems we are a part of by continually questioning them and updating the terms of our agreements with them—we can maybe find a way to keep the amber of the times we find ourselves in now from hardening around us.

I recently listened to author Reshma Saujani speak to a group of young women about how imposter syndrome was seen at first to apply only to women who were striving for high-profile jobs. I had to look this up to confirm it was true. Although today it is viewed as a syndrome that affects both men and women, Saujani said that it was initially used by men in power to distract women from their goals and to plant seeds of doubt. It made me rethink what I advised Jess Bush when she told me she wanted to direct. At the time, we had both affirmed that it was important for her not to fail, which could possibly stop other women being given the opportunity. I suggested she get in touch with Roxann Dawson, and also to prepare vigilantly before she took her shot. Now, my advice would be different. I would tell her still to connect with Roxann, still prepare, but not to strive to be perfect. What a straitjacket that is; it robs anyone of creativity and focus.

From everything I have learned about Alex Kurtzman and the people he has placed in production, I believe they will see it as part of their responsibility to give women the same chance to learn that men have had. I am hoping and betting the double competency Roxann had to have in order to learn the craft of directing won't be the same for the young women of today. Is there a worry that women who are less than serious about directing will grab the chance when it's offered and waste it? Maybe. But I saw that happen with some men who wanted to direct, back in the day. They were given the chance, and no one locked the doors on the next man in line who wanted a shot.

But going back to the beginning, it was a man who opened this impactful door we are talking about. I won't forget that. "If you see it, you can be it," Melissa Navia told me, and seeing what Gene Roddenberry imagined for women changed many people's life trajectories. Roddenberry embodied the changing mores of the 1960s. He questioned racism and sexism and softened the shock of the new by placing it safely in a far-off future.

Nichelle Nichols's Uhura was a cultural paradigm shift for women and people of color. The women from *The Next Generation*, *Deep Space Nine*, *Voyager*, and *Enterprise* encouraged women to imagine STEAM as a possible future, take leadership roles, and accept the full spectrum of their emotions and their strengths. Asian women found representation in Hoshi Sato and Keiko O'Brien, and the LGBTQIA+ community found it in the metaphors of Dax and Seven of Nine.

When we come to the "new" shows, the women and the social issues expand. First, the sheer number of shows allowed for more representation for women, people with all kinds of body types, and LGBTQIA+ actors. Whereas in the 1990s, queer subject matter had to be coded with metaphors, the present shows remove the veil. As Brannon Braga told me, the goal is to simply show change as a normal progression. I think these shows do just that: humans of infinite variety exploring space and relationships, as well as themselves.

When I asked those associated with *Discovery*, *Lower Decks*, and *Strange New Worlds* how they would categorize their workplace community, they answered work family, found family, or simply, family. There seems to be true accountability to the stories they tell. This, along with always questioning ourselves and the world around us, is the messaging the current *Star Trek* gives us. In almost sixty years, the faces of a few distinct women of *Star Trek* has turned into a small sea of diverse, individual, and complex women who live, grow, and wonder at the Galaxy, right alongside the men. Instead of effort and energy being taken up by appealing to the culturally approved version of a woman, they can put all of it toward achievement and risk-taking in their lives. When and if they choose to.

The trajectory of women in *Star Trek* hasn't always been a steady climb, but each generation's gains have been steadily built on by the next. Jad Abumrad gave a commencement speech at Caltech that spoke of the journey of the monarch butterfly. The migration starts in Vancouver, Canada, and ends in Michoacán, Mexico, almost 3,000 miles away. What scientists learned only recently is that the trip takes three to four generations of butterflies to reach the destination each way, not one as was previously assumed. If I anthropomorphize the first generation of butterflies, probably landing and ending the journey somewhere not yet Mexico, I can imagine the feeling of failure for not reaching a goal. But the fact is, each generation doing their specific leg of the journey is not only essential, but also is the only thing that guarantees the success of the butterflies that ultimately do arrive at their destination. We—all of the women of *Star Trek*—we have all been essential to the journey.

Writing this book was a journey. One I said yes to. There would be infinite variations to the conclusions that all the diverse women who could have written this would come to. What I've learned, by talking to writers, politicians, astronauts, actors, an army chaplain, authors Jess Zimmerman and Jessica Nordell, and all the rest, has focused my understanding of myself and the world around me. I understand my place among all these women much more fully, and I feel a deep connection to them.

I understand where so many women came from and how, for some, it was an almost impossible journey. I have deep respect. I was once caught in the cultural amber of the 1990s, thinking other women were my competition and their win was my loss. What an effective tool that was, from a culture that found benefit in separating women and discouraging communication between them. What an effective distraction from what our actual contribution of support could be for each other. Today, I am ready for more engagement, more learning, more opportunity. Open a channel. I can't wait to hear who speaks next.

INSPIRED AND INSPIRATIONAL

This might be the most important chapter in the book. While I was writing, I met countless women who were inspired by Star Trek—*these are people who make a real difference to the world. Some of them, like astronaut Samantha Cristoforetti or Stacey Abrams, are famous, but most of them aren't. They told me stories about how the women of* Trek *showed them what was possible and how they've taken that and used it in the real world. I wish I could include them all: Their stories are important and mean a lot to me. What follows is a small selection.*

Major Mel Baars O'Malley
ARMY CHAPLAIN

I was at a convention when a woman in an Army uniform approached me to thank me for helping her in her life. I was so struck by this person that I impulsively asked if I could take a picture of her. When I couldn't stop thinking about her and what she had told me, I knew I wanted to interview her. I did

what I have never done: I went on social media and asked if anyone knew who this young soldier was. I felt connected with her that day. It took two months and lots of paperwork for the Army to approve my interview request, but I truthfully would have waited even longer for her eloquent thoughts on her experience with the women of *Star Trek*.

Major Mel Baars O'Malley is a chaplain for the US Army. In an ever-shifting world, she has found grounding for three decades with two mentors—the character of Beverly Crusher and the woman who played her, Gates McFadden. When O'Malley was ten, she had a routine she and her parents followed every night. Home from gymnastics practice at 8:45, dinner and TNG at 9 p.m. Her parents gave her the feeling that she could do anything, but Crusher gave her the blueprint for what it would take.

She didn't have a woman in her life like Beverly Crusher, who had courage and an endless supply of solutions to try to resolve every problem. Beverly was confident, strong, and although of course she had fears, she never let them stop her. O'Malley saw the character as a mentor, and made up stories in which she was the doctor's daughter named Tiffany Lydia Crusher. To this day, childhood friends still call her that. She got deep comfort from *Star Trek*. In the difficult teenage years, Beverly and *Star Trek* were a world of hope, where people existed who had each other's backs in the workplace, working for ideals bigger than any one person alone. "I was drawn to the idea that the Galaxy…can be scary and unknown, but on the other side of those encounters is great possibility, especially when you walk into this with people you trust, people you can count on."

While she was studying at Duke University, 9/11 compelled the young theological student to serve, and the ROTC made college financially possible. She had heard that the military and the clergy were two places where women were underrepresented, and her reaction was a quick "Are you kidding?" followed by a very Crusher-like "Here we go." Although 50 percent of the Duke theological students were women, she found a very different reality when she started officer training. She felt the sting of rejection with the endless questions and comments about her becoming a chaplain. There are chaplains from all denominations in the Army; they exist "to make sure soldiers are able to exercise their freedom of religion." Some of the denominations didn't allow women to serve as chaplains, and often she would be the only woman in a room or a situation. But O'Malley said they have always found a way to work together. As was true in DS9's disparate population, diversity in a fixed environment has to lead to cooperation if anything is to be accomplished. Collectively, the chaplains think of the sick and hurting soldiers who count on them, and find a way to overcome any adversity so that they are drawn back into the work.

While she served in Afghanistan, her childhood friend sent her a Beverly Crusher action figure and reminded the young soldier to never forget the three things she got from *Star Trek*: hope, courage, and the fact that you are never alone. At twenty-eight, she was aware of the optics of a woman arriving in a Black Hawk helicopter and leading prayer in this country. She would actively and creatively use hope and courage in this hostile environment.

First, she gave her soldiers hope. She worked with a battalion of interrogators in one of the largest detention centers in the country. These young airmen and soldiers, some as young as nineteen, were tasked with getting intel to protect soldiers on the battlefield. Much of what the detainees told them was dark and disturbing. To counteract the bias and darkness, Major O'Malley developed Operation Pencil, in

which she would take interrogators out to nearby villages and hospitals to distribute school supplies, blankets, and warm clothing to Afghan children. This was often the only exposure they had to the people here, other than the detainees. These children were undersized and skinny, with white hair owing to malnutrition, but they were still children, full of hope and energy as the soldiers engaged them in soccer and other activities. The chaplain was busy planting seeds for the future, hoping that these children could see another side to the military, while the soldiers glimpsed an innocent and recognizable humanity. The chaplain told me that she hoped the soldiers could "hold that tension" between the two very different experiences of the country.

When the elders of the village wanted to thank her for her outreach with a formal ceremony, she needed to remind herself to use the courage of Crusher. She said she hadn't felt alone when she had spent some years in Africa, even in dangerous situations. The society there was run by women, and she always felt surrounded and supported by them. In Afghanistan, it was completely different, and her being a woman was a constant issue. She thought of handing the ceremonial moment over to one of the male officers. But then her mind flashed back to the five-year-old she had been playing with earlier in the day, and thought of the impact it would have for the little girl to see a woman accept the thanks from the male elders of the village. The chaplain realized her worthiness to be there in that capacity and received the thanks. Like many of the women in *Star Trek* who find themselves with the opportunity to be a role model, she found personal courage by thinking of the impact her action might have on someone else.

Chaplain O'Malley points to General Milley when she talks about the *Star Trek* messaging that we are never alone. He has said that "we rise and we fall on the content of our character and the way we come together to get the job done." *Star Trek* makes the general's words visceral; courage and collaboration during crises are some of the series' most emotionally moving sequences.

Now, O'Malley is forty years old, at one of the highest levels of chaplaincy, and working in the Sexual Harassment/Assault Response and Prevention (SHARP) program. She recently had to take the Army's new PT test for the first time. Even though she has been an athlete, at forty with two C-sections behind her and two little children to care for, she felt a legitimate worry about passing the test. With a medicine ball she had to throw four and a half meters, she said, "Do it for Beverly." She passed the test, using the thought of Beverly to get out of her head and allow her body to do what it was still capable of.

At this point in her life and career, she mentors other chaplains in how to be on a battlefield, and how to live through a single day when you could lose 10,000 or more souls. It is sobering work, and she says *Star Trek* helps to balance it. But it isn't just on the battlefield where she does emotionally taxing work. After talking to me, she was meeting with a young soldier who was a survivor of sexual trauma in the military who was contemplating suicide. In fact, she is earning a PhD on that subject. Which is where our interaction at the convention comes in.

What she calls "this special world" of *Star Trek* includes the women who played the shows' characters, and she finds strength and inspiration from them, too. Chaplain O'Malley listens to Gates's podcast *Gates Investigates,* and I had told the story of my kidnapping and rape over two episodes. It interested me that she transferred her admiration of Crusher to Gates McFadden, and I asked her about it. She said that although she would never confuse the actor's life with the character's, she can see infused in Crusher parts of the woman who played her. This led her to feel that McFadden was a mentor for this new chapter of her life. Now that Major O'Malley is the age that Crusher was at the start of TNG, she needs an older woman for guidance once again. What she sees in McFadden is someone still curious and still engaged. Because many of her real-life mentors are retiring, she wants an insight into what the next thirty years could look like.

Life in the military is very transient. It's one of the difficulties for the chaplain: She will see a soldier at one of the most desperate points of their lives, and usually never again. But she can watch a *Star Trek* episode or listen to the podcast and find the answers for the shaky ground she sometimes finds herself on while balancing a life, career, and children. She is not alone. Having a woman who has lived more life than you simply saying that life can be hard at times can normalize it. She has survived, and so can you.

The chaplain had been working on her PhD when she heard my episodes of the podcast, and she was given a living example of what she was reading in Judith Herman's book *Trauma and Recovery*. She read a quote to me: "The trauma story is part of the survivor's legacy. Only when it is fully integrated can the survivor pass it on in confidence that it will prove a source of strength and inspiration rather than a blight on the next generation." She had told me that my story had given her hope that the soldiers who had been in so much pain when she counseled them could go on to recover and find some peace. She spoke about it to a guide of hers, and they suggested she apply that hope to herself. She realizes that she has endured trauma and that it has been significant.

She said that by hearing about my recovery, she realized healing is possible for her, too. By acknowledging the trauma and working through it and not around it, she can choose to pass the strength on to the next generation, specifically her children, and not the blight. Chaplain O'Malley thanked me for the invitation to reflect on the journey she has taken in her life, and *Star Trek*'s large role in it. I cannot imagine how many soldiers she has helped with the guiding principles of hope, courage, and the reassurance that they are not alone.

Kyna

Kyna is a survivor of human trafficking who lives in Toronto. She was raised by an abusive grandmother and a drug-addicted father, so her life started badly and from high school got steadily worse. The one good memory she has of her father was when they watched *Star Trek* together when she was very little, and she has hung on to the hope that the show modeled throughout the incredibly challenging life she has led. Seeing the compassion and interest the actors exhibit on social media toward the fan base makes her hopeful for humanity as well. "Maybe this *Star Trek* stuff is achievable," she thinks, if there are that many kind people attached to it. Taking the steps to heal, she talks to her therapist about "What would Guinan do?" when they discuss response as opposed to reaction, and says, "Being nurturing doesn't mean you can't do your own goddamn thing! That's what those particular characters [Janeway and Kira] embody for me."

Dr. Lucila Rosines
GENERAL AND PEDIATRIC RADIOLOGIST

Dr. Lucila Rosines, a child of immigrants from the Dominican Republic, is a second-generation American. Her love of science was fostered by public television, by *Star Trek*, and in particular, by B'Elanna Torres. Having grown up watching *Bill Nye the Science Guy*, she was fascinated by the experiments on the show. When *The X-Files* premiered in 1993, the young Dr. Rosines was intoxicated by seeing Agent Dana Scully use science to explain the unexplained. When *Star Trek: Voyager* premiered in 1995, she had yet another female role model to look up to: fellow Latina engineer Lt. B'Elanna Torres.

"When *Voyager* premiered, I was thirteen years old," Lucila says. "I had never seen a Latina with a professional career on TV before B'Elanna. When she was promoted to chief engineer it was extremely inspiring. I saw myself every time I saw B'Elanna on TV, and every time I heard them call her name, I felt such a kinship with that character—telling myself, 'She is me and I am her.'"

Lucila received her bachelor of arts in biological sciences from Barnard College at Columbia University and her medical degree from Columbia University Vagelos College of Physicians and Surgeons. The idea that we could use sound waves, electrons, and hydrogen atoms to create

images of the inside of your body was simply amazing. She went on to specialize in the field of radiology and decided to further specialize in pediatric imaging, doing a fellowship at Texas Children's Hospital. Dr. Rosines currently works as a general and pediatric radiologist for Kelsey-Seybold Clinics in Houston.

Stephanie Perry
BSN, RN

"I'll be honest: My initial reason for wanting to be a nurse was because I'd watch *M*A*S*H* reruns with my dad, and thought I'd get to live in a tent. But *Star Trek* was what really made me start to think that I could be more than what was around me.

"I spent most of my childhood in Idaho Falls, Idaho, a 'metropolis' of about 45,000 surrounded by tiny potato farming communities. I thought I lived in a big city, and because I didn't live on a potato farm, I thought I was sophisticated. But I also knew, even in the mid-1990s, that the only real options for my life were to be a teacher, a secretary, or a nurse before I became a stay-at-home mom.

"*Star Trek* is what really made me start to think that there was something else. Because when almost everyone around you has the same skin color, religion, and ancestry as you, it can be hard to realize that there is anything else. But Beverly Crusher was a brilliant doctor, dancer, investigator, *and* a mother. Deanna Troi was a traveler, explorer, diplomat, *and* feminine.

"Ro Laren was a brave woman who stood up to oppressors *and* honored her heritage.

"Keiko O'Brien was a scientist and teacher with her own life and career *before* she ever got married. And nobody ever whispered how sad it was that she was still single, and was she even dating? And then there's Lwaxana Troi, who was loud, brazen, and beautiful, and stood up for herself and others in ways my shy little self still can't emulate.

"The women of *Star Trek* weren't there to just carry out the orders of men, like they were on *M*A*S*H*. They were complete, well-rounded people with friends, careers, and interests that were all their own. Exploring and science weren't things to do *until*, or even *or*. They were things that could be done *and*.

"I in no way want to be disparaging of women who *do* want life at home with their kids. But if everyone is the same, and stepping out of bounds or being different is looked down upon, then your society has become more like the Romulans or Cardassians than the Federation.

"I *did* become a nurse. And I have traveled and explored and advocated and rallied and learned more than that unsophisticated little girl ever imagined. I have never lived in a tent, but there's still time."

Natasha Nyaberi
PHARMACIST

"I was born, raised, and still currently live in Nairobi, Kenya. Despite growing up in a predominantly Black country, a majority of TV programs on air when I was younger were Eurocentric. So, when I watched my first episode of *Star Trek* as a preteen, and saw a Black woman in a major recurring role, I was so elated! I quickly became obsessed with the show, especially when I learned Uhura's other name was Nyota, which is the Swahili word for 'star.' I felt a kinship with her, and so I scrambled to get all the episodes I could, building a fondness of the rest of the crew as time went on. My curiosity was awakened, and I was keen on learning everything I could on various STEM-y topics mentioned or shown in the series. A scientist was born!

"I found myself really taken by McCoy's work. I often would fantasize about what post I'd hold if I was part of the crew, and the one I felt I'd be great at was his. He had the tricorder, all these other gadgets and potions, and I was so intrigued! Perhaps this was compounded by comparing the *Enterprise* to the state of health care in my developing country. But I knew that I wanted to be just like McCoy, doing my best to save lives, and began to dream of the ways tech can revolutionize health care. Now, I'm a freshly licensed pharmacist, and I truly believe I would not be where I am today if I hadn't stumbled upon Uhura, McCoy, and the rest of the crew aboard the *Enterprise*."

Kara Shemeth
CAPTAIN—EDGARTOWN FIRE DEPARTMENT

"A combination of family history and a sense of duty, cultivated by my love of Starfleet, led me to become an EMT and firefighter. I found myself drawn to service and considered the armed forces but decided being a firefighter/EMT was a better route for me after serving in AmeriCorps as a wildland firefighter in Colorado.

"I am now a captain and have found that my leadership style has been greatly influenced by the ideals and captains of *Star Trek*. I give my crew the tools they need to be successful and aim to make sure they have the experiences they need to become better firefighters and EMTs. I talk with them, not at them, and involve them in planning and execution of our duties. That being said, my life experiences have left me with the tools I need to make the difficult decisions. Part of that is upbringing and belief in our overall mission, and part of it is the influence of the leadership and humanity that characterized so many of the *Trek* captains and officers.

"Starfleet isn't foremost on my mind every shift I'm on, but I wear a Starfleet medical badge on my radio strap, and I find myself wondering, 'What would Janeway do?' more than a few times a year. Characters like Dax, Kira, and Janeway gave an awkward teen a blueprint to follow on her way to becoming a confident, compassionate leader. For that, I am eternally grateful."

Dr. Charlotte Thorley
PUBLIC ENGAGEMENT AND INCLUSION CONSULTANT

"There's no way of limiting my influences to just one woman of *Star Trek*. I love all of the series. But the one that holds my heart is *Deep Space Nine*. As a teenager, I wanted so desperately to be Jadzia, so full of wisdom and science, as happy with her female friends as with her Klingon buddies. It's no surprise then that I studied astrophysics at university, one of very few women in a field full of guys, and took pride in holding my own. Nerys was there, too, being such a leader and so strong—not traditionally feminine most of the time but still so womanly. I wanted all of that.

"Rewatching the series last year, I realized that so much more of who I am is informed by these stories. I'm a cisgender queer woman, pansexual, and I have a trans wife. Our journey has been beautiful and difficult, and we are so much stronger for it. I came to realize that teenage me didn't want to just be like Jadzia; I wanted to be with her, with all her identities. The episode "Rejoined" explored her past marriage with a woman when the Dax symbiont was hosted by Torias, and this was a crucial part of my own identity exploration.

"Seeing Nerys struggle with balancing her career, religion, the needs of her people, the government, and the needs of the Federation all with trying to be her own self really sits within me. As a working-class woman who regularly fights for the rights of vulnerable groups in meeting after meeting with stuffy men in suits, I try to channel my inner Major Kira, knowing it's OK to need softness and care after the fight.

"Nearly thirty years on, I'm still learning lessons from these wonderful characters and the women who brought them to life. And the lessons have been more far-reaching than I could have imagined. Thank you!"

Michelle Thaller
ASSISTANT DIRECTOR FOR SCIENCE COMMUNICATION AT NASA'S GODDARD SPACE FLIGHT CENTER

"As much as I love those Captain Kirk, Captain Picard figures, that's not the only way to be a leader; it's not the only way to be an effective leader. And those models were taken from men, and usually men that had really big support structures behind them, and they were raised thinking that they really belonged in this culture."

I spoke to Michelle Thaller the day after the *Perseverance* rover landed on Mars. As the assistant director for Science Communication at the Goddard Space Flight Center, she was still talking about the adrenaline of seeing ten years of work successfully realized.

As a child, she was drawn to the stars in her backyard and still brings joy and wonder into what she does and how she talks about it. She studied astrophysics at Harvard.

Michelle spoke of a leadership program taught at NASA that caused a sea change in the way she viewed gender and diversity. It was where she realized her tough, type-A exterior was not her true identity, but a tool she had used to get by in a male-oriented workplace. Some people participating in the program had high emotional intelligence, some were innovative, some introverted, and none of it seemed quantified by gender. The Darwinistic idea that survival depends on the most aggressive proved to be less effective in the program than different people bringing their personal strengths to a group that adapts together. As Michelle said, one alpha male bringing home the meat falls apart as a workable concept when you think the job at hand is going to the Moon or moving billions of people to different continents to save them from the ravages of climate change.

She watches *Star Trek* avidly, and was thrilled to see the changes that *Discovery* brought. There were tears in her eyes when she saw the opening shot of two women, Michelle Yeoh and Sonequa Martin-Green. To her, the fact that the show also had neurodiversity and LGBTQIA+ characters meant that *Trek* continues to help the culture to evolve. She loved seeing Mae Jemison appear on *The Next Generation* and said that it's a dream for a lot of people at NASA to be on *Star Trek*. The idea of the dry scientist evaporated for me when I realized how fluidly Michelle moves through wondering if being a Borg could be an ecstatic state or what would be found in the actual rock samples returned from Mars. The show also fuels hope—Michelle said that if one is devoting ten years to getting a craft to land on Mars, feeding your brain with dystopic viewpoints is counterproductive. The creativity provided by *Trek* seems to be part and parcel of the flexibility and adaptability she sees necessary to take us forward.

Dr. Erin Macdonald
STAR TREK SCIENCE ADVISOR

Erin Macdonald adds the "A" in "STEAM." Science, technology, engineering, the creative arts, and mathematics are all things she is completely fluent in. An astrophysicist, aerospace engineer, and consultant on all the *Star Trek* shows since 2019, she isn't what usually comes to mind when you think of a scholar and scientist. With an accessible personality and many, many tattoos, Erin can explain wormholes in a way that neither overcomplicates the subject nor talks down to her audience.

She is a bona fide fan who appreciates how *Star Trek* has changed the culture for women in an immediate way. Her PhD dissertation spoke of the influence "the Janeway effect" had on her becoming a scientist, but her love for the franchise started with the first iteration. She watched because she loved exploration, science fiction, good storytelling, and Mr. Spock. Fantasy and sex were definite contributing factors to her sticking with *Trek* initially. She sees them as

totally legitimate entry points for a story, which makes me think Nichelle's miniskirts may have similarly hooked young men who grew up to be important scientists as well.

Erin was twenty-five when she got her PhD and was the youngest person and only woman among older White men who expected a flirty, obsequious girl. When she didn't deliver that, she was viewed as a "bitch with an attitude" and would get marginalized. If she flirted, then the optics changed to the idea that she must have slept her way into their midst. When she got accepted into grad school, the reaction from her fellow students was that the school must've simply been meeting their quota. Erin describes creating a delicate balance between navigating toward your goals in a man's world, without compromising personal integrity, as an art form. For someone who is naturally flirty, expressive, and passionate, this meant knowing when to put up barriers and how to enter a room with "an overabundance of confidence" and to contextualize accusations of promiscuity or of being a quota filler. This is a lot more work for someone to do who got to where she is on merit alone, just like the men did.

Erin is a mainstay at conventions and does panels as a science communicator, where she was discovered by the *Star Trek* creators. "It's all been actually women who have at least been my entrée into *Star Trek*." When Michelle Paradise took over as *Discovery*'s showrunner, writers Bo Yeon Kim and Erika Lippoldt suggested she hire Erin. For someone who understands that storytelling is the perfect magic carpet to lead people to science, being the advisor on the show *Star Trek: Prodigy* excites her tremendously. By being designed for kids, the show is able to not only inspire but also teach them "who they can be, [how to] overcome obstacles, how to build networks, how to be friends, and how to discover new worlds and new civilizations, but through the eyes of children—like, literally." The franchise can not only "inspire people to become scientists and engineers and STEM professionals," but it also "inspires science itself, because those people get physics degrees because they want to build a transporter. And then they go down a rabbit hole of learning about science." Without question, this moves the cultural needle for everyone.

OPEN A CHANNEL: THE WOMEN OF *STAR TREK*

Stacey Abrams

I truly don't know where to start when talking about this incredibly impressive woman. Stacey Abrams told me that one of the most important aspects of Michael Burnham's character was that even when she wasn't the captain, she was still central to the story. "She may not be in charge, but she is the one who is responsible," and she is a lesson on how to have power when power isn't based on position, but behavior.

Abrams may as well have been describing herself. She has been nominated for a Nobel Peace Prize and an Emmy Award. A Yale University graduate, she was the first Black woman majority-party gubernatorial nominee, and the first Black woman to deliver a response to the State of the Union address. How to have power when power isn't based on position, indeed. She was House minority leader for the Georgia House of Representatives, has written thirteen books, and has co-founded several companies. Womenshistory.org sums it up by saying Abrams is "one of the most prominent African American female politicians in America." And, by the way, she's also a *Star Trek* fan.

Abrams says what she loves in *Star Trek* is that it reinforced what her parents demonstrated to their children: core sets of values that were "challenged but never broken." *Star Trek: The Next Generation* was appointment television for Stacey and her sister Andrea. When they persuaded their parents to join them one Monday, the girls discovered their parents were already *Trek* fans. Nichelle Nichols was a legend to them.

I asked Abrams to run through what struck her as important concerning the women of *Star Trek*. Starting with TNG, one episode stood out for her: Troi asks Crusher why she put herself through the rigors of becoming a bridge officer when she was already a doctor, and Crusher answers that, since she is on the spaceship, why shouldn't she be able to fly it? To Abrams, it showed that the doctor thought she "deserved to have sustained access and to be considered capable. Without ever talking about the gender expectations. Clearly, she says, 'Why wouldn't I?'"

I teased her that she is on the record for not having watched DS9 much, and she said she hated how that got characterized. I acknowledged that our show was more political, and asked if we hadn't gotten it right. "You got the politics great! That was the problem! It's what I did during the day, and DS9 didn't provide an escape from it. I love the show," she said, but it was the "most emotionally draining." I second that.

Janeway was an "exemplar of what could be." She said it was very significant that this was the first captain to be cut off from the Federation. "It's one thing to be a leader when you know you are going to be held accountable by a tribunal of your peers when you do wrong. Janeway is accountable only to who she thought she had to be. She didn't have to do the thing right, she just had to get the thing done, and watching her make that [ethically right] choice was always inspiration to me." For a woman navigating leadership and power, doing the right thing, not the convenient thing—even when no one is watching—is a concept Abrams holds dear.

Even though Seven was probably the most objectified of the *Star Trek* women, she was also "one of the most fully realized because of confronting her humanity and building her sense of self." Because of the excellence of the writing and acting of this character, this "strong, brilliant person defied objectification. Those who dismiss her are missing the point."

Abrams felt that the character of B'Elanna really came into her own when they emphasized what it was like to be a conflicted personality. "For so many people, especially people of color," the question becomes "How do you fit into a society that dismisses you because of what they see?" The way B'Elanna's story arced was valuable, she says, because "they let her learn not to be less of who she was, but to be better at who she was." That is now inked in my heart as the best description I have ever heard of how to grow oneself.

Abrams told me that *Star Trek* has staying power because it deals in universal subjects, and at its core has always "recognized, centered, and situated women in positions of power and opportunity, but never negated their responsibility or their capacity for leadership, for mistakes, and for challenges. Their competency was never gendered. That's what's so enduring."

ESA/NASA

OPEN A CHANNEL: THE WOMEN OF *STAR TREK*

Samantha Cristoforetti

There is an image that could define the word "meta." A young woman smiles at the camera, wearing a Starfleet uniform. But she isn't at a convention—she's in space. She is astronaut Samantha Cristoforetti, engineer, fighter pilot, fluent in nine languages, and most recently, commander of the *International Space Station* (*ISS*). When she was a girl, the original *Star Trek* led to her imagining going boldly and exploring space. When she was a teenager, the women of *Deep Space Nine* and *Voyager* served as her virtual mentors. She told me months before another stint on the *ISS* that "I'm not sure that I would be on this path had it not been for *Star Trek*."

Cristoforetti grew up in a small village in the Italian Alps. She was a child who didn't quite fit in: There weren't other kids in her village reading physics books and dreaming of space travel. Access to *Star Trek* was extremely limited, and she dreamed of coming to the United States, where there were opportunities like Space Camp and seemingly free-flowing episodes of *Star Trek*. When given the opportunity to become an exchange student in the United States at seventeen, "it was like this land of abundance in terms of being a *Star Trek* fan." It didn't matter so much to her that the women in the original episodes weren't the principal ones having the adventures. The show was enough to connect her to the idea that there must be others who loved the mystery of space as much as she did. She only saw episodes of *The Next Generation* sporadically, but she identified with the character of Data as an outsider. In the United States, she was able to watch *Deep Space Nine* and *Voyager*.

DS9 strikes Cristoforetti as the show that speaks to what the world still needs today. Acknowledging that "perfectly noble, nice people can still have conflicting views" encourages the idea of compromise. It occurs to me that being an astronaut on the *ISS* is a social experiment of sorts. I have stood in the mock-up station in Germany. Conflict of any sort would have all sorts of bad outcomes in that hugely limited area.

The character of Dax was her avatar. "She was so mysterious and had so much depth and so much wisdom," and wasn't binary because her symbiont had lived lives as a man. There wasn't a cultural box to put a character like this in, so anyone who felt like an outsider could find representation in her.

Cristoforetti loves the fact that every *Star Trek* iteration has had a character who struggles with identity and belonging: Spock, Data, Dax, and Seven. When I asked how she felt about Seven's costume, she ascribed it to just the way TV was at the time, and not all that important to her. But the arc of Seven's journey to find herself was.

Janeway was a revelation to the young Cristoforetti. Not only was the captain a woman in charge, but she was also a trained scientist. It raised the position of scientist in her eyes from the expert who can only give an informed insight, to the one making the decisions. Our ultra-military idea of astronauts comes from the early days when they were war-experienced pilots. The culture of the astronaut corps today, says Cristoforetti, is "very much a balance of stereotypically male and stereotypically female characteristics." Both men and women need to be "disciplined, tough, and strong," but there's also "a lot of emphasis on being empathetic."

That B'Elanna was such a competent engineer was inspirational. That she was also uncompromising and opinionated gave the young Cristoforetti the freedom to realize that she shared these qualities, which led to her eventually modulating them as she got older.

The first time we talked, Cristoforetti was going into space for several months. She had just told me that the only time she felt the cultural drag of expectations of her as a woman was after she had children. And yet, I asked, "Who helps you with your children while you are in space?" She answered that they were her husband's children, too, and of course during that time he would be the primary caregiver. I suddenly felt like a fossil caught in the cultural amber of 1990s expectations of women. From that moment, I stopped asking my husband for "help" in the kitchen. Instead, I now suggest we each put in twenty minutes of cleanup. It's one of those realizations you can't unsee.

INSIGHT
EDITIONS

PO Box 3088
San Rafael, CA 94901
www.insighteditions.com

Find us on Facebook: www.facebook.com/InsightEditions
Follow us on Instagram: @insighteditions

ISBN: 979-8-88663-301-6

PUBLISHER: Raoul Goff
VP, CO-PUBLISHER: Vanessa Lopez
VP, CREATIVE: Chrissy Kwasnik
VP, MANUFACTURING: Alix Nicholaeff
PUBLISHING DIRECTOR: Ben Robinson
ART DIRECTOR: Matt Girard
EDITOR: Ben Robinson
PROJECT EDITOR: Stephen Fall
SENIOR PRODUCTION MANAGER: Greg Steffen
SENIOR PRODUCTION MANAGER, SUBSIDIARY RIGHTS: Lina s Palma-Temena

FRONT COVER ILLUSTRATION: Tom Ralston

INTERIOR DESIGN BY: Malea Clark-Nicholson

ROOTS of PEACE   REPLANTED PAPER

Insight Editions, in association with Roots of Peace, will plant two trees for each tree used in the manufacturing of this book. Roots of Peace is an internationally renowned humanitarian organization dedicated to eradicating land mines worldwide and converting war-torn lands into productive farms and wildlife habitats. Roots of Peace will plant two million fruit and nut trees in Afghanistan and provide farmers there with the skills and support necessary for sustainable land use.

Manufactured in China by Insight Editions

10 9 8 7 6 5 4 3 2 1

I want to thank all the people who shared their stories with me, and the ones who waited patiently to talk, and were kind even when we ran out of time. A million thanks to all the actors and writers who shared their perspectives so generously and my apologies to anyone we weren't able to include. I want to thank writer Jessica Nordell, whose book *The End of Bias: A Beginning*, changed my paradigm, and Jess Zimmerman, whose book *Women and Other Monsters* resonated so, so deeply with me. Huge thanks to my editor, Ben Robinson, who knows more about *Star Trek* than anyone I know and guided me gently through the process. Thank you to Risa Kessler, Marian Cordry, and John Van Citters at CBS for all their hard work. And thank you to my husband Matthew Rimmer, who did everything from getting people coffee, to sending me back downstairs to my office when I would get overwhelmed with how big the assignment was. As the Chaplain said, *Star Trek* teaches us to have courage, hope, and to know none of us are alone. This experience has reinforced that for me, ten times over.